D1604144

Shadows and Illuminations

For Laura, my wife,
who along with many of the writers I discuss here
reminds me that often the best way to find the
illuminations within the shadows is by
keeping a good sense of humor

Shadows and Illuminations

Literature as Spiritual Journey

JOHN NEARY

sussex
ACADEMIC
PRESS
Brighton • Portland • Toronto

Copyright © John Neary, 2011.

The right of John Neary to be identified as Author of this work has been asserted in accordance with the Copyright, Designs and Patents Act 1988.

2 4 6 8 10 9 7 5 3

First published in 2011 by
SUSSEX ACADEMIC PRESS
PO Box 139
Eastbourne BN24 9BP

and in the United States of America by
SUSSEX ACADEMIC PRESS
920 NE 58th Ave   Suite 300
Portland, Oregon 97213-3786

and in Canada by
SUSSEX ACADEMIC PRESS (CANADA)
90 Arnold Avenue, Thornhill, Ontario L4J 1B5

British Library Cataloguing in Publication Data
A CIP catalogue record for this book is available from the British Library.

Library of Congress Cataloging-in-Publication Data
Neary, John, 1952–
Shadows and illuminations : literature as spiritual journey / John Neary.
p. cm.
Includes bibliographical references and index.
ISBN 978-1-84519-431-4 (acid-free paper)
  1. Psychology and literature. 2. Revelation in literature. 3. Self-consciousness (Awareness) in literature. 4. Spiritual biography—History and criticism. I. Title.
PN56.P93S53 2011
809′.93353—dc22

Papers used by Sussex Academic Press are natural, renewable and recyclable products from well-managed forests and certified in accordance with the rules of the Forest Stewardship Council.

Typeset and designed by Sussex Academic Press, Brighton & Eastbourne.
Printed by TJ International, Padstow, Cornwall.
This book is printed on acid-free paper.

Contents

Preface

Journey to Darkness as Journey to Enlightenment

This book elaborates and builds on a literary paradigm that I developed some time ago: the "dark-side" narrative. During an initial viewing of Stanley Kubrick's film *Eyes Wide Shut*, I observed (with the help of my wife, Laura, as I will explain later) that the film was uncannily similar to Nathaniel Hawthorne's classic short story "Young Goodman Brown." In each case a limited, somewhat naive protagonist goes out, at night, into the darkness (the streets of New York in the case of Kubrick's protagonist, the New England forest in the case of Hawthorne's) and discovers things about himself and the world that he previously was unaware of. It is a disturbing discovery of deep imperfection and apparent perversity, an encounter with what Jungian psychology names "the shadow." But it is also an experience of what Christian theologian Paul Tillich calls "depth," which he considers an experience of ground-less mystery that is no less than an encounter with whatever it is we refer to when we use the word "God." This struck me as a stunning paradox: that a discovery of apparent perversity may be an enlarging experience of, in the broadest sense, the divine. And indeed, many Jungians—including Robert Bly, an important voice in this project—now see the "shadow" not just as a bundle of repressed negativity but as a harbinger of growth and soul, a doorway to spiritual illumination.

I found this idea so provocative, and its potential application so interesting, that I developed a literature course at St. Norbert College, where I work, in which we explored "shadows and illuminations" within a variety of literary texts, many of which I treat here; this book grew from that course, and I owe many of its insights to the thoughtful students who have contributed to the course over the years.

As I developed the ideas that led to the course and then this book, I initially intended to dichotomize, as I describe in my first chapter: to look first at the "shadows" and then at the "illuminations." But this idea quickly fell apart, as my *Eyes Wide Shut* experience should have alerted me that it would. Helped by Tillich's idea of depth, by Bly's notion of the shadow, and by insights from other thinkers—Buddhist nun Pema Chödrön, and especially archetypal psychologist James Hillman—I realized that dichotomizing simply would not do. The shadows truly are the illuminations, and the illuminations are filled with shadow. So this book, far from emphasizing polarities, resists them; I have tried to break down the oppositions, seeing not antinomies but what Hillman calls "shaded differentiations." And my companions on this journey—Hillman, Chödrön, Tillich, Bly, and most particularly the literary writers, Dante, Shakespeare, Hawthorne, Stevenson, and the wonderful contemporary novelists Toni Morrison, Jane Hamilton, Jonathan Safran Foer, and Yann Martel—have provided me with great depth and illumination. I am thankful to all of them, and I hope they provide you with a meaningful journey too.

Acknowledgments

I wish to thank the following publishers, who have granted me permission to use extended quotations from copyrighted works. Excerpts from Toni Morrison's *Sula*, copyright © 1973 by Toni Morrison, are used by permission of Alfred A. Knopf, a division of Random House, Inc.; in the UK *Sula* is published by Chatto and Windus, and is quoted by permission of The Random House Group Ltd. Excerpts from Jane Hamilton's *The Book of Ruth*, copyright © 1988 by Jane Hamilton, are used by permission of Houghton Mifflin Harcourt Publishing Company; in the UK *The Book of Ruth* is published by Black Swan, and is quoted by permission of The Random House Group Ltd. Excerpts from Jonathan Safran Foer's *Everything Is Illuminated*, copyright © 2002 by Jonathan Safran Foer, are reprinted by permission of Houghton Mifflin Harcourt Publishing Company, and in the UK by permission of Penguin Books (Hamish Hamilton, 2002). Excerpts from Yann Martel's *Life of Pi*, copyright © 2001 by Yann Martel, are reprinted by permission of Houghton Mifflin Harcourt, and in the UK by permission of Canongate Books Ltd, 14 High Street, Edinburgh, EH1 1TE, and by permission of the author.

Passages from Pema Chödrön's *When Things Fall Apart*, copyright © 1997 by Pema Chödrön, are reprinted by arrangement with Shambhala Publications, Inc., Boston, MA (www.shambhala.com). Excerpts from *A Little Book on the Human Shadow*, by Robert Bly and edited by William Booth, copyright © 1988 by Robert Bly, are reprinted by permission of HarperCollins Publishers. Excerpts from James Hillman's *Re-Visioning Psychology*, copyright © 1975 by James Hillman, and from Hillman's *The Dream of the Underworld*, copyright © 1979 by James Hillman, are reprinted by permission of HarperCollins Publishers. And permissions to quote from James Hillman's books *Insearch* and *Healing Fiction* and from Hillman's essay "Alchemical Blue and the Unio Mentalis" have been granted by Spring Publications, Inc.

Portions of "Glow in the Dark" originally appeared in the Winter 2006–2007 edition of *Religion and the Arts*, Boston College, Chestnut Hill MA 02467.

I wish also to thank the St. Norbert College Faculty Personnel Committee for graciously granting me a sabbatical leave to work on this book. In addition, I am grateful to Jeffrey Frick, St. Norbert's Dean of the College and Academic Vice President, David Duquette, Associate Dean of Humanities and Fine Arts, and my English discipline colleagues, for generously finding funds to help me complete this project. And I wish to thank my wife, Laura, for giving me the idea that Stanley Kubrick's *Eyes Wide Shut* is a modern reimagining of Nathaniel Hawthorne's "Young Goodman Brown"; it was that idea that spurred this project. And finally, I am thankful to the students at St. Norbert College who have taken my course "Shadows and Illuminations"; the ideas that emerged in those class discussions are the sources of much that I have written here.

Glow in the Dark
The Journey to Hades

Shaded Differentiations

When I first imagined a study of literature of and as spiritual journey, my inclination was to dichotomize: the spiritual journey can be *either* dark *or* light; it can go *either* down into pain and fear *or* up to rapturous exhilaration. Shadows *or* illuminations.

But I found myself much more enthused about the dark half of this dichotomy. Young Goodman Brown's trek into the haunted forest, Marlow's voyage to the Heart of Darkness, portrayals of the Jungian "shadow": these things gripped me more powerfully than stories of the unalloyed light (if there are such things). And then I found myself bombarded by wise voices, thinkers and spiritual teachers whom I deeply respect, urging me to dissolve this dichotomy. I will present some of these voices in much greater detail later, but I will briefly present three.

The first, Pema Chödrön, is an American Buddhist nun whose "wisdom of no escape" — a Tibetan Buddhist spirituality of gentle, loving, good-humored acceptance of all of life — will appear from time to time in these pages. Chödrön explicitly merges the seeming opposites I am examining, claiming that the apparent shadows and the apparent illuminations are "all mixed together," that they "interpenetrate each other" and *together* make up the "basic creative energy of life":

> Now, sometimes the teachings emphasize the wisdom, brilliance, or sanity that we possess, and sometimes they emphasize the obstacles, how it is that we feel stuck in a small, dark place. These are actually two sides of one coin: when they are put together, inspiration (or well-being) and burden (or suffering) describe the human condition. . . .
>
> We see how beautiful and wonderful and amazing things are, and we see how caught up we are. It isn't that one is the bad part and one is the good part, but that it's a kind of interesting, smelly, rich, fertile mess of stuff. When it's all mixed together, it's us: humanness. . . . Both the brilliance and the suffering are here all the time; they interpenetrate each

other. . . . The basic creative energy of life — life force — bubbles up and courses through all of existence. It can be experienced as open, free, unburdened, full of possibility, energizing. Or this very same energy can be experienced as petty, narrow, stuck, caught. (*No Escape* 21)

The second of the voices that urge me to blur the lines between shadows and illuminations is that of Catholic theologian John S. Dunne, whose "Parable of the Mountain Man" reverses the stereotypical notion of what a journey to God would look like. For Dunne, although the spiritual journey includes a detour to a sublime mountaintop, it ultimately points downward into shadows, into the valley of human "cares and concerns," which surprisingly is where God actually resides:

Man, let us say, is climbing a mountain. At the top of the mountain, he thinks, is God. Down in the valley are the cares and concerns of human life, all the troubles of love and war. By climbing the mountain and reaching the top man hopes to escape from all these miseries. God, on the other hand, is coming down the mountain, let us say, his desire being to plunge himself into the very things that man wishes to escape. Man's desire is to be God, God's is to be man. God and man pass one another going in opposite directions. When man reaches the top of the mountain he is going to find nothing. God is not there. . . . [M]an learns that climbing was a mistake and that which he seeks is to be found only by going down into the valley. He turns around, therefore, and starts going down the mountain. He sets his face towards love and war, where before he had turned his back upon them. (14)

Dunne says that the trek up the mountain in search of enlightenment, of shadowless illumination, is a "mistake," but it is a necessary mistake. The mountaintop is a place of escape from the web of bodily and relational humanity, a place of pure reason, of the Aristotelian God ("a knowing of knowing") and of the Hegelian "autonomous human spirit" (17). It is a sterile place, however, a place of "madness — not the madness that consists in having lost one's reason, but a madness that consists in having lost everything except one's reason" (18). This withdrawal to the mountain of light is a needed halt, an awakening to consciousness. But for Dunne it is an illumination in desperate need of shadows: the traveler's "realization that he has lost everything except his reason, that he has found pure humanity but not full humanity, changes his wisdom from a knowledge of knowledge into a knowledge of ignorance. He realizes that he has something yet to learn, something that he cannot learn at the top of the mountain but only at the bottom of the valley" (19).

The third voice calling for a blurring of the lines between shadows and illuminations is that of James Hillman, the post-Jungian psychologist whose radical insights about the wisdom that comes through the darkest of life experiences has to a large degree inspired this study. In a provocative defense of psychologist Alfred Adler, Hillman asserts that "oppositional thinking . . . is a pampering safeguard against the true reality of the world, which in Adler's view is one of shaded differentiations and not oppositions" (*Healing Fiction* 100). All oppositions, Hillman says, are grounded on "the male/female pair" (*Healing Fiction* 101). The psyche — the soul — is, Hillman claims, hermaphroditic, many-shaded and male-female. But our literal-minded egos cannot handle such ambiguity, and we embrace oppositions as a neurotic defense. In particular, as a bulwark against supposed weakness and inferiority, our culture — patriarchically biased — has made male and female not just biological descriptions but rather qualitative oppositions: strength vs. weakness, superiority vs. inferiority, certainty vs. ambivalence. Illuminations vs. shadows.

Psychological healing, Hillman says, amounts to "restoring psychological hermaphroditism"; "any disjunctive move is contra-indicated" (*Healing Fiction* 102).

Hillman provides us here with an important thesis: "any disjunctive move is contra-indicated." I wish in these pages to embark on an exploration of literary texts as verbal portrayals of and even sacramental experiences of spiritual journeys, and these journeys will necessarily take us to places of darkness and light both — to shadows *and* illuminations. What Chödrön, Dunne, and Hillman suggest, however, is that this is not a hierarchical opposition: the shadows are not bad stuff that we have to encounter and overcome in order to get to the good stuff, the illuminations. Indeed, these are not oppositions are all, but "shaded differentiations." Perhaps we will find that the spiritual journey is precisely (precisely? no, nothing will be very precise in this journey) fueled by a kind of light/dark hermaphroditism. The spiritual journey, the journey of the soul, is an immersion in shadowy illumination or illuminated shadowiness.

If Pema Chödrön is correct, then all the events of our lives are holy; all contain the "basic creative energy of life — life force," which "bubbles up and courses through all of existence." As John S. Dunne's parable neatly suggests, an authentic, spiritual, soul-enriching journey is not a process of escaping from bad stuff and jumping or climbing or flying up to the good stuff. However, there must be something to differentiate a spiritual journey from other activities and events, and here again James Hillman suggests a place to start. For Hillman a spiritual journey — or a journey of the *soul* (a word he prefers to "spirit," since it is richer, male-female rather than male, light and dark both rather than all ethereal light) — is marked not by specific kinds of events but rather by a perspective on, a relationship with, those events; perhaps this is analogous to Dunne's temporary trek up the mountain, not for divine illumination but for *perspective*. Human life, for Hillman, is a barrage of events, but we enter the realm of soul when "events" (external facts, happenings) become deeply felt ("digested") *experiences*: "An event becomes an experience, moves from outer to inner, is made into soul, when it goes through a psychological process," Hillman says (*Healing Fiction* 26). This process can be philosophical (Plato's dialectic method is aimed at facilitating a spiritual journey) or erotic (loving another is a journey to soul) or religious (rituals create a sense of the holy). Or poetic: making or, I would strongly suggest, reading literature can effect this psychological process.

Indeed, for Hillman, literature is the prototypical way to transform "events" into "experiences." Hillman evokes the romantic poet William Wordsworth; Wordsworth famously claimed that poetry, by which he meant all literature, requires that the artist *recollect in tranquility*, and Hillman claims that it is just such a "digestive operation" that transforms events (facts) into experiences (soul): "Ingestion slows down the happenings for the sake of chewing" (*Healing Fiction* 27). A "tenet" of Hillman's "faith" is that "soul slows the parade of history; digesting tames appetite; experience coagulates events" (*Healing Fiction* 27). This psychological process is like Buddhist meditation — it slows down, attends, is mindful. But unlike at least some Buddhist meditation, it tells and receives *histories* (that is, *narratives*, always fictionalized in the retelling), which are "an equivalent for soul-making, as a digestive operation" (*Healing Fiction* 27). Narratives slow events down, as Tristram Shandy discovers when he tries, in Laurence Sterne's great eighteenth-century novel, to tell his whole life story and finds that the events wildly outpace the telling, and after some eight-hundred pages he has scarcely gotten himself born. And this respect for the slow, the fully digested, leads Hillman to praise the god of dark, leaden depression, Saturn, and Hillman gives us a glimpse at the possibility that stories of soul-making — stories told by and of the soul — are dark, discomforting, steeped in the blues: "I worship psychologically at the altar of the God of historical time and slowness, Saturn, the archetypal swallower, who teaches us the art of internal digestion through the syndrome of his magistral depressions" (*Healing Fiction* 28). While many psychotherapies return to the past and retell the story in order to transcend the past, to help the ego break from its entanglement in the muck of its past story, Hillman returns — recollects in tranquility — to steep in the past and brew up a story, as tea leaves steep in hot water, darkening and darkening and darkening the water, making it an ever-richer tea.

So here is a place to start: the spiritual journey is about experience, not just events; it digests, recollects in tranquility. In this process, facts steep in the water of tranquil reflection, becoming story. Let us look at some other ways of understanding this darkly illuminating journey, a journey to depth, it appears; we will look at such writers as Dante, Protestant theologian Paul Tillich, and Catholic theologian Michael Himes as well as more deeply explore the insights of Hillman and Chödrön. Then we will experience the insights more directly by diving into some prototypical "dark-side" works: in this chapter we will perform spiritually tilted close readings of Nathaniel Hawthorne's short story "Young Goodman Brown" and Stanley Kubrick's film *Eyes Wide Shut*; and in subsequent chapters we will look at the shadow or doppelgänger motif, we will examine family as a kind of dark-side journey, and we will end by returning to storytelling itself as a spiritual journey.

Into the Inferno

"The dread and resistance," says Carl Jung, "which every natural human being experiences when it comes to delving too deeply into himself is, at bottom, the fear of the journey to Hades" (qtd. in Hillman, *Dream* vii). The journey to Hades or Hell or the land of the dead has been part of human mythology at least since Homer sent Odysseus down to the underworld; for a variety of reasons Orpheus, Aeneas, and of course Jesus also undertook infernal voyages. But it was Dante who explicitly depicted the journey to Hell in a way that captures Jung's vision that this is a metaphor for the dreadful, resisted experience of delving deeply into the self. And the fact that the structure of Dante's Divine Comedy is a lengthy recollection of such delving ties this great poem to the later Wordsworthian notion of literature as a recollection in tranquility, a remembering, a storying, that is itself a kind of spiritual journey into the imagination.

Dante the mature and enlightened poet, the speaker of the Comedy, begins by recollecting his midlife crisis, or more specifically the midlife crisis of his remembered self, his pilgrim self, prior to the illumination that his spiritual journey brought him to. This midlife crisis is *dark*, and Dante poetically presents it not just in vague feelings but in specific images; the spiritual journey, as Hillman asserts, is insistently metaphorical, imaginal, literary, narrative, and that is just how Dante says he experienced it. "Midway on our life's journey," Dante says,

> . . . I found myself
> In dark woods, the right road lost. To tell

> About those woods is hard — so tangled and rough
>
> And savage that thinking of it now, I feel
> The old fear stirring; death is hardly more bitter. (*Inferno* 3)

The spiritual journey begins, for Dante, in the dark, but it is intrinsically metaphorical, imaginal (in dark *woods*); and it evokes an encounter with limit, the ultimate limit, death. The experience is also dreamlike, another prototypical characteristic of a dark-journey narrative:

> how I came to enter
> I cannot say, being so full of sleep
> Whatever moment it was I began to blunder
>
> Off the true path. (*Inferno* 3)

James Hillman, as we saw, claims that such a frightening experience tends to create a "pampering" compulsion to dichotomize, to immediately imagine a light to escape to from this darkness — in John S. Dunne's terms, an urge to climb up a mountain, out of the valley of human cares and concerns. And the pilgrim Dante tries to do just that:

> when I came to stop
> Below a hill that marked one end of the valley
> That had pierced my heart with terror, I looked up
>
> Toward the crest and saw its shoulders already
> Mantled in rays of that bright planet that shows
> The road to everyone, whatever our journey.
>
> Then I could feel the terror begin to ease. (*Inferno* 3)

Thinking he can quickly escape this dark, wooded valley, Dante starts to climb the hill toward the light. But his "delving . . . into himself," his "journey to Hades," is not to be shirked so easily. A leopard blocks Dante's way; "she made me turn about / To go back down," he says (*Inferno* 3). But he still has "hope," provoked by the

> fair sun rising with the stars attending it
>
> As when Divine Love set those beautiful
> Lights into motion at creation's dawn. (*Inferno* 3–5)

But discovering that a lion and a she-wolf also guard the hill, "I lost hope of the crest," Dante says (*Inferno* 5). And, indeed, his journey instead will take him through a portal over which are inscribed the words, "ABANDON ALL HOPE, YOU WHO ENTER HERE" (*Inferno* 19). Though he has a wise mentor, the poet Virgil, and a promise that he ultimately will make his way to Heaven, the midlife spiritual journey begins, at least, as a journey down (Jung's "journey to Hades") rather than up.

The *recollection*, too, is a return to — a reanimation of — this descent to the dark side. Early in the telling of his tale, Dante the present, enlightened poet invokes the Muses as those who, in James Hillman's terms, have allowed him to "digest" the fearsome events of Hell and turn them into experience, the substance of soul. "O Muses, O genius of art, O memory," Dante apostrophizes, saying that Muses/genius/memory is the one "whose merit / Has *inscribed inwardly* those things I saw" (*Inferno* 11, emphasis added); and now he says that "flawless memory will redraw" those things (*Inferno* 11).

So the necessary, healing journey is a double-darkness for Dante. Dante the pilgrim's way was a way through Hell, not a quick jaunt up the sunny hill. And even now, Dante the poet must delve into another shadowy Hades, the inner world of memory, of recollection in tranquility. Foreshadowing another great romantic poet, Samuel Taylor Coleridge, Dante seems compelled to stop us readers, to slow us down, to reiterate a dark story and turn us, too, into "sadder but . . . wiser" people (Coleridge, "Rime of the Ancient Mariner").

Now I must admit that I am cheating a bit. Dante is ultimately a serene Thomist and his poem is a *commedia*. As we will see, the literature that best incarnates the spiritual vision I am attempting to describe will *stay* in the dark — or rather, will find shadows and illuminations stubbornly and ambiguously mixed rather than dichotomized. But Dante the pilgrim, of course, makes it *through* Hell, climbs up *through* Purgatory, and ends up with a vision of absolute light in Heaven. Dante the storytelling poet, too, seems to escape the dark of inner imagining and earn a rest as he leaves his pilgrim persona engulfed in Light and Love:

> Here my powers rest from their high fantasy,
> but already I could feel my being turned —
> instinct and intellect balanced equally
>
> as in a wheel whose motion nothing jars —
> by the Love that moves the Sun and the other stars. (*Paradiso* 365)

This difference from my own model of the interpenetration of shadows and illuminations seems to me absolutely fundamental and merely incidental both at the same time. Yes, in one sense Dante has fully dichotomized light and darkness, in the orthodox Christian fashion: the Light that saturates Dante the pilgrim and silences Dante the poet appears to be utterly without shadow, as the Christian God is utterly without imperfection. James Hillman, to the contrary, endorses a sort of psychological polytheism that resists postulating such a singular, absolutely perfect Divine Being. But Hillman's theology is a poetics, a play of interconnected metaphors, and as a work of poetry rather than dogma Dante's comedy is the same thing, I believe. In Dante as in Chödrön, Dunne, and Hillman, the light and darkness are both part of the whole. The poem cannot do without either dimension. Yes, propositionally Dante's Light is entirely without darkness; poetically and narratively, however, the dark-side journey is as fundamental to the poem as the final rapture. Indeed, Dantean scholar John Freccero argues that "rapture" is not the final place that the poem rests but that, rather, Dante delicately, poetically weaves together the divine and the human, the light and the dark, even in the ecstatic final lines: the final scene, Freccero says, is

> a return to the darkness of this world for its own good and a reintegration of poetry into society. . . . The restless drive of Dante's verse reaches its climax and its repose with the word "Love" in the last verse, just as the desire that is in human terms insatiable finds its satisfaction in the Love of God. What follows after the word represents a fall to earth, which is to say to us, after the ecstatic moment. . . . Spatially, to speak of the Sun and stars is to return to our perspective, looking up at the heavenly bodies. . . . The word "Love" is therefore the link that binds heaven to earth and the poet to his audience, containing within it the substance of the poem. (xxi)

Freccero's analysis makes the end of Dante's great poem resonate with John S. Dunne's Parable of the Mountain Man, returning Dante to "our perspective," not on the mountaintop but in the valley of humanity. For Dunne however, if not quite for Dante, this is actually where the incarnate God dwells; the Catholic Dunne as much as the post-Jungian Hillman sees darkness as always, not just temporarily, part of the spiritual journey, and I am not sure that Dante ultimately agrees. But there is no question that Dante the pilgrim must at least *initially* travel into the shadows to achieve spiritual illumination; the Divine Comedy is an excellent first prototype of those literary works that portray — and in a sense *are*, for teller and reader both — the spiritual journey as a delving into self that is a journey to the dark, to Hades. Let us now examine the ways Christian theologians Paul Tillich and Michael Himes provide explicitly theological models for understanding the spiritual journey in the sense I am discussing it.

Cracking the Surface — Paul Tillich

For Paul Tillich, the spiritual journey can be imagined as a journey to darkness — or, paradoxically, to illumination in and through darkness — because of the resonant power of the metaphor of *depth*. In his famous essay/sermon "The Depth of Existence," Tillich says:

> The words 'deep' and 'depth' are used in our daily life, in poetry and philosophy, in the Bible, and in many other religious documents to indicate a spiritual attitude, although the words themselves are taken from a spatial experience. Depth is a dimension of space; yet at the same time it is a symbol for a spiritual quality. (59)

Although Tillich's commitment to metaphors is more provisional and utilitarian than that of James Hillman, who considers poetic metaphor the very constitutive basis of soul, Tillich nonetheless asserts that "We are and we remain sensuous beings, even when we deal with spiritual things," that there is "a great wisdom in our language" (59), and that the metaphor of depth is therefore worth unpacking. This spatial metaphor, spiritual development as a journey to *depth*, provides Tillich with a striking, existential portrayal of the encounter with the divine as a descent down into the dark.

This descent is preceded by modern humanity's superficiality, our barren, routine lives lived "on the surface":

> Most of our life continues on the surface. We are enslaved by the routine of our daily lives, in work and pleasure, in business and recreation. . . . We are in constant motion and never stop to plunge into the depth. We talk and talk and never listen to the voices speaking *to* our depth and *from* our depth. We accept ourselves as we appear to ourselves, and do not care what we really are. Like hit-and-run drivers, we injure our souls by the speed with which we move on the surface; and then we rush away, leaving our bleeding souls alone. We miss, therefore, our depth and our true life. (62)

It is only, Tillich says, when the surface cracks — "when the picture that we have of ourselves breaks down completely, . . . when we find ourselves acting against all the expectations we had derived from that picture, and . . . when an earthquake shakes and disrupts the surface of our self-knowledge" — that we "are willing to look into a deeper level of our being" (62–63). This is our Dantean dark-wood experience; we find ourselves "In dark woods, the right road lost," and despite all our resistances we find that we must make the descent to Hades.

Tillich goes on to make a strong theological claim about the value of such an experience. "The wisdom of all ages and of all continents," he says, "speaks about the road to our depth. . . . [A]ll those who have been concerned — mystics and priests, poets and philosophers, simple people and educated people — with that road through confession, lonely self-scrutiny, internal or external catastrophes, prayer, contemplation, have witnessed to the same experience" (63). But, he says, "the so-called 'psychology of depth'" (that of Freud, Jung, Adler), although it "can help us to find the way into our depth," cannot "help us in an ultimate way, because it cannot guide us to the deepest ground of our being and all being, the depth of life itself" (63). It is important to Tillich to affirm that the journey to depth is nothing less than the journey to God: "The name of this infinite and inexhaustible depth and ground of all being is *God*. That depth is what the word *God* means" (63).

Tillich's rich, non-reductive vision of what the word "God" refers to links him, I think, to the Buddhist writer Pema Chödrön and to post-Jungian James Hillman, if not to the more scientific Freud, Jung, and Adler (though I think he is probably a bit unfair to them as well). After making his theological claim, that depth is what the word "God" means, he breaks open any absolutist definition of that word:

> And if that word has not much meaning for you, translate it, and speak of the depths of your life, of the source of your being, of your ultimate concern, of what you take seriously without any reservation. Perhaps, in order to do so, you must forget everything traditional that you have learned about God, perhaps even that word itself. For if you know that God means depth, you know much about Him. You cannot then call yourself an atheist or unbeliever. For you cannot think or say: Life has no depth! Life itself is shallow. Being itself is surface only. If you could say this in complete seriousness, you would be an atheist; but otherwise you are not. He who knows about depth knows about God. (64)

So right at the outset of our own journey, Tillich holds up two equally important warnings: first, this spiritual journey into the dark depths is profoundly important, since it is nothing less than a journey to God; but second, naming it as a journey to God does not prejudge the outcome, since "God" is not a referent that refers to anything to which we have clear, certain, univocal, absolute access.

Nor does the fact that this is a journey to "God" mean that it will be sweet and edifying. The dark-side journeys that I intend to explore in literature and film are often, perhaps usually, edgy and disturbing; the two examples in this chapter alone will include a devilish ritual and a sexual orgy. Can these be avenues to God? Well, yes, Tillich says, and he invokes what he calls an "old and beautiful myth: when the soul leaves the body," he says, "it must pass over many spheres where daemonic forces rule" before it can reach "the ultimate depth of the Divine Ground. . . . Everyone has to face the deep things of life. That there is danger is no excuse" (67–68). The way of depth is a way of suffering, Tillich says, a way that jars us — often violently — out of our comfort zones: "the road runs contrary to the way we formerly lived and thought" (68). Indeed, Tillich goes on to say, "When this breaking away occurred in men like Paul, Augustine, and Luther, such extreme suffering was involved that it was experienced as death and hell. But they accepted such sufferings as the road to the deep things of God, as the spiritual way, as the way of truth" (69). I have no idea whether Tillich would be willing to refer to the journeys to the dark side undertaken by the characters in "Young Goodman Brown" and *Eyes Wide Shut* as "the spiritual way, as the way of truth," but Tillich's very non-fundamentalist vision of depth and "God" at least allows us to take seriously the possibility of a religious dimension in the disturbing journeys I wish to talk about.

Tillich provides us with a language and a powerful existential understanding of the spiritual journey as a way of depth. I believe that his view complements those of Pema Chödrön and James Hillman, adding a sophisticated, non-fundamentalist Christian framework for our governing metaphor. However, Chödrön, Hillman, and Jung himself all, in different ways, worry that because Christianity has so dichotomized light and darkness, God and Satan, Christian approaches to the spiritual journey cannot maintain the hermaphroditic wholeness of soul and tend to collapse into dichotomies. Does Tillich's view of surface-versus-depth succumb to this dichotomizing? Perhaps. In a sermon collected in the same volume as his "Depth" piece, "We Live in Two Orders," Tillich sharply contrasts the "human order, the order of history" (27) — marked by "growing and dying" (27), "sin and punishment" (28), "finiteness and sin" (28) — with the "divine order" (29):

> men are like grass, but the word of God spoken to them shall stand forever. Men stand under the law of sin and punishment, but the divine order breaks through it and brings forgiveness. Men faint, falling from the height of their moral goodness and youthful power, and just when they have fallen and are weakest, they run without weariness and rise up with wings as eagles. God acts beyond all human assumptions and valuations. (29)

But I believe that, in a paradoxical way, Tillich qualifies the dichotomizing to some extent. For him postulating a divine order precisely prevents the illusion of human perfection that Pema Chödrön criticizes by gently calling for "the wisdom of no escape" from the human condition. Tillich says that modernity has suffered under the illusion that modern civilization can conquer (escape from) "finiteness, sin, and tragedy" (31), and Tillich espouses his own version of a wisdom of no escape. Yes, Tillich also says that we participate "in something infinite, in an order which is not transitory, not self-destructive, not tragic, but eternal, holy, and blessed" (31), but I believe that he, like John S. Dunne, says that this participation in the infinite is worked out not on a victorious mountaintop but in the valley of human brokenness. "What is new in the prophets and in Christianity," Tillich says, ". . . is that the eternal order reveals itself in the historical order" (32). The way to the divine is a descent to depth, not a flight to the angelic. Is this vision exactly the same as Hillman's, Chödrön's, Dante's, Dunne's? No — but neither are all of these others the same. We are dealing with more "shaded differentiations," and all are wise supplements of each other. Let us look at the Catholic theological approach of Michael Himes and then revisit Hillman and Chödrön to get a deeper look at this vision of "no escape." Then we will proceed into the dark woods with Young Goodman Brown and into the dark city with *Eyes Wide Shut*'s Bill Harford.

Mystery, Metaphor, and Sacrament — Michael Himes

The Catholic sacramental framework provides another, complementary way of seeing the spiritual journey as a journey down into illuminating darkness. It is this theology, stressing sacramental images and an incarnational God, that underlies John S. Dunne's Parable of the Mountain Man; it is a viewpoint that is summed up beautifully by the great Jesuit poet Gerard Manley Hopkins:

> The world is charged with the grandeur of God. . . .
>   It gathers to a greatness, like the ooze of oil
> Crushed. ("God's Grandeur" 1–4)

Hopkins' point here is similar to Dunne's: God's grandeur or grace, he is saying, is not like a lightning bolt from up in the sky or from a mountaintop. Rather, it rises up from the valley of human cares and concerns, oozing out of the earth like the oil from a squeezed olive ("like the ooze from oil / Crushed").

Michael Himes, in his essay "Finding God in All Things," elaborates on Hopkins' point, beginning with his own assertion that for him, as for Tillich, God is not some huge being who dwells high up above humanity: "When the Christian tradition speaks of God, it does not mean a great big person out there somewhere, older, wiser, stronger, than you and I. That is Zeus, not God" (94). Rather, for Himes "'God' is theological shorthand that we use to designate the Mystery which grounds and undergirds all that exists. One could call it something else, perhaps, but 'God' is handy" (91). Thus, language about God must leave room for shadow, for darkness, for unknowability: "Any language about God that is perfectly clear is certainly wrong. We are, after all, daring to speak about ultimate Mystery, and whatever we say, we must not, under pain of blasphemy, lose a profound sense of awe before the Mystery that undergirds all that exists" (92). But we cannot resist raising the *question* of God (no absolutely certain, shadow-free answers, please), and this question — rather than shooting us up to the sunny mountaintop — plunges us into John Dunne's valley of human cares and concerns: "Christian statements about God," Himes says,

> are ways of answering the question, "Do you think that there are meaning, purpose, and direction to your life, and do you think that you are not the one who decides that meaning, purpose, and direction?" That question, however it is answered, is the question of God. . . . We cannot *not* ask that question, implicitly or explicitly. It cannot be answered finally, but it is too impossible not to answer it in some way. That is where we find ourselves in religious language, in language about Mystery. (94)

So we *have* to talk about God, even though we *cannot* speak of God adequately. For Himes, therefore, we must "do what the great users of language — poets — do when trying to say the unsayable: we pile up metaphors" (94). Thus, says Himes, "we say that God is creator, judge, parent, spouse, shepherd, king, lawgiver, rock, leader in battle, savior, and on and on. We pile image on image on image on image, metaphor after metaphor after metaphor" (95).

Already it should be clear how and why God-talk for Himes — as for Hopkins and, in a different way, for Tillich — is earthly and even earthy. Metaphors are sensuous; God is the oozing of olive oil. But Himes goes on to say that the "fundamental metaphor for God in the Christian tradition," which is "suggested over and over again in the New Testament, but [which] finds its clearest, sharpest, most succinct statement in one of the last documents of the New Testament collection written, what we call the First Letter of John," is *God is love* (96).

Himes explicates the word *love* here ("agape" in Greek) as "self-gift":

> The whole Christian doctrinal tradition is an expansion of this funda-
> mental claim, that God, the Ultimate Mystery which undergirds the
> existence of all that is, is least wrongly thought of as pure and perfect
> self-gift. . . . The central point of the doctrine of the Trinity is that God is
> least wrongly understood as a relationship, as an eternal explosion of
> love. . . . This is what Christians mean when they talk about God: from
> all eternity the Mystery at the root of all that exists is endless self-gift,
> endless outpouring of self. (96–97)

Himes claims that because this self-gift, this "grace," explodes everywhere — it pours out "like the ooze of oil / Crushed" — we do not notice
it: "if grace is omnipresent, grace is likely to go unnoticed" (99). And
that, for Himes, is the value of *sacraments*: "We require occasions when
grace is called to our attention, when it is made concrete for us, when
that which is always the case is made present in such a way that we
cannot help but notice it and may either accept or reject it and, if we
accept it, celebrate it" (99). Himes is, of course, using the word "sacrament" in a broad rather than specific way, referring not just to the "seven
great public rituals that Catholics celebrate" (99) but to *any* thing that
rises to the level of religious metaphor, causing us to *attend*, to *see what
is there*: "By *sacrament* I mean any person, place, thing, or event, any
sight, sound, taste, touch, or smell, that causes us to notice the love
which supports all that exists, that undergirds your being and mine and
the being of everything about us" (99). This is why, I believe, a descent
into the valley of darkness is a good way of talking, metaphorically,
about the spiritual journey. It is not that the ultimate Mystery that
grounds existence is not on the mountaintop; Being *is*, everywhere, of
course. The issue, rather, is that a metaphor of a holy mountaintop can
perpetuate the idea that this Mystery, this grace, this self-gift, this illumination comes only in rarefied, pure-seeming places like
mountaintops; hence, the illuminating-mountaintop metaphor can actually misrepresent the spiritual journey that I am trying to talk about in
these pages. *Seeing what is there* means *attending to*, being *mindful of* (in a
way that Buddhist nun Pema Chödrön would smile about), all the dark,
juicy, neurotic, wonderful mess of the valley of human cares and
concerns. "The whole Catholic sacramental life," Himes says, "is a
training to be beholders. Catholic liturgy is a lifelong pedagogy to bring
us to see what is there, to behold what is always present, in the convic-
tion that if we truly see and fully appreciate what is there, whether we
use the language or not, we will be encountering grace. We will see the
love which undergirds all that exists" (100).

From Himes' viewpoint, the shadows and the illuminations are *not* separate; they are mixed together. We are back to James Hillman, for whom "any disjunctive move is contra-indicated" (*Healing Fiction* 102). We are back to Pema Chödrön, who says, "It isn't that one is the bad part and one is the good part, but that it's a kind of interesting, smelly, rich, fertile mess of stuff. . . . The basic creative energy of life — life force — bubbles up and courses through all of existence. . . . It involves not just the parts we like, but the whole picture, because it all has a lot to teach us" (*Wisdom of No Escape* 21, 23). Night journeys to a witch festival or to a ritualized orgy, which the characters in "Young Goodman Brown" and *Eyes Wide Shut* respectively embark on, can be "training to be beholders." It is not that there is no such thing as evil, and that all the goings-on in Nathaniel Hawthorne's short story, in Stanley Kubrick's film, and in the other works we will look at are moral and should literally be engaged in. As narratives, however, these journeys to the dark side operate as powerful metaphors that correct a view that only pure, saintly, antiseptic journeys create and deepen the soul. Indeed, Michael Himes goes so far as to claim: "There is nothing that cannot be a sacrament, absolutely nothing — even, as St. Augustine observed, sin. Within the context of repentance, sin can become an occasion when we discover how deeply loved we are. . . . There is nothing that cannot become a sacrament for someone, absolutely nothing" (99).

In the Destructive Element Immerse

Paul Tillich, as we saw, claims that "the so-called 'psychology of depth'" provides useful strategies for traveling to depth, but that its agnostic scientism prevents such a psychological approach from being fully spiritual and religious. I believe that Tillich has a point, and his claim that the fully religious goal of the journey to depth is "the depth of life itself" (63), which he says is what the word "God" refers to, establishes the stakes of this journey as very high. Michael Himes and John S. Dunne, with a more Catholic/sacramental vision of God's (sometimes dark) grandeur, make much the same argument. This is about something bigger than individual therapy: escaping neurosis, defeating depression, feeling better. That is why, in my discussion of literary journeys into illuminating shadows, I find post-Jungian psychologist James Hillman so helpful. His project is psycho-logical not in the individual therapeutic sense but in the root sense of the term: his *logos* is *psyche*, i.e., *soul* (a rich, complex, unscientific, religious word). Hillman's goal is not feeling better, defeating depression and other unpleasant head-problems, but rather (using John Keats' lovely term) "soul-making." Though Hillman would perhaps disagree in some important ways with the Christian theologians I have been invoking, I believe that "soul-making" names as a process what Tillich names as object: "the depth of life itself," which is God. Both are ways of describing the spiritual journey in more than therapeutic terms, as a trafficking with ultimate reality.

And this may help explain a Hillman concept that I consider key to this study, a strong claim about what will and will not happen in a spiritual journey to illuminating darkness: *"The true revolution,"* Hillman says, *"begins in the individual who can be true to his or her depression"* (*Re-Visioning* 98, Hillman's emphasis). Be *true* to depression? Yes, exactly — so fully does Hillman reject a feel-good model of therapeutic self-help that he calls not for jumping out of depression but for authentically attending to it as a dimension of soul-making.

Hillman claims that his "true revolution" is a rejection of the "Christian myth," but I believe that what he is primarily rejecting is a *secularized* use of the Christian story as a kind of psychological Band-Aid: "Because Christ resurrects," he says, we have mistakenly come to think that "moments of despair, darkening, and desertion cannot be valid in themselves. Our one model insists on light at the end of the tunnel" (*Re-Visioning* 98). So therapy, Hillman claims, imitates (secularizes and literalizes, I would add) this program "in ways ranging from hopeful positive counseling to electroshock" (*Re-Visioning* 98), and the "individual's consciousness" does the same: "Our stance toward depression is a priori a manic defense against it. . . . More personal energy is expended in manic defenses against, diversions from, and denials of it than goes into other supposed psychopathological threats to society: psychopathic criminality, schizoid breakdown, addictions" (*Re-Visioning* 98). In place of these "manic defenses" — leading to "cycles of hoping against despair, each productive of the other" (*Re-Visioning* 98) — Hillman prefers exactly the kind of spiritual journey *into* illuminating darkness that I am examining in these pages, and for just the same reason. Depression, he says, can be a way into depth, the way *of* soul-making, a process-focused manner of describing what Tillich sees as a way *to* the depth of life itself. Clearly, "depression" here means more than a specific personal, psychological problem; Hillman is using the term and concept and painfully familiar experience of depression as a kind of metaphor, pointing toward the spiritual journeys our literary texts will undertake. Through depression, Hillman says,

> we enter depths and in depths find soul. Depression is essential to the tragic sense of life. It moistens the dry soul, and dries the wet. It brings refuge, limitation, focus, gravity, weight, and humble powerlessness. It

reminds of death. . . . Neither jerking oneself out of it, caught in cycles of hope and despair, nor suffering it through till it turns, nor theologizing it — but discovering the consciousness and depths it wants. So begins the revolution in behalf of soul. (*Re-Visioning* 98–99)

Relatedly, Hillman rehabilitates Death as another metaphor for the descent to the underworld, that journey we have to make in order to be in touch with and even make soul: "it is in the face of death that we ponder and go deep and sense soul, and then build our fantasies for housing it" (*Dream* 70). Just as I said that depression for Hillman is a resonant metaphor rather than only a literal pathology, so with death. It is difficult for us to understand that death "could be metaphorical"; the ego — "the great literalist, positivist, realist" — resists metaphors, and as a result we "easily lose touch with the subtle kinds of death" (*Dream* 64). But the spiritual journeys we are talking about here, which are descents into a darkly illuminating underworld, are a death: the death of "our daylight notions": "*Death* is the most profoundly radical way of expressing this shift in consciousness," Hillman asserts (*Dream* 66).

But maintaining a perspective that values the metaphors of depression and death is difficult, Hillman says, and it is hard for us to see the value of what I am calling the dark-side journey, the journey to "death." Our "sunny viewpoint," however, has a price, Hillman claims:

death and the fear of it become the fount of psychology's negative predications: 'evil,' 'shadow,' 'unconscious,' 'psychopathic,' 'regressive,' 'stuck,' 'destructive,' 'cut off,' 'unrelated,' 'cold,' as well as the familiar minus sign pasted onto one side of each complex — do these words and signs not mean "tinged with death," as enemies of life and love? (*Dream* 66)

Hillman's vision of "depth psychology" — a sort, as I have said, that has a religious orientation toward Tillich's "depth of life itself," *ultimate depth* — is that it has "brought Death back from its exile . . . — back to its main place in the midst of the psychological life of each individual, which opens into depth at every step" (*Dream* 67). This is a death that does not wait until the end of bodily life, a depression that is not clinically diagnosable and treatable: "There is an opening downward within each moment, an unconscious reverberation, like the thin thread of the dream that we awaken with in our hands each morning leading back and down into the images of the dark" (*Dream* 67). The "concern with depth," Hillman says, "leads us in practice to pay attention to *whatever is below*" (*Dream* 139, Hillman's emphasis).

Hillman weaves another metaphor for this deep, deathlike, depressive soul-making venture; he draws it from alchemy, the medieval activity that so interests Jungians. For our study of literary depictions of the spiritual journey, this is perhaps the most fruitful of his metaphors. The metaphor is simply the color *blue*, the transitional color in the transformation of lead (black) to silver (white):

> The blue transit between black and white is like that sadness which emerges from despair as it proceeds toward reflection. Reflection here comes from or takes one into a blue distance. . . . This vertical withdrawal is also like an emptying out, the creation of a negative capability, or a profound listening — already an intimation of silver. ("Alchemical Blue" 154)

The in-between color blue, not absolute black, is the color of the dark journey, of depression: "As even the darkest blue is not black, so even the deepest depression is not the *mortificatio* which means death of soul" ("Alchemical Blue" 154). This terrible "death of *soul*," by the way, is not the metaphorical death of ego — of the rapacious "me" — that Hillman, as we just saw, uses as a positive metaphor for soul-*making*; that positive death of ego would, I take it, be a *blue*-blackness, marked by reflection, "the blues," rather than by utterly opaque oblivion. The blues, unlike the death of soul, entail the reflective pulling back ("vertical withdrawal") and the openness to ambiguity ("negative capability") of sad (depressed) wisdom.

But "sadness is not the whole of it," says Hillman. Blue includes "turbulent dissolution," which a narrow daylight moralism would proscribe with Blue Laws: "blue movies, blue language, *l'amour bleu*, bluebeard, blue murder. . . . When these sorts of pornographic, perverse, ghastly, or vicious animus/anima fantasies start up" — as they do in "Young Goodman Brown" and especially in *Eyes Wide Shut*, as we will see — "we can place them within the blue transition" ("Alchemical Blue" 154).

Blue holds the seeming opposites together, makes them soul-filled, shaded differentiations: there are "bits of silver in the violence," on the one hand, but on the other, "Blue protects white from innocence" ("Alchemical Blue" 154). Even the "dark blue of the Madonna's robe bears many shadows, and these give her depths of understanding, just as the mind made on the moon has lived with Lilith so that its thought can never be naive, never cease to strike deep toward shadows" ("Alchemical Blue" 154). Blue, in other words, is the color of hermaphroditism, bridging white (pure spirit) and black (pure inert matter), bridging races and traditions ("Among African peoples . . . black includes blue: whereas in the Jewish-Christian tradition blue belongs rather to white" ["Alchemical Blue" 154]). The movement into blue is a movement into reflective feeling:

> Blue misery. So, with the appearance of blue, feeling becomes more paramount and the paramount feeling is the mournful plaint (Rimbaud equates blue with vowel O; Kandinsky with the sounds of flute, cello, double bass and organ). These laments hint of soul, of reflecting and distancing by imaginational expression. Here we can see more why archetypal psychology has stressed depression as the via regia in soul-making. ("Alchemical Blue" 155)

The "sense of soul," Hillman says, "appears first in the blued imagination of depression" ("Alchemical Blue" 155).

In teaching about the spiritual journey in literature, I have found that *blue* is an enormously helpful image for students. And, precisely to exercise their capacities for metaphor rather than literalism, I use musical, not visual, examples of blue to demonstrate Hillman's point. First I play nearly "black" music (*absolute* black, unreflective opacity would be musically unattainable), a piece of radical underground experimentation, a barrage of low-pitched electronic noise. Then I play nearly "white" music: Julie Andrews singing "My Favorite Things" in *The Sound of Music* (the single "blue" moment — "When the dog bites, / When the bee stings / When I'm feeling sad" — is very quickly whitened: "I simply remember my favorite things"). Finally, I play Billie Holiday singing "Lady Sings the Blues." And the students easily sense the in-between space that Holiday inhabits, the depressed-reflective-wise-soulful *blue* space.

Students also then grasp the idea that is perhaps the main point of these introductory pages: that this blue space, the space into which the darkly illuminating spiritual journey travels, the space of "death" and "depression," is not evil or sick. "My Favorite Things" is, on its own terms, quite wonderful, but no one would complain that Billie Holiday would be better if only she sang exactly like Julie Andrews. Holiday's *blue* is a gift, a blessing, as the spiritual journey into blue is.

"Blue" is the space of deep wisdom, John Dunne's *valley* and even, in a sense, Paul Tillich's *depth*. It is the space that the wise mentor Stein recommends to Joseph Conrad's would-be hero Jim in the novel *Lord Jim*, Conrad's reflection on and subversion of the myth of heroism. Jim, in this novel, wants to be perfect, but he fails badly, commits a moral atrocity, and is crushed by guilt. And he finds some serenity only after visiting Stein, who tells him not to try harder, not to attempt to master his weakness and climb out of the valley of human imperfections.

Rather, Stein tells Jim to go down — into the dark, into the mess, into blue. "A man that is born," Stein says, "falls into a dream like a man who falls into the sea. If he tries to climb out into the air as inexperienced people endeavour to do, he drowns — *nicht wahr?* . . . No! I tell you! The way is to the destructive element submit yourself, and with the exertions of your hands and feet in the water make the deep, deep sea keep you up. . . . In the destructive element immerse" (154).

The resonance between Joseph Conrad's Stein's prescriptions for spiritual wholeness and Hillman's is, I believe, fairly obvious. Both are urging a journey down into a kind of dark Hades rather than up to perfect light. "In the destructive element immerse," says Stein; "this formative imaginative work is always at the same time deformative, destructive," says Hillman (*Dream* 140), and Hillman also claims, almost directly echoing Stein, that "Depression is worst when we try to climb out of it, get on top of it" (*Inter Views* 20). But like a good bridging metaphor — like *blue* — Stein's mandate also links up nicely with the prescriptions of Christian writers Tillich and Dunne, who speak of the journey to depth and of the spiritual trek down into the valley of the cares and concerns of human life.

And, finally, Conrad's Stein brings us back to the Buddhist teachings of Pema Chödrön. Just as Stein's point is that Jim's desire to "climb out into the air," to be perfect and angelic, is futile and debilitating, so Chödrön urges us to descend into the "juicy" mess of our own dark sides; more gently than Hillman and Conrad, Chödrön too suggests that the spiritual journey goes downward into (in Hillman's words) "*whatever is below*":

> This is not an improvement plan; it is not a situation in which you try to be better than you are now. . . . [O]ur hangups, unfortunately or fortunately, contain our wealth. Our neurosis and our wisdom are made of the same material. If you throw out your neurosis, you also throw out your wisdom. Someone who is very angry also has a lot of energy; that energy is what's so juicy about him or her. That's the reason people love that person. The idea isn't to try to get rid of your anger, but to make friends with it, to see it clearly with precision and honesty, and also to see it with gentleness. . . . So whether it's anger or craving or jealousy or fear or depression — whatever it might be — the notion is not to try to get rid of it, but to make friends with it. That means getting to know it completely, with some kind of softness, and learning how, once you've experienced it fully, to let go. (*No Escape* 14–15)

Journeys to the Dark Side

Stanley Kubrick almost broke up my relationship with my wife. For years I had told her how great Kubrick's film *A Clockwork Orange* is, but then, when we finally saw it together, she was appalled — at the movie, at Kubrick, and especially at me for liking it. So it was with some trepidation that I went with her, many years later, to see Kubrick's final film, *Eyes Wide Shut*. Was Kubrick going to put me in the doghouse again?

Fortunately not. During the infamous ritual-orgy scene, my wife, like me a teacher of literature, turned to me and whispered, "This is 'Young Goodman Brown'!" My first thought was relief; she *liked* this Kubrick film, edgy as it was. But my second thought was that she was really onto something. Though its explicit source is a 1926 German novella by Arthur Schnitzler, *Eyes Wide Shut* is a nearly exact re-imagining of Nathaniel Hawthorne's short story "Young Goodman Brown," down to the dark religious rituals at the works' centers. The two works have opened each other up for me in enlightening ways, and have helped me describe a significant sub-genre that I call the "dark-side narrative," stories of the illuminating descent to the shadows that I am describing in these pages. In both "Young Goodman Brown" and *Eyes Wide Shut*, a protagonist initially leads a shiny, naive existence at the surface of life. But the surface cracks. The characters fall through, cross the threshold from their surface world of ego and travel down into the underworld of the larger, and morally ambiguous, soul. Each has an encounter with his own shadowy potential that leads him to an expanded view of reality, an experience of the divine not as transcendent and kingly and unambiguously good but rather, in Paul Tillich's terms, as *depth*.

"Young Goodman Brown" begins with the daylight already fading and its protagonist already crossing his literal threshold, already slipping beneath his safe surface: "Young Goodman Brown," the story begins, "came forth, at sunset, into the street at Salem village, but put his head back, after crossing the threshold, to exchange a parting kiss with his young wife."* But Hawthorne supplies details to suggest that these newlyweds have been living at an unexamined surface level, in the Christian daylight of 17th-century Salem, unaware of the implications of their town's nightmarish, witch-hunting underside. Brown wears his society's title for "Mister" — "Good-man" — with an apparent lack of

* Hawthorne's "Young Goodman Brown" is frequently anthologized, and each edition is differently paginated; thus, I have not indicated page numbers in my text.

irony, and his wife, we are told, is "aptly named" Faith. As Goodman Brown leaves home at the story's start, Faith thrusts "her pretty head into the street, letting the wind play with the pink ribbons in her cap"; clearly the narrator is insisting on, even perhaps gently laughing at, the purity of this young woman and of the household that Goodman Brown is leaving.

But leave he does; the action of Hawthorne's story is Goodman Brown's trek into the wild, dark forest to witness a witchcraft ritual, and perhaps to become a Satanist himself. The sunny purity of the pink-ribbon-bedecked Brown world is dimmed over the course of the tale — indeed, is exposed as always having been sunny only on its shallow surface.

Who or what, however, is exposed here? Some critics have argued about whether in "Young Goodman Brown" it is humanity in general or Goodman Brown in particular who is exposed as deeply corrupt beneath an innocent surface. Answering such traditionalists as Q. D. Leavis and Harry Levin, who assert that Hawthorne is exposing humanity's general depravity, such critics as Paul J. Hurley opine instead that the story is about Goodman Brown's own very particular perversity and not about humanity as a whole. The story, Hurley says, reveals "a distorted mind"; it is "a revelation of [Goodman Brown's own] individual perversion" (411). The story's ambiguity (is it a dream? do the events truly occur or does Goodman Brown merely imagine them?), which I consider constitutive of the story and therefore irreducible and undecidable, is to Hurley only apparent. Hurley confidently describes Goodman Brown's night adventure as a hallucination — "an ego-induced fantasy, the self-justification of a diseased mind" (419).

With a bit more subtlety, I think, Michael Tritt similarly assumes that the night adventure is Goodman Brown's fantasy, but he uses the language of Freudian *projection* to talk about this hallucinated experience as Goodman Brown's neurotic defense against his own guilt: "Brown's compulsive condemnation of others, along with his consistent denial of his own culpability, illustrates a classically defined case of projection. . . . First, Brown locates his own evil in others. Second, . . . Brown believes himself to be without guilt," though in fact his guilt remains active in his subconscious (116).

Hurley's and Tritt's respective psychologizings of Goodman Brown's dark adventure both have the value of focusing on Brown's inner experience. But they fail, I believe, to see that the dark experience has a kind of heuristic value — that it *illuminates*, and not just in relation to Brown's own private perversions. There *is* a Big Picture that Goodman Brown is encountering; the more traditional critics' emphasis on the story's revelations about "humanity in general" is not unfounded. My approach, I believe, differs from Hurley's and Tritt's because it is founded not on Freudian depth *psychology* but on a depth *spirituality*, for which I am indebted to the likes of Tillich and Hillman. For Hillman a conventional idea of psychological projection, an imposition on others of one's own private flaws, is founded on a reductive world view, "based on a system of private experiencing subjects and dead public objects" rather than on a concept of "nothing less than the world ensouled" ("Anima Mundi" 77); in other words a visionary experience, according to Hillman, may be a glimpse of something deeply real rather than just a picture show manufactured by the private subconscious. Hence, what looks like a "projection" of merely personal contents, a picture projected onto an opaque screen, can actually be a window into insight. Similarly, an encounter with a reflection (a projection) of the Jungian "shadow," that part of the self that the ego finds repulsive, can be more than just an encounter with personal twistedness; as we will discuss much more fully in the next chapter, the emergence of the shadow fuels a journey to Self — to deep, even ultimate, reality.

Those critics who see Hawthorne's story as an exposure of Goodman Brown's private depravity point out that from the very start Brown is conscious of where he is going and of what is going to happen there, what "work is to be done": "Methought as she spoke," Goodman Brown thinks after leaving his wife, "there was trouble in her face, as if a dream had warned her what work is to be done to-night." So Faith may be naive, trapped in simple surfaces, but Goodman Brown, it appears, is not; he is depraved from the start. But such a reading ironically gives Goodman Brown too much credit. Brown begins the story almost as ignorant, as surface-entrapped, as his wife. Even though his conscious goal tonight is to visit the dark side — to attend this ritual in the wild forest outside the apparently safe and civil village of Salem — he is initially naive about this, deceived by surface appearances. "My father never went into the woods on such an errand, nor his father before him," he tells the devilish "fellow-traveller" he encounters on the road. "We have been a race of honest men and good Christians since the days of the martyrs; and shall I be the first of the name of Brown that ever took this path . . ."

But the traveller sneers at Goodman Brown's naivete and informs him that he has hobnobbed with Brown family members for generations. This devilish figure is an overt embodiment of that Jungian "shadow" which I just mentioned, an image in the outer world of repugnant aspects of the ego that the ego hides from itself. However, Goodman Brown has barely seen this dark side in himself ("shall I be the first of the name of Brown that ever took this path") and has definitely not seen it in the other Salem Puritans; until he meets this demonic fellow in the forest, who may or may not be a hallucinatory invention, Brown has not yet begun the activity of Freudian *projecting* that Michael Tritt attributes to him. It has never occurred to Brown that his Christian family's intolerance and persecution of others was a service to Satan rather than to God. He has not seen the narrowness — the rigid surface — of his Christian community.

He is about to see it, however. Despite some qualms, Goodman Brown takes the plunge; the surface of his simplistic world cracks open, and he steps in. He walks on into the forest, seeing his catechism teacher, his deacon, and his minister all going on the same night journey, until he gets to a clearing and sees "A grave and dark-clad company": all the "good" people of his town side by side with the criminal and "dissolute," singing hymns and ritualistically celebrating a spiritual reality rather different from that which they think they worship back in Salem. "Depending upon one another's hearts," intones the presider, "ye had still hoped that virtue were not all a dream. Now are ye undeceived. Evil is the nature of mankind. Evil must be your only happiness. Welcome, again, my children, to the communion of your race." When Goodman Brown sees that even his wife is here, he cries, "My Faith is gone!" The surface has shattered.

I have used this story in many literature classes, and students have frequently been perplexed. In order to suggest the nightmarish quality of the experience — indeed, eventually Goodman Brown is not sure whether he has "only dreamed a wild dream of a witch-meeting" — Hawthorne narrates the story in general and the ritual scene in particular in a rather vague, misty way, with the details lost in chiaroscuro, and students often have no clear idea what is going on in that forest. But when I show the film *Eyes Wide Shut* right afterward, telling students to watch for a parallel narrative structure, they suddenly grasp what kind of scene Goodman Brown has come upon. At the center of his own night journey, Dr. Bill Harford, the character played by Tom Cruise in Kubrick's film, makes his way to a ritualized heart of darkness. Using the password "Fidelio" — *Faith*, Goodman Brown's wife's name, which Goodman Brown screams out at the witch-meeting — Bill Harford gains entrance into a ceremony very similar to the one attended by young Goodman Brown. The event in Kubrick's film is specifically a sexual orgy, but the ritualistic accoutrements of the scene indicate that sex is merely the vehicle — probably due to the Freudian era of the film's literary source, which presents sex as *the* dark-side experience par excellence. Hawthorne's worshipers sing a hymn, "a slow and mournful strain, such as the pious love, but joined to words which expressed all that our nature can conceive of sin, and darkly hinted at something more," and the ambience of Kubrick's scene is similar: the incense, the vestments, the chanting all suggest something more mystical than sexual. The lure of shadowy depth has pulled Bill Harford into an underworld far beneath the cracked surface he used to inhabit.

Bill has begun in an ego world of surfaces that is established even more insistently than in Hawthorne's story, and much more insistently than in the Schnitzler novella. Kubrick uses the attractiveness of his actors, Tom Cruise and Nicole Kidman, exploiting their clean-scrubbed, glamorous surface images. The movie notoriously begins with Kidman dropping her dress, becoming nude, but this is not an erotic moment but rather a purely pragmatic one: her character, Alice Harford, is getting dressed for a party. "How do I look?" she asks Bill. "Perfect," he answers, checking his own appearance in the mirror and not looking at Alice at all. "Is my hair OK?" Alice asks. "Great," Bill says distractedly.

The party they attend at the New York mansion of the filthy-rich and shady Victor Ziegler, played by Sydney Pollack, is similarly all pretty surfaces. Alice flirts with a suave Hungarian and two attractive but seemingly mindless young women flirt with Bill, but nothing comes of either of these flirtations; they are mere surfaces. Even Bill's profession as a physician is revealed as keeping him at the surface of things. Ziegler calls Bill upstairs to attend to a beautiful, naked woman who has overdosed on drugs, and Bill's examination of her body — like his medical examinations of other women later in the film — is detached and clinical. This is entirely appropriate, of course, but that is the point: like Goodman Brown, Bill Harford is a man who, prior to his dark-side journey, behaves appropriately, unthinkingly, at the surface. In a film in which the cracking of the surface and the ensuing night journey will be effected by the eruption of the erotic, Bill is initially established as lacking any kind of dark eros.

Two characters begin to make the sleek image crack. First, at the Ziegler party, Bill encounters an old medical-school friend named Nick Nightingale, a typical Jungian "shadow" figure. Apparently this Nightingale and Bill were once birds of a feather, but Nick has left the "doctor business," as he calls it, and has become something more, well, Dionysian: a pianist, who performs at clubs like the Sonata Café in the Village, where he invites Bill to come see him play. The invitation will ultimately lead Bill to the "Fidelio" orgy, where Nick is the hired musician.

The second shatterer of Bill's surface is Alice herself. The night after the party, Alice — high on marijuana — tears into Bill, asking him if he had sex with the two young women at the party and taunting him with her flirtation with the Hungarian. Bill's responses are typically conventional and clichéd, at the surface of things. "We both know what men are like," Bill says of the Hungarian and his motives; but he says that he himself is an "exception" because, as he puts it, "I happen to be in love with you and because we're married"; he has no erotic feelings for beautiful female patients because, he says, "It's all very impersonal and you know there is always a nurse present"; and his female patients certainly don't think about sex because, well, "women don't . . . they basically don't think like that." That does it. Alice, angry at his naive stereotyping (and stoned), decides to blast away Good-man Bill's shiny, comfortable surface. She emotionally stabs him by telling him about a young naval officer she once had an intense sexual fantasy about, and Bill — as stunned and shaken as Goodman Brown when he discovers his wife, Faith, at the witch-meeting — goes out into the street, into the night, into the dark-side adventure at the heart of which will be hooded worshipers, incense, otherworldly music, and the word "Fidelio."

So what is the result of this cracked surface? For Jungians, as we will see in the next chapter, the encounter with the repressed shadow can be the first step toward an expansion of the personality beyond ego to a relationship with the Self, the wise voice of the soul. And throughout this chapter I have talked of the way illumination occurs not from a climb out of the dark but from a descent into it. I believe that "Young Goodman Brown" and *Eyes Wide Shut* powerfully embody Paul Tillich's notion of *depth*, even including the truly religious dimensions of this expansion downward into soul-filled darkness. These works also illustrate Michael Himes' notion of sacrament as a special image or experience reminding us of grace — not on an ethereal mountaintop but in John S. Dunne's valley, quite unsavory in these cases, of human care and concern.

"Most of our life continues on the surface," Tillich says, as I have already quoted (55). (He could be talking about Goodman Brown or Bill Harford — or, perhaps, most of us.) "We talk and talk and never listen to the voices speaking to our depth and from our depth. We accept ourselves as we appear to ourselves, and do not care what we really are" (56). Tillich claims that, living at the surface of our lives, we "miss . . . our depth and our true life." It is only, he says, when the surface cracks — "when the picture that we have of ourselves breaks down completely, . . . when we find ourselves acting against all the expectations we had derived from that picture, and . . . when an earthquake shakes and disrupts the surface of our self-knowledge" — that we "are willing to look into a deeper level of our being" (56). The relevance of this analysis to "Young Goodman Brown" and *Eyes Wide Shut* should be obvious. Goodman Brown and Bill Harford find themselves acting against all their expectations about themselves; earthquakes shake and disrupt their easy surfaces. But Tillich, as we saw, goes on to make a strong claim about the value of such an experience. For Tillich, the depth experience is a window into "the deepest ground of our being and of all being, the depth of life itself" (57). Indeed, he says that "The name of this infinite and inexhaustible depth and ground of all being is *God*. That depth is what the word *God* means" (57).

It may seem a strange claim to suggest that a "witch-meeting" and a ritual orgy are avenues to God. But as we have seen, Tillich takes up exactly this issue. "The depth in religious language," he says, "is often used to express the dwelling place of the evil forces, of the daemonic powers, of death and hell" (60). Tillich is invoking here the very tradition I am discussing in these pages, the journey of and to soul inevitably experienced as a journey to Hades. This is the "old and beautiful myth" that we earlier saw Tillich refer to: the myth of the soul passing over "many spheres where daemonic forces rule." And, he says, "only the soul that knows the right and powerful word" — *Fidelio*? — "can continue its way to the ultimate depth of the Divine Ground" (61). In a sense, this is the "myth" governing my entire exploration of the shadowy spiritual journey; perhaps "finding the right and powerful word" is a metaphor for the sacramental perspective that finds illuminations in the shadows, the depth of the valley of human care and concern as "the ultimate depth of the Divine Ground."

So Goodman Brown's and Bill Harford's flirtations with the "daemonic" would, for Tillich, have a genuine and potentially positive religious dimension. And it is important to note, in response to those critics who consider Goodman Brown (and, by implication, Bill Harford) personally immoral and perverse, that the narratives stress the characters' *visions* of evil rather than their actual *behavior*. They do indeed pass over "spheres where the daemonic forces rule," but their disturbing adventures are more about seeing than doing. The insistence in each work that the experience is *like* a dream, may even *be* a dream, as well as the fact that these protagonists are more observers than actors (though each finds himself in an extremely compromised situation, neither Goodman Brown nor Bill Harford ever quite commits a morally heinous act), makes it plausible to describe the night journeys as valuable, expansive encounters with depth, descents toward wild but vital soul or Self or divine ground.

But it is up to the characters to integrate the experiences into their lives, to find "the right and powerful word" that changes daemonic depth to ultimate depth, and this Bill Harford does but Goodman Brown seems not to do. His surface Christianity shattered, Goodman Brown spends the rest of his life in bitterness and cynicism. "And when he had lived long," Hawthorne tells us, "and was borne to his grave a hoary corpse, followed by Faith, an aged woman, and children and grandchildren, a goodly procession, besides neighbors, not a few, they carved no hopeful verse upon his tombstone, for his dying hour was gloom." But at the end of *Eyes Wide Shut* Bill and Alice Harford renew, however shakily, their marriage at a deeper level; they are no longer the merely glamorous Beautiful People they were at the film's start. Alice, it turns out, has had a harrowing, jarring dream of an orgy exactly like the one Bill attended, and Bill then tearfully confesses to Alice how he spent the night. And then, in a toy store with their daughter, surrounded by gaudy and glittery commercialism (the world of *surfaces*), they tentatively articulate the troubling but important depth that Bill's journey has brought them to. "Maybe, I think," Alice says, "we should be grateful — grateful that we've managed to survive through all of our adventures, whether they were real or only a dream." "Are you — are you sure of that?" Bill asks. "Am — am I sure?" Alice says, and then she stumblingly states an important understanding of depth as always receding, never coalescing into a frozen surface: "Umm — only — ," she murmurs, "only as sure as I am that the reality of one night, let alone that of a whole lifetime, can never be the whole truth." "And no dream is just a dream," Bill adds. "The important thing," Alice says, "is that we're awake now and hopefully for a long time to come." She hesitates to say that they are now awake "forever" because, I think, that would entrap them in another overly confident surface. This final conversation is nervous and uncertain, but it is groping and searching and deep in ways that Bill and Alice's conversations have not previously been. And even the movie's final shock word — Alice ends by saying that as soon as possible she and Bill need to "Fuck" — has a resonance it does not often have in a movie.

So we are left with something mysterious and disturbing. Goodman Brown and Bill Harford undergo similar experiences, versions of the prototypical experience of Dante, who opens his poem not with his own private midlife crisis but with that of all of us: "Midway on our life's journey," Dante says — *our* life's journey, not just his own — "I found myself / In dark woods, the right road lost." Brown and Bill both, like Dante, descend to an Inferno; in Tillich's words, their souls "pass over many spheres where daemonic forces rule." Yet one returns from the journey deepened, perhaps even enriched by "the ultimate depth of the Divine Ground," while the other returns bitter and desolate, and we are told that even "his dying hour was gloom." What is the key, the "right and powerful word," that seems to lead Bill Harford to one kind of destination and Goodman Brown to another? I will end this chapter, this initial look at the dark-side journey, by arguing that the difference between them is *everything* and *nothing*.

The Difference an Ending Makes

First, everything. In one sense there is all the difference in the world between the conclusions of the two stories, Goodman Brown's and Bill Harford's. And the difference, I would suggest, is related to whether or not the character is able to relinquish *certainty*. The "right and powerful word" may turn out, ironically, to be a humble silence in the face of mystery.

Michael Himes begins his fine discussion of the sacramental imagination with what may appear to be a digression: a discussion of the meaning of the word "God." But this is no digression at all. For Himes, as we saw, sacramentality is built on a vision of metaphor; "God" is a word pointing toward ultimate mystery, something about which we know, in the final analysis, nothing. Invoking Ludwig Wittgenstein, Himes says that one wise attitude before such radically impenetrable mystery is silence. "'Of that about which we can say nothing, let us be silent,'" Himes quotes Wittgenstein as saying, from which Himes infers, "If God is Mystery, then let us not natter on about God like we know what we're talking about" (92). However, Himes also invokes T. S. Eliot, who said with passion equal to Wittgenstein's "that there are some things about which we can say nothing and before which we dare not keep silent" (93). As we have seen, Himes says that in the face of divine mystery, about which we can say nothing definitive but before which we cannot be silent, we must "do what the great users of language — poets — do when trying to say the unsayable: we pile up metaphors" (94). The deepest Christian insight, "God is love," on which Himes builds his entire vision of earthly and earthy sacramental reminders of God's graciousness, is a metaphor, not an absolute statement of fact. The first virtue, it appears, necessary for our "training to be beholders" of the grace-filled creation, is humility, an acknowledgement that in some fundamental way we do not know what we are talking about.

Paul Tillich calls for a similar kind of humble openness and lack of certitude in his own definition of "God." Indeed, in one sense Tillich's "depth" is reached when a surface-level view of God — as what Himes calls "a great big person out there, somewhere, older, wiser, stronger, than you and I" (94) — cracks open and we see that "God" is not a Zeus-like person but rather, Tillich says, "the deepest ground of our being, the depth of life itself. . . . That depth is what the word *God* means" (63). And this, I believe, is what John S. Dunne means when he says, in his metaphorical parable, that God has left the sunny mountaintop, "his desire being to plunge himself into the very things that man wishes to escape" (14).

Furthermore, Dunne specifically describes *darkness* as humanity's necessary and valuable lack of certitude, our not-knowing. Dunne asserts that he sees not only the light but also

> the darkness in which I live, which conceals my fate from me, as a gift. I could communicate both gifts to others too, the insight that lights the way and the sense of adventure which goes with the darkness and the lack of foreknowledge. Both of these, the light and the darkness, are essential to the journey. Without the light a man would lose his way; without the darkness, if he already knew his fate, there would be no adventure. (210)

For Dunne, this darkness of not-knowing is a version of James Hillman's metaphorical death, not a cessation of biological life but an always-already reality that needs to be accepted, even embraced; it is a darkness that is a part of "God." Dunne has proposed that "everything which belongs to an individual's life shall enter into it," and that includes the dark side. As Pema Chödrön says, a human life is not divided into good parts and bad parts, but all is "a kind of interesting, smelly, rich, fertile mess of stuff" (*No Escape* 21), and everything that occurs in our lives "is not only usable and workable but is actually the path itself" (*When Things Fall Apart* 123). And this insight, says Dunne,

> speaks of the triumph of God's dark purpose. This triumph comes about again and again in the course of a man's lifetime. Each transition from one stage of life to another involves the defeat of a certain kind of human consciousness and of the purposes which were based upon it. The immediate awareness of the child proves inadequate to the demands of youth, the existential awareness of the youth inadequate to the demands of manhood, and the historic awareness of the man inadequate to the demands of further growth. The dark purpose which is triumphing is one which seems to have man's being as its aim. It is a purpose which is dark but creative. (215–216)

In these terms, it seems to me clear that Goodman Brown and Bill Harford differ significantly at the end of their respective works: Goodman Brown has not truly opened himself up to "darkness," while Bill Harford, in relinquishing certainty, has.

In an essay spinning a thesis about dark-side narratives that is similar to my own, John S. Hardt suggests that these journeys are encounters with "doubts and uncertainties" and that the protagonists return home "with reduced confidence in what [they] can know about [their] world." They move, Hardt says, "from a false confidence in their knowledge to a realization that full knowledge is in fact not possible" (249). Although the examples Hardt uses, including "Young Goodman Brown," are all journeys into "rural settings" with "paradisal associations," I believe that Hardt's analysis is equally relevant to the urban *Eyes Wide Shut* — and it resonates remarkably well with John S. Dunne's discussion of the dark dimension of a life journey as "the defeat of a certain kind of human consciousness and of the purposes which were based upon it." Analyzing "Young Goodman Brown," Hardt says that Goodman Brown begins the story with a "misplaced trust in appearances" (253) and that his forest experience breaks this trust down. Brown encounters the ambiguity beneath smooth surfaces, the depth that Tillich speaks of. And Hardt points out, as I have, that this truth beneath the appearances is not the same as a revelation of outright immoral activity. As I have noted, Brown, like Bill Harford, does not actually commit any heinous acts, and even the townspeople in his dream/vision/experience do not actually *do* anything terrible either; they simply stand together and sing some disturbing songs. "His forest experience," Hardt says, "has caused Brown to perceive discrepancies between appearances and reality, between reputation and performance, between form and meaning, between action and intention" (254).

What Brown fails to do — in James Hillman's terms — is to digest the experience, to turn it into soul, into depth (into God?). "We can use everything that happens to us," Pema Chödrön says, "as a means for waking up" (*When Things Fall Apart* 123), but this is just what Goodman Brown does not do with his troubling forest experience; he stubbornly keeps his eyes closed to anything that will shake his cut-and-dried absolutes. Brown is not able to sort out the discrepancies he encounters in the forest, says Hardt, *"because of his simplistic faith in absolutes"* (254, emphasis added). This is Hardt's key insight. Brown, I believe, is crushed not by the dark-side experience itself, but by his failure to digest it. His initial superficiality, his dwelling at the surface, is precisely due to the "black-white distinctions" — the "simplistic faith in absolutes" — that Hardt says are at the core of "Brown's (and the Puritans') outlook" (254).

His "night in the forest," Hardt continues, "has blurred such distinctions for him, leaving him faithless, unknowing in a gray world" (254). But no, that is not quite it; if his distinctions had really "blurred," then perhaps Brown would have eluded his Puritan black-and-white world and achieved depth and soul. So Hardt, immediately and appropriately, backtracks: "Not even partially is Brown able to accept the limitations of his own knowledge," Hardt says (254). This is the problem; it is not that the dark-side journey has damaged Brown's outlook, but that it has failed to do so. Goodman Brown does not budge from his "black-white" outlook. At the end of the story, far from having become humbly uncertain, Brown has replaced naivete (absolutely certain faith) with self-righteousness (absolutely certain condemnation of others). Back from the forest where he saw — or dreamed he saw — the townspeople at the witchcraft ritual, Brown avoids the minister, mentally condemns the deacon, and snatches a child away from the catechism teacher "as from the grasp of the fiend himself." When he attends church on Sunday and sees all the people, minister and congregation alike, with whom he had attended the ritual, Brown turns "pale, dreading lest the roof should thunder down upon the gray blasphemer and his hearers." And he shrinks from his wife; he scowls at her and mutters and gazes "sternly" at her, and then turns away. What is notable about all these reactions is that Brown does not include himself among the sinners whom he condemns; the "blasphemer" and "hearers" upon whom the roof will "thunder down" are the *other* people in church, not Brown. Considering that his forest experience may have been a dream or hallucination, which would mean that *only* Goodman Brown was "there" at the (imagined) ritual, this confident condemnation of everyone else is especially ironic. Despite the limitations of Michael Tritt's discussion of Freudian projection, Tritt analyzes Brown's ultimate self-righteousness very aptly: "Brown consistently focuses his attention outwards," Tritt says. "There is loathing, but it is manifestly not self-loathing. . . . Brown never glimpses his own image as something fearful and iniquitous" (115–116). If a dark-side adventure is an encounter with "doubts and uncertainties," Goodman Brown has somehow missed out; his ego has come out of its ordeal tougher and more certain than ever.

So Brown's ultimate bitterness, I suggest, is not due to his having fallen into a dark pit; the issue is not that a dark-side journey has destroyed him. Rather, the problem seems to be that he has *not* fallen deeply enough, that he has not fully undergone a depth experience. He has, instead, returned to the surface, despite what John S. Dunne might call the "gift" of darkness that he has been offered. Dunne talks of the need for the gift of darkness in terms similar to those with which Tillich talks of the need for depth; Dunne thinks that an encounter with darkness subverts the very limitation that plagues Brown, a certainty about *what humanity is* and *what God is*. The gift of darkness, says Dunne, breaks open this shallow certainty and leads to a wise silence, which I take to be not a literal lack of speech but a relinquishment of mentally noisy certainty:

> Silence goes with the realization that man does not know what man is and what God is. Living in silence like this would be quite different from

living in doubt or in disbelief. Instead of doubt and disbelief there is in this silence a sense of boundless depths. (232)

It is this transformative, boundless, deep "silence" that Brown misses out on.

But in *Eyes Wide Shut* Bill Harford, along with his wife, Alice, achieves exactly such a "silence." They both end up in a nervous, uncertain place that seems to me exactly the place of *depth* and *darkness*, perhaps of Hillman's *blue*. This is the soft, shaky uncertainty that for Pema Chödrön characterizes spiritual awakening: "To stay with that shakiness — to stay with a broken heart, with a rumbling stomach," she says, ". . . that is the path of true awakening. Sticking with that uncertainty, getting the knack of relaxing in the midst of chaos, learning not to panic — this is the spiritual path" (*When Things Fall Apart* 10).

As we have seen, Bill begins Kubrick's film all slick surface (a good-looking society doctor with ridiculously wealthy patients and a movie-star-beautiful wife) and full of clichéd certainties: "We both know what men are like. . . . It's all very impersonal and you know there is always a nurse present. . . . [Women] don't think like that." But the final conversation between Bill and Alice in the toy store, after the dark-side adventure, is a model of *un*certainty; we can almost feel the characters' broken hearts and rumbling stomachs as they haltingly address each other. "Are you — are you sure of that?" "Am — am I sure?" And yet they stick with that uncertainty; they do not run from it; they seem to be "getting the knack of relaxing in the midst of chaos." And they draw some real, if uncertain, insight from their experience. "[T]he reality of one night, let alone that of a while lifetime, can never be the whole truth." "And no dream is just a dream." The hesitations — the stammering — the mixing of dream and reality — the resistance to the word "forever": these are precisely indications that Bill and Alice have received, as Goodman Brown has not, the "gift of darkness," the kind of metaphorical "silence" that "goes with the realization that [a person] does not know what [humanity] is and what God is" (Dunne 232). But the fact that the not-knowing brings the couple together suggests that this is something more, deeper, than despairing agnosticism; this is — perhaps — the stomach-rumbling uncertainty of the spiritual path. "Instead of doubt and despair," says Dunne, "there is in this silence a sense of boundless depths" (232).

And yet . . . I fear that I am myself guilty of excessive certainty by ending this discussion of "Young Goodman Brown" and *Eyes Wide Shut* with such clear-cut dichotomizing: Bill Harford, I have just said, uses his dark-side adventure as he *should*, while Goodman Brown misuses his adventure, fails to digest it, acts in a way he *should not*. And then I find Pema Chödrön saying this: "My experience is that by practicing without 'shoulds,' we gradually discover our wakefulness and our confidence" (*When Things Fall Apart* 140–141). Parker Palmer, a spiritual writer from the Quaker tradition, similarly warns against "shoulds" and "oughts" in the spiritual journey. In a book about a person's "vocation," which he sees as a spiritual journey very much in the terms we have been discussing, Palmer criticizes the "conventional concept of vocation, which insists that our lives must be driven by 'oughts.'" Rather, he says,

> we do not find our callings by conforming ourselves to some abstract moral code. We find our callings by claiming authentic selfhood, by being who we are. . . . The deepest vocational question is not "What ought I to do with my life?" It is the more elemental and demanding "Who am I? What is my nature?" (15)

Palmer relates his image of God to this idea, drawing on the Tillich tradition of seeing "God" as the name of the depth and ground of all *being* — of what *is*, not what *ought* to be:

> The God I was told about in church, and still hear about from time to time, runs about like an anxious schoolmaster measuring people's behavior with a moral yardstick. But the God I know is the source of reality rather than morality, the source of what is rather than what *ought to be*. . . .
> One dwells with God by being faithful to one's nature. One crosses God by trying to be something one is not. Reality — including one's own — is divine, to be not defied but honored. (50–51)

It is not too great a leap from Palmer's assertion to a warning against dictating in advance what the result of a spiritual journey ought to be — in literature no less than in life. Perhaps the sacramental act of *seeing what is there*, of *being a beholder*, or the Buddhist stance of *mindfulness*, includes a kind of generosity even to fictional characters: a willingness to let go of *oughts* even in relation to fiction and to allow Goodman Brown to be Goodman Brown. Perhaps, in a way, Hawthorne has simply brought Brown to the authentic conclusion — however painful — of his own particular dark-side journey, as Kubrick brings Bill Harford to the conclusion of his. Maybe I need to avoid overstating the dichotomy and just settle with this is-ness.

Perhaps most relevant to my argument, the dichotomizing itself (Bill gets it right, Brown gets it wrong) is problematic, in light of my initial caution against dichotomies. Perhaps there is a way that the dissimilarity between the endings of "Young Goodman Brown" and *Eyes Wide Shut* is a matter of "shaded differentiations" rather than of absolute right and wrong; otherwise we are back to sharply opposing a kind of "light" from a kind of "darkness." So we need to experiment with the possibility that the difference the endings make is nothing, not important, that the point of the journey is the journey, not some predetermined positive destination.

"This is not an improvement plan," Pema Chödrön says of the spiritual journey; "it is not a situation in which you try to be better than you are now" (*No Escape* 14). How depressing: is all this trouble for naught? But this is where Chödrön goes on to say that our hangups contain our wealth and that our neuroses and our wisdom are integrally bound together; hence, ferreting out hangups and neuroses is not necessarily desirable. She also points out that seeing the spiritual journey as a self-improvement plan requires that it have a clear, certain goal, when actually, as we have seen, it tends toward the *relinquishment* of certainty. If the goal has to be the emergence of a better, happier, more connected Goodman Brown, this sounds more like a slick technique from an infomercial than like a journey grounded on wise, shadowily illuminated mystery. The spiritual path, Chödrön says, is "uncharted":

> The path is not Route 66 — destination, Los Angeles. It's not as if we can take out a map and figure that this year we might make it to Gallup, New Mexico, and maybe [eventually] we'll be in L.A. The path is uncharted. It comes into existence moment by moment and at the same time drops away behind us. It's like riding in a train sitting backwards. We can't see where we're headed, only where we've been. (*When Things Fall Apart* 143)

Yes, Chödrön's is a Buddhist vision; Christianity is normally seen as a more linear, historical, and hence goal-oriented tradition, so perhaps a Christian spirituality will have a different emphasis. But many Christian writers agree with Chödrön — Parker Palmer, as we have seen, is one. And surely in Catholic theologian John S. Dunne's view, the "boundless depths" offered by God's "gift" of darkness precisely prevent us from prejudging where the journey ought to take us; rather, Dunne's spiritual vision leaves open "the sense of adventure which goes with the darkness and the lack of foreknowledge" (210). For a Christian too, then, it is appropriate to think that the goal is the path itself. Hence it is risky to dichotomize "Young Goodman Brown" and *Eyes Wide Shut* by saying that in one work the protagonist follows the spiritual path incorrectly and in the other he does so correctly.

Perhaps it is better to think of the two works — the two stories, and especially the two endings — as supplementing each other, with all the possible supplements being infinite in number. Each is a metaphor, a narrative, an artifice picturing one particular version of a dark-side journey; these are not prescriptions to be followed literally. So one depiction ends with sadness and grimness — and pain without easy remedy *is* part of the mystery of the dark-side. Another ends with tentative serenity — and some respite from pain is also part of the mystery. But again, the point is the journey itself. The glory of literature is that it allows us to experience vicariously the many dimensions of human possibility; collectively, literary depictions of the journey of and to soul supplement each other, and in doing so they remind us that the ending of the journey is unpredictable. Theologian Paul Tillich himself warns against seeing "depth" as some kind of stable goal that is reached definitively. The seekers of depth, Tillich says,

> have found that they were not what they believed themselves to be, even after a deeper level had appeared to them below the vanishing surface. That deeper level itself became surface, when a still deeper level was discovered, this happening again and again as long as their very lives, as long as they kept on the road to their depth. (63)

Tillich here points out in his own way how the goal is the path itself. As the path opens up, the surface cracks and the person descends to depth, but then that depth can become another surface. This is one way of understanding what happens to Goodman Brown at the end of his story: perhaps, rather than illustrating a failed journey to depth, Brown simply exemplifies the partiality, the incompleteness, of the depth journey — which after all allies him with the ultimately tentative and uncertain Bill Harford. Yes, it is valid to criticize Brown for failing to keep "on the road to [his] depth," for allowing the journey to petrify into grim absolutism and despair. But it is equally important to balance this critique with an appreciation of the way Hawthorne has used Goodman Brown's story, quite non-judgmentally, to illustrate the potentially tragic and mysteriously unpredictable trajectory of a dark-side journey. There is no guarantee that everyone will end up with an unequivocal Dantesque vision of "the Love that moves the Sun and the other stars." If Michael Himes is correct, that Love is always there, since it is nothing less than Being itself, but it may not be apparent or consciously grasped.

Whatever the seeming contradiction, this warning against "oughts" and dichotomies does not cancel out my previous argument that an authentic dark-side journey tends to lead to a relinquishment of certainty, which occurs in *Eyes Wide Shut* but not in "Young Goodman Brown." I am not trying to erase all differences in literary works; on the contrary, I am trying to open up the world of spiritual-journey narratives as one of great and unpredictable variety. We can appreciate the ways these narratives present the opening up of boundless mystery, and at the same time we can accept that in some cases the authentic ending is tragic paralysis (or worse) rather than peaceful reconciliation. And the most deeply affirmative, even sacramental, reading of all this is that either result is, in a deep way, all right, all part of James Hillman's wide spectrum of blue, a mysterious space in which illuminations are shadowy and shadows are illuminating.

Works Cited

Chödrön, Pema. *When Things Fall Apart: Heart Advice for Difficult Times*. 1997. Boston: Shambhala, 2000.

———. *The Wisdom of No Escape and the Path of Loving-Kindness*. 1991. Boston: Shambhala, 2001.

Conrad, Joseph. *Lord Jim*. 1900. New York: Oxford University Press, 2002.

Dante Alighieri. *Inferno*. Trans. Robert Pinsky. New York: Farrar, Straus & Giroux, 1996.

———. *Paradiso*. Trans. John Ciardi. New York: New American Library, 1970.

Dunne, John S. *The Way of All the Earth*. New York: Macmillan, 1972.

Freccero, John. Introduction. *Paradiso*. By Dante Alighieri. Trans. John Ciardi. New York: New American Library, 1970. Ix–xxi.

Hardt, John S. "Doubts in the American Garden: Three Cases of Paradisal Skepticism." *Studies in Short Fiction* 25, no. 3 (Summer 1988): 249–259.

Hillman, James. "Alchemical Blue and the Unio Mentalis." *A Blue Fire: Selected Writings by James Hillman*. Ed. Thomas Moore. New York: HarperCollins, 1989. 154–156.

———. "Anima Mundi: The Return of the Soul to the World." *Spring* (1982): 71–93.

———. *The Dream and the Underworld*. New York: Harper & Row, 1979.

———. *Healing Fiction*. 1983. Woodstock, CT: Spring Publications, 1996.

———. *Inter Views*. 1983. Dallas, TX: Spring Publications, 1992.

———. *Re-Visioning Psychology*. 1976. New York: HarperCollins, 1992.

Himes, Michael J. "'Finding God in All Things': A Sacramental Worldview and Its Effects." *As Leaven in the World: Catholic Perspectives on Faith, Vocation, and the Intellectual Life*. Ed. Thomas M. Landy. Franklin, WI: Sheed & Ward, 2001. 91–103.

Hurley, Paul J. "Young Goodman Brown's 'Heart of Darkness.'" *American Literature* 37, no. 4 (Jan. 1966): 410–419.

Palmer, Parker. *Let Your Life Speak: Listening for the Voice of Vocation*. San Francisco: Jossey-Bass, 2000.

Tillich, Paul. *The Shaking of the Foundations*. 1949. Middlesex, UK: Penguin, 1962.

Tritt, Michael. "'Young Goodman Brown' and the Psychology of Projection." *Studies in Short Fiction* 23, no. 1 (Winter 1986): 113–117.1.

And What Can Be the Use of Him is More Than I Can See

The Shadow

In talking about shadows and illuminations — indeed, shadows *as* illuminations, the visit to the dark side as the necessary journey to spiritual healing — I am at least implicitly invoking a key concept of Carl Jung: *the shadow*, which I briefly talked about in the previous chapter. Jung and his followers write a great deal about the "shadow," for which Jung's colleague Marie-Louise von Franz provides a straightforward, traditional Jungian definition; the shadow, says von Franz, is made up of "aspects of one's own personality that for various reasons one has preferred not to look at too closely" ("Process of Individuation" 174). It is a truism of Jungian thought that spiritual healing requires that the shadow be "realized" — made real, confronted, brought to consciousness in some way — and that when its contents languish in the unconscious they do damage to self and others. And it is almost as much a truism that the arts, especially literary storytelling, are often related to this realization of the shadow, whether the shadow-realizing process be described at its source, biographically, as the imaginative engine that drives the creative work, or at its reception as the transformative effect the work has on its reader (or viewer or hearer), or inside the work as a theme governing the play of images in the text.

It is the latter, structural and formal and thematic, approach that I wish primarily to take. Many literary works utilize themes and images of doubling — doppelgängers, if you will — within their structures and plots, and I would like to examine two novels that seem to me especially potent and revelatory: Robert Louis Stevenson's *Strange Case of Dr Jekyll and Mr Hyde* (perhaps the urtext in this regard) and Toni Morrison's *Sula*. Both of these novels illustrate the importance of "the realization of the shadow" for spiritual wholeness, but they also illustrate how paradoxical, loopy, and indefinitely deferred this "realization" process is. They reveal that an embrace of the shadow is spiritually necessary but never completed, and that the never-completed is itself the shadow behind any quest to realize the shadow. As we have seen in the previous chapter, the spiritual journey is indeed a journey, not a goal.

In this chapter our journey begins not with the literary works them-selves but with another — equally shadowy, equally illuminating, equally fascinating and frustrating — adventure: the search for the concept of the shadow itself. And as befits an image that is itself image-*less* (isn't a "shadow" exactly what I do *not* see?), the writings about what I am seeking when I embark on a quest for the shadow are elusive and even contradictory, but I believe thrillingly illuminative. I will follow a thread through the concept of the shadow that takes us from the classic, primarily negative definition espoused by Jung himself and by his careful interpreter Marie-Louise von Franz, through poet Robert Bly's and psychologists Connie Zweig and Steven Wolf's more positive views of the shadow as something to be embraced and "romanced," to the paradoxical and radical concepts of post-Jungian James Hillman and deconstructionist Jacques Derrida. For all these writers, the shadow requires the nuances and metaphors of the arts because metaphor, unlike abstract thought, allows hiddenness (shadows, the non-literal) to be part of illumination.

Jung, Von Franz, and the Shadow

Marie-Louise von Franz reports that once, in annoyance with students who "were too literal-minded and clung to his concepts and made a system out of them and quoted him without knowing exactly what they were saying," Jung threw over his technical definition of the shadow and said, "This is all nonsense! The shadow is simply the whole uncon-scious" (*Shadow and Evil* 3). But when Jung is sticking to his technical anatomy of the human person, as in his key book *Aion: Researches into the Phenomenology of the Self*, he is more specific than this and claims that the shadow is something much more particular: "the most accessible" of all the archetypal images floating around in the unconscious, beneath the ego.

As with Freud, the ego is Jung's word for the conscious subject; it "'rests' on the total field of consciousness" — on all the psychic material that "I" can bring to mind when I direct my conscious gaze. The ego is the conscious subject that, as I will discuss, is decentered by postmod-ernism. But the ego is already pretty well decentered by Jung:

the ego is never more and never less than consciousness as a whole. As a conscious factor the ego could, theoretically at least, be described completely. But this would never amount to more than a picture of the conscious personality; all those features which are unknown or unconscious to the subject would be missing. . . . [T]he most decisive qualities in a person are often unconscious and can be perceived only by others, or have to be laboriously discovered with outside help. (5)

The "total personality" — ego and all that the ego is unconscious of — is what Jung calls "the *self*"; "though present," this self "cannot be fully known" (5). Jung claims that the ego was formerly (prior, presumably, to Freud) considered to be "the centre of the personality," and "the field of consciousness" was considered the whole of the psyche (6). With the discovery of "a psyche outside consciousness," the "position of the ego, till then absolute, became relativized. . . . It is part of the personality but not the whole of it" (6). The rest of the personality, Jung says, is made up of two unconscious (or "extra-conscious") levels: "an 'extra-conscious' psyche whose contents are *personal*, and an 'extra-conscious' psyche whose contents are *impersonal* and *collective*" (7).

The "personal" unconscious is made up, Jung says, of contents that "are acquired during the individual's lifetime" (8); that is, this portion of the unconscious is the storeroom for material that has been forgotten or for some reason repressed. And then, beneath that personal layer are "archetypes that were present [in the unconscious] from the beginning" (8). This is Jung's well-known theory that all humans have access to a "collective unconscious," a reservoir of psychic material, the imagistic equivalent of universal species instincts. And Jung claims that the shadow, which he calls "the negative side of the personality" (10), is right on the border between the personal and the collective. He describes the shadow as a kind of inner devil, which shows up, he says, throughout world mythology and hence is archetypal, universal. But its particular contents are mostly personal: "it represents first and foremost the personal unconscious, and its content can therefore be made conscious without too much difficulty" (10). In his classic elaboration — which, as we have seen, is only one version of the concept, a version that Jung himself undermined in the petulant outburst recorded by von Franz — Jung reveals the Victorian-era roots of depth psychology; the shadow in this version is the repressed id-self, sexual and passionate, all that socialization into a polite, sexually repressed society forces us to clamp down. We can infer this view of the shadow from Jung's description of its uncontrolled emotionalism:

Closer examination of the dark characteristics — that is, the inferiorities constituting the shadow — reveals that they have an emotional nature, a kind of autonomy, and accordingly an obsessive or, better, possessive quality. Emotion, incidentally, is not an activity of the individual but something that happens to him. Affects occur usually where adaptation is weakest, and at the same time they reveal the reason for its weakness, namely a certain degree of inferiority and the existence of a lower level of personality. On this lower level with its uncontrolled or scarcely controlled emotions one behaves more or less like a primitive. . . . (8–9)

The "moral problem" that the shadow elements of the self pose is the need to bring this nasty material to consciousness so it will not wreak havoc behind our backs, so to speak: "To become conscious of [the shadow] involves recognizing the dark aspects of the personality as present and real. This act is the essential condition for any kind of self-knowledge, and it therefore, as a rule, meets with considerable resistance" (8). Such self-knowledge, as we saw, is exactly what is thrust on Young Goodman Brown in Hawthorne's story; Goodman Brown does indeed resist, and even reject, this self-knowledge.

All of this shadowy ("inferior," "emotional," "primitive") psychic material is what Jung considers the "personal" shadow, the messy, wild parts of myself that I have relegated to my psychic basement. (This presumes, of course, that I was raised in an era or family that suppresses such aspects of the self; Jung seems not to have anticipated modern and postmodern permissiveness, and it appears that in his primmer moods he would have found such permissiveness distasteful.) But the personal points toward something archetypal, Jung thinks; individual immorality bleeds into radical evil: "With a little self-criticism one can see through the shadow — so far as its nature is personal. But when it appears as an archetype, one encounters . . . difficulties. . . . In other words, it is quite within the bounds of possibility for a man to recognize the relative evil of his nature, but it is a rare and shattering experience for him to gaze into the face of absolute evil" (10).

Relative evil in my own nature . . . absolute evil . . . In both its personal and collective aspects, the shadow is sounding quite thoroughly wicked, something one needs to be conscious of but not yet — as it will become for later writers influenced by Jung's idea — something golden to be embraced and "romanced."

Marie-Louise von Franz sits on the cusp between traditionally negative and more positive views of the shadow and its role in spiritual growth. She does acknowledge, in her book *Shadow and Evil in Fairytales*, the broader notion of the shadow — "simply the whole unconscious" —

that she quotes Jung as tossing out. And she states there that for someone "who knows nothing about psychology . . . the shadow is simply a 'mythological' name for all that within me about which I cannot directly know" (3). But for knowledgeable people, von Franz asserts a much more focused and particular definition of the shadow. In her essay "The Process of Individuation," published in a collection of writings edited by Jung himself, von Franz supplies the classic Jungian definition I have already quoted: the shadow is made up of those aspects of my personality that I have "preferred not to look at too closely" (174). And like Jung, von Franz talks frequently about the shadow as something that needs to be encountered in order to be kept in check: "the shadow may be base or evil, an instinctive drive that ought to be overcome" (234). This is exactly the kind of heroic, triumphalist attitude that writers like Bly and Hillman will disagree with.

But von Franz even more than Jung complicates the story. Yes, insofar as the repressed shadow contents represent a merely "instinctive drive," she believes they need to be made conscious but held in check. In her discussion of the way the ego is enriched by the larger, deeper "Self," however, she talks of the shadow as having other possible functions and contents, much more positive ones. She describes the ego as a sort of stuffy administrator, concerned with measurable outcomes and strategic planning. But the development of the full self is more organic than the ego can imagine, more of a grace than a plan, and spiritual growth can feel like an affront to the ego's confident designs:

> This creatively active aspect of the psychic nucleus [i.e., the Self] can come into play only when the ego gets rid of all purposive and wishful aims and tries to get to a deeper, more basic form of existence. The ego must be able to listen attentively and to give itself, without any further design or purpose, to that inner urge toward growth. (164)

Especially in our culture, obsessed with efficiency but not rooted in the soul, "it is necessary," von Franz says, "to give up the utilitarian attitude of conscious planning in order to make way for the inner growth of the personality" (164).

As a result, the deeper soul emerges in a way that seems to the ego jarring, disturbing, *shadowy* — the "call" to depth begins with a "wound" (what Hillman calls "symptoms": depression, anxiety, etc.). Von Franz describes the ego's painful encounter with a seeming obstructionist that is actually a healer:

> The actual process of individuation — the conscious coming-to-terms with one's own inner center (psychic nucleus) or Self — generally begins

with a wounding of the personality and the suffering that accompanies it. This initial shock amounts to a sort of "call," although it is not often recognized as such. On the contrary, the ego feels hampered in its will or its desire and usually projects the obstruction onto something external. . . . Thus it seems as if the initial encounter with the Self casts a dark shadow ahead of time, or as if the "inner friend" comes at first like a trapper to catch the helplessly struggling ego in his snare. (170)

So the Self itself — that Jungian version of the *imago dei*, the divine wisdom that humans carry within them and that links them to all being — casts a shadow on the ego. "I" am relativized by something larger and deeper and wiser than the "I." This is the context within which von Franz proceeds to lay out the Jungian anatomy of unconscious factors, the first of which is the "shadow." And she does — as an orthodox follower of Jung — define the shadow as the first layer of nasty, immoral, "instinctive" (read *appetitive*, especially sexual) contents that need to be realized in order to be held in check: "The shadow is not the whole of the unconscious personality. It represents unknown or little-known attributes and qualities of the ego — aspects that mostly belong to the personal sphere and that could just as well be conscious" (174). But if the deep, wise Self itself casts a shadow, then *that* "shadow" is not just one layer of specific, repressed badness; it *is* the whole of the unconscious personality, or at least the bellwether of that potential wholeness. So which shadow are we dealing with? — the shadow as a collection of antisocial urges that need to be tamed, or the shadow as that which curbs the utilitarian ego in favor of deeper meaning? Von Franz is forced by her own story of the wounding "call" to complicate her definition, to introduce ambiguities that Bly, Hillman, and others will pick up and run with. Thus, in her attempt at an orthodox Jungian anatomy of the psyche, von Franz says this: "When Jung called one aspect of the unconscious personality the shadow, he was referring to a relatively well-defined factor." (This "factor" is made up of the instincts and passions, which supposedly need to be discovered and controlled — though Bly and Hillman, not to mention William Blake, might demur.) "But sometimes," von Franz tellingly goes on, "everything that is unknown to the ego is mixed up with the shadow, including even the most valuable and highest forces" (183). This situation poses von Franz a problem: how are we to separate out the animalistic urges of the shadow from the angelic "call" of the Self? "The fact," she says,

that the shadow contains the overwhelming power of irresistible impulse does not mean . . . that the drive should always be heroically repressed. Sometimes the shadow is powerful because the urge of the Self is pointing in the same direction, and so one does not know whether it is the Self or the shadow that is behind the inner pressure. In the unconscious, one is unfortunately in the same situation as in a moonlit landscape. All the contents are blurred and merge into one another, and one never knows exactly what or where anything is, or where one thing begins and ends. (183)

Though on a theoretical level von Franz maintains that "the shadow" and "the Self" do not overlap, to her credit she does not lay out a dogmatic program for differentiating one from the other. She acknowledges unclarity and doubt:

> When dark figures turn up in our dreams and seem to want something, we cannot be sure whether they personify merely a shadowy part of ourselves, or the Self, or both at the same time. Divining in advance whether our dark partner symbolizes a shortcoming that we should overcome or a meaningful bit of life that we should accept — this is one of the most difficult problems that we encounter on the way to individuation. . . . In such a situation all one can do is accept the discomfort of ethical doubt. . . . (184)

In "The Process of Individuation," published in 1964, von Franz's Jungian orthodoxy will not permit her to go further than this; von Franz is determined, here, to assert the theoretical distinction between the bad, passionate shadow and the good — even if sometimes shadowy — Self, a distinction challenged by Bly, Hillman, Derrida, and, I believe, the literary works I am examining.

But von Franz was aware that this distinction is muddy, and so, as we saw, was Jung himself. What exactly are we talking about when we talk about "the shadow"? Is it a particular cluster of personal characteristics, which is only one part of the large unconscious self? Or is "the shadow" a term pointing toward the whole unconscious realm, all of ourselves — and even the world — that is outside the spotlight of our meager egos? Probably both ways of looking at the shadow have value. Too technical and focused a definition would pin down what we have already seen to be mystery, Paul Tillich's large, shadowy concept of "depth." But a completely open definition — "shadow" as everything that our ego does not (yet) grasp — may leave out the fearsome dangerousness that must be part of the concept.

Eating the Shadow: Robert Bly

The first of our remaining theoretical writers, Robert Bly, supplements the definitions of Jung and von Franz by offering a more positive view of the shadow — for Bly this is most definitely *not* the part of a person that is wicked and needs curbing — while still maintaining its dangerous, disturbing mysteriousness. And Bly also discusses the retrieval of the shadow in very helpful ways; his recipe for "eating the shadow" insightfully finds a third way between repression of the dark side and all-out immersion into it.

Bly's concept of the shadow is founded on a view of the human person as originally, naturally good and full of life. "When we were one or two years old," he says, "we had what we might visualize as a 360-degree personality. Energy radiated out from all parts of our body and all parts of our psyche. A child running is a living globe of energy. We had a ball of energy, all right" (17). Bly restates this vision in the form of an evolutionary drama, and he heightens its neo-romantic optimism by quoting Wordsworth:

> The drama is this. We came as infants "trailing clouds of glory," arriving from the farthest reaches of the universe, bringing with us appetites well preserved from our mammal inheritance, spontaneities wonderfully preserved from our 150,000 years of tree life, angers well preserved from our 5,000 years of tribal life — in short, with our 360-degree radiance. . . . (24)

But society, Bly says, rejects this sphere of throbbing energy, and we are forced to slice off chunks of it and thrust them into the unconscious, which he compares to a long bag that we drag behind us: "Behind us we have an invisible bag, and the part of us our parents don't like, we, to keep our parents' love, put in the bag. . . . Then our teachers have their say. . . . Then we do a lot of bag-stuffing in high school. This time it's no longer the evil grownups that pressure us, but people our own age" (17). Eventually, Bly says, "out of a round globe of energy the twenty-year-old ends up with a slice" (18).

What goes into the bag differs from culture to culture, but "In a Christian culture sexuality usually goes into the bag," Bly says, and along with sexuality "goes much spontaneity" (18). Men in Western culture, furthermore, stuff their feminine sides in the bag, and women stuff their masculine sides. Despite cultural differences, however, Bly for the most part thinks, as Marie-Louise von Franz does, that the material pushed down into the "personal shadow" is id-appetite: "appetites well preserved from our mammal inheritance," which for Bly are essentially positive and valuable — "spontaneities wonderfully preserved from our 150,000 years of tree life" (24).

Overall, Bly thinks of the contents of the shadow "as threefold": some of the shadow, at least in the twentieth-century United States, "hides in the sexual area"; some resides in "a hunter and hermit area" ("a desire to live in the woods, a desire to kill animals and smear their blood on our faces, a desire to get away from all profane life and live religiously like an Australian aborigine"); and some of the shadow is related to strong emotions — "hatred, fear, anger, jealousy" (50). None of these contents are inherently wicked, however; in this regard Bly disagrees with von Franz and Jung in their most traditional moods (though, as we have seen, they also acknowledge a larger and less intrinsically negative definition of the shadow). Bly's inner drama includes an account of how the shadow elements begin as positive energy but turn bad. The "bag" for Bly is a place in which initially healthy energies, cut off from a healthy maturation process, fester, become tainted, and turn hostile:

> when we put a part of ourselves in the bag it regresses. It de-evolves toward barbarism. Suppose a young man seals a bag at twenty and then waits fifteen or twenty years before he opens it again. What will he find? Sadly, the sexuality, the wildness, the impulsiveness, the anger, the freedom he put in have all regressed; they are not only primitive in mood, they are hostile to the person who opens the bag. (19)

Thus, Bly's thesis about the shadow's fierceness, its apparent wickedness, is this: "Every part of our personality that we do not love will become hostile to us. We could add that it may move to a distant place and begin a revolt against us as well" (20).

Intrinsically, then, shadow contents are vital energy, good stuff (though, as we will see, Bly eventually doubts that they should ever be given completely free rein). Pragmatically, however, these contents are dangerous because they have festered in the bag; hence, their reemergence — either by being projected on people and things outside or just by bursting out into consciousness after years of fermenting — needs to be wisely managed. And here Bly offers his version of Jung's and von Franz's prescription for a "realization of the shadow." For Jung and von Franz, as we saw, much of the shadow is truly "base or evil, an instinctive drive that ought to be overcome" (von Franz, "Process of Individuation" 234). But von Franz also sees another part or face of the shadow as a bellwether of the healing, enlarging Self, which needs to be delicately nurtured and integrated. Since Bly's "shadow" is all good energy, one might expect that he would encourage an all-out, wholesale embrace of it rather than Jung and von Franz's delicate dalliance. But because its time in the "bag" has tainted the spiritual energy that is now shadow, in practice Bly encourages a care and delicacy in dealing with the shadow that is rather similar to von Franz's prescription, even if for slightly different reasons. Bly recommends neither repressing the shadow when it reemerges nor expressing it; rather, he talks in a poetic, even sacramental way about *eating* the shadow.

Energies, Bly says, do not disappear when they go into the bag, and they remain active, largely by projecting themselves outside onto other people and things, usually our significant others or other people toward whom we feel strong emotions, positive or negative. (Bly considers this projective mechanism valuable; it draws us out of ourselves and engages us in the world. But maturity demands that we eventually call these projections home and move to more authentic relationships.) At a certain point, Bly says, the projection wobbles: I realize that the mask I have imposed on the other does not really fit him or her or it. At that point I am tempted to repress all the harder, to force the mask to fit, using all the pressure of self-righteous moral certainty; this is the source of personal bigotry and cultural xenophobia — forcing others to carry my own distasteful shadow, and then punishing them for doing so. Or I can become conscious, recognizing how much of myself I have shoved into the bag and then projected on others, and deeply feeling how diminished I am, how much of my 360-degree ball of energy I have lost: "Suppose that one day, exhausted, one gives up for the moment the struggle to make the mask hang onto the other person. At that moment the eyes break contact; we suddenly look into ourselves and see our own diminishment. We recognize how diminished we have been for years" (35–36). At that point we are able to take in what we have lost, to reverently "eat" it.

In other words, for Bly the "realization of the shadow," which he calls "eating the shadow" (38) to distinguish this from indiscriminate immersion in the shadow, is not a grand, intense Dionysian return to full original energy. Rather, it is a saturnine, melancholy — deep and rich, but sad — experience: "When the person begins to bring in rejected or projected authority, for example, and eat that, Saturn enters, and our passion deepens, and melancholy, always a mark of Saturn, and of retrieved shadow, brings its sorrow in, and its opening to the spirit" (39). So, Bly says,

> the person who has eaten his shadow spreads calmness, and shows more grief than anger. If the ancients were right that darkness contains intelligence and nourishment and even information, then the person

who has eaten some of his or her shadow is more energetic as well as more intelligent. (42)

Bly's muted, melancholy approach to the shadow is a call for retrieval of the shadow as wise mourning and grieving for the lost energy rather than thoughtless intoxication with it. His *A Little Book on the Human Shadow*, a compilation of his thoughts on this subject, is actually a collection of writings, speeches, and interviews spanning from the 1970s through the 1980s, and looking back to the 1960s as well; the book demonstrates that Bly's unbridled enthusiasm for the 360-degree energy ball has tempered over time. Obviously his "drama" of the repression of energy, unlike von Franz's claims that "base" instincts need to be curbed, represents a critique of social restraints on the instincts and a seeming call for greater permissiveness. But in the most recent piece in the book, Bly acknowledges the failure of "permissive theories of childrearing" (51) that allow young people to express — act out — anger, sexuality, etc. Bly's most nuanced position calls for a balance between ego and shadow:

> it's as if there were some kind of game being played here between the ego and the shadow. When permissive educators come in and tell children to express their anger, it's like giving the shadow side fifteen balls and the structure side none. Permissiveness is a misunderstanding of the seriousness of that game. George Leonard, in his book called *The End of Sex*, describes himself as having been enthusiastic about the complete expression of sexuality during the sixties. He now feels that such expression results eventually in some humiliation of the ego, and the psyche as a result loses some of its interest in sexuality; it loses some of its eros.
>
> The culture has a longing for primitive modes of expression as an antidote to repression. Nazi youth groups emphasized a kind of back-to-nature primitivism. Obviously Nazism involved a state insanity, and not all back-to-nature movements involve insanity; most embody health. And yet we can understand through Kurtz's experience in *Heart of Darkness* that the Western longing for the primitive is dangerous to the psyche. The ego becomes unable to hold its own among the primitive impulses and dissolves in mass movements, vanishes like sugar in water. (51–52)

Bly, then, considers "spontaneity" and even wildness to be positive, but they are different from unleashed "expression" and "acting out," which are savage, violent, and oppressive toward others. He considers the Grimms' "Iron John" fairy tale (the root of his famous "men's movement" book) to endorse exactly this balance between unbridled expression and unhealthy repression: "the image [in that fairy tale] of the wild man describes a state of soul that allows shadow material to return slowly in such a way that it doesn't damage the ego" (53).

Bly complains that Western culture dualistically sees expression and repression as the only choices; once again, as with James Hillman in the previous chapter, we see an attempt to avoid dichotomizing:

> Either one represses anger or one expresses it. For example, it could be said that Richard Straus is repressing certain negative emotions, whereas punk rock is expressing them. But expressing is not any more admirable than repressing. The Western man or woman lives in a typical pairing of opposites that destroys the soul. (56)

Bly's eating of the shadow, he claims, *honors* shadow material: "eating" the shadow entails taking it in deeply, feeling the shadow's anger, aggression, sexual desire. But instead of then acting out, expressing these feelings willy-nilly, one who eats the shadow acts *on* the shadow material with care and discrimination — humorously, playfully, subtly, meditatively, and especially artistically. When honoring the shadow by eating it, Bly says, a person "does not aim to act out the aggressive energies as we do in football or the Spanish in bullfighting, but each person aims to bring them upward into art: that is the ideal" (20). Indeed, in a statement that is obviously of great importance for this study, Bly claims that *all literature* is an engagement with the shadow, the dark side, eating and honoring but not acting out: "All literature, both of the primitive and the modern peoples, can be thought of as creations by the 'dark side' to enable it to rise up from earth and join the sunlit consciousness again" (63).

According to Bly humans have a great deal at stake here, individually and even globally. We saw in the previous chapter that a visit to the dark side can leave a person enriched, as I believe it enriches Bill Harford in *Eyes Wide Shut,* but it can also leave him or her bereft and bitter, like Young Goodman Brown at the end of Hawthorne's story. Bly's shadow theory offers a helpful explanation of these alternate possibilities:

> If the shadow's gifts are not acted upon, it evidently retreats and returns to the earth. It gives the writer or person ten or fifteen years to change his life, in response to the amazing visions the shadow has brought him. . . . [B]ut if that does not happen, the shadow goes back down, abandoning him, and the last state of that man is evidently worse than the first. (80–81)

The Shadow as a Henchman of the Self

Despite the seemingly celebratory title of their 1997 book *Romancing the Shadow*, psychologists Connie Zweig and Steve Wolf may *romance* the shadow but they do not *romanticize* it. They compare the shadow and its development to the painting of Dorian Gray in Oscar Wilde's novel:

> Each of us is like Dorian Gray. We seek to present a beautiful, innocent face to the world; a kind, courteous demeanor; a youthful, intelligent image. And so, unknowingly but inevitably, we push away those qualities that do not fit the image, that do not enhance our self-esteem and make us stand proud but, instead, bring us shame and make us feel small. We shove into the dark cavern of the unconscious those feelings that make us uneasy — hatred, rage, jealousy, greed, competitiveness, lust, shame. . . . Like Dorian's painting, these qualities ultimately take on a life of their own, forming an invisible twin that lives just behind our life, or just beside it, but as distinct from the one we know as a stranger. (3–4)

Cut off from our conscious, and deceptive, persona, the shadow operates as a malicious saboteur, "the one within who feels as if it cannot be tamed" (4), who pushes us to engage in a host of self-destructive behaviors: addictions, eating disorders, depression, abusiveness. Yes, Zweig and Wolf claim that there is "gold in the dark side" (6), but they never quite claim that the shadow's basic material is utterly good, remnants of a magnificent 360-degree ball of energy.

Indeed, in 1997 they are fully aware of cultural tendencies to relish and glorify the dark side. What Robert Bly touches on when he refers to the excessive expression of negative emotions by punk rock has become, for Zweig and Wolf, the danger of full-fledged sensationalism: "Millions of us read terrifying gothic novels with great appetite, regularly visiting domains of cruelty, lust, perversion, and crime. Or we sit for hours transfixed by films about cold, vengeful, bloody behavior that, in the outside world, would be deemed inhuman" (7). This "strange obsession" (7) with the dark side is, for Zweig and Wolf, the flip side of a new, repressed conservatism that is equally unhealthy: neo-conservatives, they claim,

> believe that we need more protection from the lures of the shadow — stricter morals, higher fences. They wish to bring back old fundamentalisms to shield us against forbidden feelings, ambiguous choices. They seek to widen the split between good and evil, between Jesus and his dark brother Satan, between the followers of Allah and the heathens,

between the members of their religious cults and the rest of fallen humanity. Longing to remain on god's side, they refuse to engage the darkness in their own souls. (6–7)

Zweig and Wolf call for a balance of these extremes, a version of Bly's "eating" of the shadow, respecting it, finding its gold, but not deliriously plunging into it:

> We cannot afford to look away from the beast in denial, pretending that a naive, trusting stance will protect us from it "out there." And we cannot afford to look too directly at the beast for too long, for we risk numbing our own souls. Instead, we need to cultivate an attitude of respect toward the shadow, to see it honestly without dismissing it or becoming overwhelmed by it. (7)

So what exactly is this "beast," the shadow, according to Zweig and Wolf? Like our other writers, they consider the shadow to be made up of contents judged distasteful by the ego. And Zweig and Wolf have their own narrative about how this shadow is created, similar to Bly's drama of an energy ball but with a somewhat less exuberantly romantic tone.

As with Jung and von Franz, what Zweig and Wolf name "the Self" is each human's *imago dei* — "the 'God within,' the transpersonal realm within the personal life" (16). The Self is the whole, the Tao or dharma (or voice of God), larger and wiser than the ego; the Self is an inner healer, and the healing spiritual journey is the ego's voyage toward harmony with this Self. But at the start of the journey the ego, say Zweig and Wolf, is necessarily inauthentic, "the result of many inevitable adaptations to forces that cannot tolerate the authentic expressions of the Self" (17). So helplessness, rage, sensuality, and depression get "stuffed into a trunk in the cellar," forming the shadow, and the ego fosters inauthentic compensations for these lost qualities, replacing helplessness with seeming hyper-competence, rage with false demureness, sensuality with rigidity, depression with addictive palliatives (17). So although the qualities relegated to Zweig and Wolf's "cellar" are not quite as glorious as Robert Bly's bagged energies, the result is the same: an impoverished ego.

And as von Franz describes the shadow, though not itself positive, as sometimes operating as a bellwether for the Self, so Zweig and Wolf claim that shadow eruptions are the "Henchmen" of the Self. Using an old Sufi story as a parable, Zweig and Wolf describe the ego as a rigid, controlling Butler that has taken over the house of the Master, the Self; in order to bring back harmony, the Master has to reestablish its centrality in the house, and to do so it needs to dislodge the usurping

Butler. So the Master/Self sends in Henchmen (shadow symptoms like anger, depression, feelings of futility) to obstruct the Butler/ego, to nudge the Butler out of its place of control. Thus, these "Henchmen," these seemingly negative symptoms, are actually trying to usher the Self back into its rightful place. The shadow, in other words, is not for Zweig and Wolf itself "good" — it brings great pain — but it has a positive purpose. The shadow, according to Zweig and Wolf, "knows its purpose: It seeks to make the unconscious conscious; it tries to tell its secret" (18).

I believe that this is perhaps Zweig and Wolf's most important contribution to our conversation about the shadow, which we will soon watch unfold in two literary works. Despite their use of the loaded, dark term "shadow," which has all sorts of risks in a majority-Christian and majority-Caucasian society, Zweig and Wolf call for a conceptual shift away from light-and-dark thinking, similar to those other warnings against dichotomizing that we have seen:

> Because most of us are trained as children to split off God from Satan and good from evil, we cannot hold the tension of these opposites: light side and dark side. Instead, we tend to seek out untarnished, idealized heroes in an attempt to remain optimistic and hopeful. Or another part of us, which is jaded and cynical, expects the worst of others. (18)

In place of this dualistic splitting, Zweig and Wolf call for a way of knowing that holds "light side" and "dark side" together: "To practice light side/dark side thinking is to practice holding opposites, a subversive act in our either/or culture: (18). Zweig and Wolf remain plagued, as this study does, by the "light" and "dark" metaphors, but at least they have tried to strip these metaphors of moral judgment. The metaphors do serve a purpose — "light" as the already grasped, visible; "dark" as the not-yet-known, not-yet-seen. But the metaphors, and the psychological concept of the shadow, need a bit more unpacking before we watch them unfold in our literary works. Let us turn to two more elaborations of the concepts, one by post-Jungian psychologist James Hillman and the other by postmodern philosopher Jacques Derrida.

Shadow and Soul: James Hillman

The most paradoxical and even intentionally self-contradictory of the theoretical analyses of the shadow that we are looking at is James Hillman's *Insearch: Psychology and Religion*. First published in 1967, this is a relatively early Hillman work and his most systematic examination of the concept of the shadow. But the book's 1994 revised edition includes a postscript in which Hillman significantly critiques his own earlier ideas. The combination of his detailed exposition of the shadow and his later deconstruction of this exposition makes the book vibrate with the kind of untamable energy that the shadow itself gives off, as do the literary works we will look at. So it is helpful to look at Hillman's initial injection of a religious dimension into the concepts of the psyche and especially the shadow, as well as his later de-Christianization and de-internalization of these ideas.

Drawn from lectures Hillman originally gave to Christian ministers and pastoral counselors, *Insearch* is Hillman's attempt to bring "soul" back to psychology, and especially to theology (which in the 1960s was going through its "death of God" phase, rationally demythologizing religious imagery for a scientific era, a very different situation from the evangelical turn of the 1990s and early twenty-first century). "Soul," as we saw in the previous chapter, is Hillman's word for a locus of imma-nent spirituality, one that views the spiritual journey as a journey *down* into human experience rather than *up* into transcendence. As the churches emptied, Hillman writes, "the clinics filled, and the depth psychologists — especially Jung — seemed to find soul and a living God-image in the midst of their work. So theology is now looking in another direction, down to the 'ground of being.' . . . The new mysticism is one of descent" (49).

A mysticism of descent leads, Hillman says, not to light but to the dark unknown and to the "things which have been put down through the ages" (those things that society judges to be inferior and thrusts into the "bag," the "cellar"):

> If we discover the place of the soul — and the experience of God — to be darkly within and below, we must reckon with a perilous voyage. The lower positions (the dark, the down, and the deep) are the realm of the devil and his horde of demons. The way of descent means the way through the labyrinth, and even theological tradition tells us that the descending path means a confrontation with all things which have been put down through the ages. . . . This is of course the classical route of analysis, the return to the repressed. (49–50)

The spiritual journey down leads to the psychological shadow. Conversely, says Hillman, the plunge into the personal psyche leads to God:

> As one penetrates into the essentials of oneself, one feels that personal problems take on a general human dimension and that the essential truths about oneself become universal, quite like the statements of

> theology. It would appear that deep analysis leads to a strange dark center where it is difficult to differentiate the unconscious from the soul and from the image of God. (54)

Neither psychology nor religion is primary, Hillman says; each leads to the other: "The symbolic attitude of psychology arising from the experience of soul leads to a sense of the hidden numinous presence of the divine, while the belief in God leads to a symbolic view of life where the world is filled with significance and 'signs'" (65). This is the psychological/religious framework in which Hillman, in 1967, sketches out his high-stakes concept of the shadow and how to "realize" it.

Hillman's concept of the shadow has similarities to all those other definitions we have looked at so far, but even in its more traditionally Christian formulation in 1967, his description is perhaps the least dogmatic, the most open and undecidable. Indeed, in his critique of Freudian dream interpretation, Hillman argues that an overly specific analytical interpretation of psychic material is an imposition of ego on the larger Self, a warning that applies to precise definitions of the shadow as well:

> To give dream the meanings of the rational mind is just to replace the id with ego. . . . It is an attitude of wanting from the unconscious, using it to gain information, power, energy, exploiting it for the sake of the ego: make it mine, make it mine. This attitude breaks apart the symbol, which is a joining of the two sides of the psyche. . . . Then the unconscious becomes mine enemy which must be worked on or propitiated with analytical techniques, or observed and watched from clever vantage points. But above all it must be depotentiated. (59)

As Robert Bly invoked Romantic poet William Wordsworth's parable of preexistence (we are born "trailing clouds of glory"), so Hillman is implicitly echoing Wordsworth's claim that egoistic analysis carves up vital being and hence kills it. As Wordsworth succinctly puts it in his poem "The Tables Turned":

> Our meddling intellect
> Misshapes the beauteous forms of things —
> We murder to dissect.

(We will see another important Wordsworthian turn in Hillman's 1994 postscript to *Insearch*, so this earlier echoing of Wordsworth is very significant.)

Hillman's reluctance to grant the ego too much power by overly pinning down psychic contents is underlined by his view, similar to Zweig and Wolf's, of how the shadow produces painful symptoms to relativize the ego, to put it in its place so that "soul-awakening" can occur. Painful symptoms — depression, anxiety, and the like — make me feel bodily, incarnate, bringing my head out of an egotistical heaven and reminding me that I am mortal: "a prolonged occupation with suffering, with the incarnation of oneself in flesh which is tormented for apparently no reason, . . . is a humiliating, soul-awakening experience. Symptoms humiliate; they relativize the ego. They bring it down" (55). Quick medical symptom-removal, Hillman says, represses these shadow-messages from the soul: "Cure of symptoms may but restore the ego to its former ruling position" (55). Symptoms are humbling, and humility — which comes from the word humus, earth, so humility brings us down to earth — is

> the traditional mark of the soul. . . . Because symptoms lead to soul, the cure of symptoms may also cure away soul, get rid of just what is beginning to show, at first tortured and crying for help, comfort, and love, but which is the soul in the neurosis trying to make itself heard, trying to impress the stupid and stubborn mind — that impotent mule which insists on going its unchanging obstinate way. (55–56)

Hillman is not a masochist, nor does he endorse martyrdom. But he does think, like each of our other writers but perhaps most explicitly, that the most healing stance toward the psyche is *attention*, and that the harshness of the shadow is often what it takes for the ego to wake up and attend to the deep and important realities:

> Through the symptom the psyche demands attention. Attention means attending to, tending, a certain tender care of, as well as waiting, pausing, listening. . . . Just this same attitude is what the soul needs in order to be felt and heard. So it is often little wonder that it takes a breakdown, an actual illness, for someone to report the most extraordinary experiences of, for instance, a new sense of time, of patience and waiting, and in the language of religious experience, of coming to the center, coming to oneself, letting go and coming home. (56)

So Hillman, too, sees the shadow as a kind of herald or bellwether, something to be listened to. But despite his reluctance to interpret and his preference for simply attending-to, Hillman does provide some helpful descriptions of the shadow, which we should ourselves attend to before looking at his and Derrida's deconstructions. Hillman begins, though, by warning that the shadow is exactly what cannot be seen, that darkness is dark (a point that will become even more important when he redefines the shadow in his 1994 postscript): "The unconscious . . . cannot be conscious; the moon has its dark side, the sun goes down and cannot shine everywhere at once, and God has two hands. Attention and focus require some things to be out of the field of vision, to remain in the dark" (72). But Hillman, at least in 1967, says that he can explain *why* the dark side is dark, and this allows him obliquely to define the shadow. He says that there are two reasons for the shadow's darkness, and thus two areas of shadow. The first is familiar to us at this point, a repetition of the concept of the shadow we have seen again and again: "it is necessarily repressed — the world which Freud so carefully investigated . . . the darkness of the Past" (72). But the second area is new; Hillman claims that the shadow also includes "the darkness of the Future": "it is dark because it has not yet had time nor place to emerge into the light. This, too, is the inner darkness, the earth or ground of one's new being, that part which is *in potentia*" (72). For Hillman the "moral problem" posed by the shadow is based on *both* of these aspects of the hidden self. In the first case, "we are specifically responsible for specific actions and for specific character traits which stand contradictory to the light side of ourselves" (73). But we are also responsible for our unfulfilled potentialities, relegated to the psychic basement by a priggish, controlling ego:

> When one has a moral obligation to oneself, figures appear in the shadow which represent positive possibilities of one's own nature, potentialities that have not been given a chance. I am guilty not only toward the past, but toward my own potentialities. . . . The one-sided light of ego-consciousness implies that darkness means neglect. And it is the neglected elements which appear in the shadow. . . . Then these potentials must appear as outlaws, misfits, even cripples or lunatics. Healing these, the blind and the lepers, raising the dead, becomes an inner necessity to bring health to the personality. (74–75)

For Hillman a key paradox is "that rotten garbage is also fertilizer, that childishness is also childlikeness, that polymorphous perversity is also joy and physical liberty, that the ugliest man is at the same time the redeemer in disguise" (77). It is this paradoxical aspect of the shadow that most compellingly emerges, as we will see, in Morrison's *Sula*.

And finally, at least prior to Hillman's self-critical postscript, we have his prescription for healing, care of the shadow, which comes down to what we have already seen to be Hillman's "cardinal psychological virtue" (119): *attention*. Hillman does not romanticize the shadow; much more than Bly, the Christian Hillman of 1967 thinks that a great deal of the shadow's contents *is* immoral and needs to be atoned for and curbed. But atonement and curbing are not repression and indeed are possible only if repression is lifted: "The cure of the shadow is on the one hand a moral problem, that is, recognition of what we have repressed, how we perform our repressions, how we rationalize and deceive ourselves, what sort of goals we have and what we have hurt, even maimed, in the name of these goals" (75–76). But paradoxically, the "cure of the shadow" is also "a problem of love. How far can our love extend to the broken and ruined parts of ourselves, the disgusting and perverse? How much charity and compassion have we for our own weakness and sickness?" (76). Attention means care, which entails carrying, carrying the shadow along with us; this, says Hillman, is what "the old Puritans" did so well, "daily aware of their sins, watching for the Devil, on guard lest they slip" (76). But unlike these Puritans, Hillman says that care also involves "loving all of oneself, including the shadow where one is inferior and socially so unacceptable" (76). So in addition to carrying the shadow, we must joyfully, laughingly accept it. (Laughter, we will see, figures largely in *Sula*.) Thus, for Hillman "cure" is

> a paradox requiring two incommensurables: the moral recognition that these parts of me are burdensome and intolerable and must change, and the loving laughing acceptance which takes them just as they are, joyfully, forever. One both tries hard and lets go, both judges harshly and joins gladly. Western moralism and Eastern abandon: each holds only one side of the truth. (77)

Like Bly, Hillman rejects both repression and acting out, calling them "two sides of the same coin" (83). In their place he calls for his own version of a third way: "internalization, or symbolization, or living-in" (83). That is, the key again is *attention* — meditative, imaginative, poetic, playfully and creatively carrying and laughing.

Despite his positive view of shadow symptoms, Hillman is no naïve optimist. Like Jung and von Franz, he believes that there is yet another area of shadow darkness that is *not* a herald of healing. There are, he says, "experiences of evil which cannot be humanized and which have been represented by devilish powers in the various religions of the world" (89); he mentions Nazism, the treatment of African Americans in the United States, and other examples. But even in this case of the shadow as radical evil, Hillman maintains that a humble attention to the shadow is what is called for. He claims that the devil's power grows "not in our shadow but from our light. He gains when we lose sight of our own destructiveness and self-deception" (91). If the great sin is pride, then the humus of attention to the shadow is its best antidote:

pride is a denial of the personal shadow and a blind fascination with the dazzle of one's own light. Therefore the best protection is not the reinforcement of the good and the light, but familiarity with one's own shadow, one's own devil-likeness. Homeopathic dosage of lesser evils as bitter pills of moral pain may be prophylactic against the greater evil. (91)

So goes James Hillman's discussion of the shadow and its care, in 1967 to Christian ministers. But his 1994 postscript to *Insearch* represents a rather stunning reconsideration and even rejection of some of his earlier ideas, and I believe that this postscript offers a perspective that it would be perilous to overlook in a study of the shadow and its stories. Hillman asserts, in his postscript, that his earlier view of the shadow was too enmeshed in a Christian suspicion of bodily, especially sexual, desire and in a psychoanalytic obsession with the inner world. He suggests other areas of shadow darkness and other, less moralistic ways of thinking about that darkness. In doing so he makes the concept of the shadow even more vibrantly ambiguous than it has already been, and he points us toward a truly postmodern undecidability that makes it necessary for us to allow Derrida also to have a say.

In the postscript, Hillman is put off by the "moral earnestness" of his 1967 book, its "parasitical relation with Christianity" (130). He now sees his book as too focused on the (implicitly Christian) salvation of the individual's soul, accomplished by "moral work on oneself" (131). He proceeds to broaden the notion of where the journey to soul leads, and hence where soul and shadow are located; in doing this, he poses a significant and important challenge to this work and adds a resonance to our experience of the literary texts.

The image that Hillman most vigorously critiques is verticality. A shift of the soul-journey from an upward to a downward direction is perhaps valuable, but it maintains the verticality of a certain kind of conventional Christianity, Hillman now thinks. Verticality, whether upward or downward, turns attention, Hillman says,

> away from what is around us, the actual life shared with the environment, to what's above and below — the characteristic foci of Christian eschatology, Heaven and Hell. This emphasis upon the two poles above and below leaves the great wide world as mainly a dangerous ladder between them, a ladder from which one may fall at every step. The world is thus turned from a place of beauty and learning into a horizontal battlefield of moral struggle. (131)

Hillman, in the postscript, suggests that, *pace* Jung, modern humanity has not lost the soul; we are just looking in the wrong place:

What's missing is the inside "out there": in the trees, in the finches and squirrels in the trees, in the soil and stones, and even in the panes of glass that you see through to the trees, the squirrels, and the stones. . . .

Might it not be far simpler just to step outside, or walk around your room, and do what the Psalmist said: "O taste and see." Soul is in, or is, the very first matter to hand. (130)

"Soul" is not, or not just, *my* world, and my *inner* world; it is all around. Hillman's reorientation seems to me very important, though it is not entirely unique among the voices we have been looking at, including two Christian ones. For instance Michael Himes, cited in our previous chapter, proposes a horizontal vision of Christian sacramentality that I consider quite well attuned to Hillman's revised ideas; Himes, as we saw, describes *sacrament* as a poetic, metaphoric reminder of the explosion of love throughout all that is. And Paul Tillich's image of "depth" is not about psychoanalytic inward-looking, but rather about recovering a sense of the shared ground of the being of all being. "Taste and see," indeed.

In any case, Hillman is arguing for an enlarging of the idea of "soul" beyond the individual human person, a stance that he shares with, for example, the great romantic poets. An utterly rational, "enlightened" viewpoint may consider that it is pure projection to ascribe "human" feelings and spiritual energy to the nonhuman world, but William Wordsworth, like Hillman, did not think so. Having lost touch with a living soul, Wordsworth did engage in meditative inner soul-searching, but he also looked outward to the natural world. One of his most profound experiences is recorded in his great poem "Lines Composed a Few Miles Above Tintern Abbey," in which Wordsworth describes his own healing as occurring when he went out to nature and experienced a soul "out there" that was in deep harmony — shared the same "ground of being," perhaps — with his own inner self:

> And I have felt
> A presence that disturbs me with the joy
> Of elevated thoughts; a sense sublime
> Of something far more deeply interfused,
> Whose dwelling is the light of setting suns,
> And the round ocean, and the living air,
> And the blue sky, and in the mind of man;
> A motion and a spirit, that impels
> All thinking things, all objects of all thought,
> And rolls through all things.

What has this expanded view of soul to do with the shadow? Hillman's answer is that a broader view of the spirituality of the world out there, not just of the self in here, is the *shadow* side — the unseen, the unattended-to — of an overly self-saving and inward-looking theology and psychology. A decentered view of soul, therefore, also decenters our way of defining "shadow," suggesting that "the" shadow is not only an inner, psychological entity, existing in the same way in all people at all times. Our way of conceptualizing and discoursing shapes our definitions of things, so our concepts of shadow leave aspects of the shadow in a shadow. For a broader view of the shadow, Hillman says, we "would have to inquire into the way in which our discourse about shadow determines the nature of shadow" (132). Hillman concludes that "the entire shadow issue so basic to Jungian psychology and therapy is a by-product of its Christian moral theology" (132); that is, the very discourse about "the shadow" has been framed by a particular cultural/religious idea of sin. So that may be why the shadow always seems mixed up with sex. But what happens when a cultural group — today's young people, perhaps — does not repress sexuality? Does the shadow go away? Well, certainly many things still remain in the dark; clearly, then, our definition of shadow needs to be stretched, and that is what Hillman is trying to do in this postscript. He suggests, for example, *structural* rather than moralistic concepts of the shadow.

We could, he says, examine "our theories of perception and cognition (more in the manner of Wittgenstein), raising doubts about our senses, what they are selecting, ignoring, distorting. How do the patterns of our thought determine the world we behave in and adapt to?" (132). Or we could look at "language and the shadows of our discourse (more in the manner of Derrida)" (132). Or, if our psychologizing has made us too inwardly focused, perhaps "the psychopathological shadow at its fundamental level is neither evil, devil, nor lovelessness, but the shadow of psychology itself, the psychopathological lacuna in its theory that neglects the soul out there" — the finch chirping in the tree outside, "altogether neglected by the shadow integration" (136).

Lifting repression may have less to do with "opening the cellar door and releasing the sexual libido," letting loose "permissive behavior," and more to do with the not-seen in *all* seeing — "the fateful and ever-present unconsciousness in all consciousness, that whatever consciousness casts light upon at once creates a shadow. The moment we see more clearly, we become more blind and cannot see behind what we see, the other side of what we see. Seeing and not seeing go together, concurrently, co-relatively" (133). Shadow, says Hillman now, is not only a moral issue; it is also the penumbral life that lives with life as the never-ceasing darkening of the light in every search, a darkening of the light of certainty, the light's own sense that however an "I" searches for soul, that same "I" is inherently biased against the object of its searching and therefore biases the methods it employs for its search. Shadow both keeps us searching and prevents us finding. It is the obstruction that does not want to find what it's looking for. Embedded in the very consciousness that is the instrument of our insearch, shadow is the unconsciousness of consciousness itself. (134)

So the shadow cannot, for Hillman, be "realized," cannot be made to go away. There is no "bag" that can eventually be emptied so that "I" can be "whole." Such a picture of the spiritual journey is too heroic, too self-centered. Rather, shadow "is an inevitable necessity of the human condition, an indelible psychological fact of all perception and behavior" (135). Shadow *is* related to humility, humus, but in a large structural way, not just a personal way. After all, the Greek mandate to "Know Thyself" was not about psychological "insearching"; it was a reminder that I am mortal, limited. Such is the shadow, says Hillman in 1994: "Like ancient Greek fate that keeps us mortal, flawed, humanely limited, shadow guards us from the *hubris* of blindly trusting our own awareness, and as such, shadow is a blessing. Perhaps it is a gift from Hades" (135).

What's the Différance?

It is far beyond the scope of this study to analyze the difficult, extensive work of Jacques Derrida, the founder of the philosophical approach to knowledge called deconstruction. But since James Hillman has broadened the definition of the shadow beyond the concept of a "bag" of repressed psychological contents, and in doing so has invoked Derrida, it seems worthwhile to give Derrida's work a look. And indeed, Derrida's concept of *différance*, as well as some particular ideas he presents in his book *The Gift of Death*, one of his most explicitly religious works, deepens and enriches Hillman's suggestion that the idea of "the shadow" really indicates the darkness of unknowing that frames all our experiences.

Différance is a word Derrida coined to suggest precisely this lack-of-knowing-fully that is, for him and Hillman both, part of the structure of the human situation. A combination of "difference" and "defer," the word has to do with how language works (or works-without-working): words, Derrida suggests, are always *different* from that which they attempt to signify, and the actual presence to us of that-which-is-signified is always *deferred*. Words, therefore, are located within a kind of culturally circumscribed tapestry. Each word exists in relation to other words in the tapestry; all are interrelated with each other, and none are outside the fabric. (Unlike the writer of the gospel of John, Derrida does not postulate some original "Word" at "the beginning," outside the interwoven web.) There is no way out of this web of text to a certain grasp of the "real presence" of the signified. There is internal difference between one word and another: each word is related, via difference, to each other word. But the absolute reality of the signified, its presence, is not accessible but is always deferred. This presence is a beckoning "other," which I would suggest is a kind of *shadow*, haunting language but never brought into the light. And since we all live and think inside such a cultural/linguistic web, it is not just words but it is we ourselves, our very subjectivities, for whom the other — truth, each other, the singing finch described by Hillman, even ourselves — is never quite grasped, is in shadow as well as light. (The fact that this shadowiness of *différance* includes my own self, deferring even the "I," has led to the postmodern idea of "the death of the subject." But, as I have noted, even the psychological ideas of the unconscious, the shadow, and so forth have dislodged the ego from its sovereignty.)

Otherness of all kinds calls us but is always beyond, the concept of *différance* suggests. So every other is infinitely sought for but infinitely unreachable (enshadowed); this leads Derrida to a playfully serious formula: "*tout autre est tout autre*," "every other (one) is every (bit) other" (*Gift of Death* 82). But "every (bit) other" means *wholly other*, which is what God is called; thus, Derrida suggests that God is what is (not) glimpsed in all our (non-)encounters with the other:

> The trembling formula "every other (one) is every (bit) other" can also be reproduced. It can do so to the extent of replacing one of the "every others" by God: "Every other (one) is God," or "God is every (bit) other." Such a substitution in no way alters the "extent" of the original formulation, whatever grammatical function be assigned to the various words. In one case God is defined as infinitely other, as wholly other, every bit other. In the other case it is declared that every other one, each of the others, is God inasmuch as he or she is, like God, wholly other. (87)

The description of *différance* and otherness generates a Derridean structural definition of *shadow*, shadow as a fundamental aspect of the human situation, and certainly an aspect of any experience of what is "out there" beyond the self. And *voilà*, by a turn of language that is more than a linguistic trick, this structural shadow is — or points toward — or embodies the (unhearable) call of (language limps here, of course) *God.* No wonder the discussion of the shadow always takes a religious turn.

This overall situation — humanity in darkness — is the backdrop for Derrida's specific religious reflections and his reflections on shadow in *The Gift of Death*, one of his later works, written as he became increasingly drawn to religious thought. In this book Derrida discusses a series of ways that some kind of shadow is *carried* (to use Hillman's word), each of which deserves a look: Christianity carries a shadow; the self carries the shadow of death, and also of its own invisibility; each act we do casts a moral shadow; and finally, even the explosive "gift" of love (like that described by Michael Himes) is darkly shadowed.

From the viewpoint of morality, one can think of a number of ways that Christianity carries a shadow: the Crusades, for instance, or the Inquisition, or the Catholic church's contemporary sex scandal. But since these horrors come to mind so easily, they are not really shadow; they are blights, but well-known ones. Derrida, however, points out more hidden shadows carried by the Christian religion, which might tend to unite his ideas with those of the Jungian theorists of the shadow: Christianity, says Derrida, represses but maintains, invisibly, in its tapestry of text two forms of holy death — a loss of ego in the orgiastic raptures of the ancient mystery religions, and a loss of body in the Platonic flight from the physical into the light of reason. The idea that Christianity carries these past mysteries ("the buried memory or crypt of a more ancient secret" [9]) suggests that shadow is part of cultural texts themselves, not just something in a personal psychological repository.

But indeed the self carries shadows too — the shadow of death, which ironically constitutes the self, as well as the shadow of the self to itself (the "death" of the subject).

Death constitutes the self by, in a sense, demarcating the self, framing it, giving it identity. The self is "irreplaceable" really only in one way: in *dying* — because no one can replace me in death, no one can die in my place. And this single form of irreplaceability gives the self an identity as that-which-is-going-to-die: "The sameness of the self, what remains irreplaceable in dying, only becomes what it is, in the sense of an identity as a relation of the self to itself, by means of this idea of mortality as irreplaceability. . . . The identity of the oneself is *given* by death, by the being-towards-death that *promises* me to it" (45). But because I know of my own death only by learning that *others* die, so the shadow of my death — which establishes my self-identity — is formed by my encounter with the other, toward whom the "hello" is always shadowed by a potential, ultimate "goodbye" (every parent knows how true this is). So I know *I* am (one who has demarcation because my story will end) because I know I must say goodbye to *you.*

But this self-definition trembles with shadows not only because I carry my own death as a shadow, but also because of my own lack of self-knowledge. This is what Derrida calls "The question of the self: 'who am I?' not in the sense of 'who am I' but 'who is this "I"' that can say 'who'? What is the 'I,' and what becomes of responsibility once the identity of the 'I' trembles *in secret*?" (92). The very fact that "I" can talk about "me" — that the subject can split itself and make itself an object — means that there *is* no stable, absolute subject. One shadow of the "I" is simply "me"; this shadow is part of the very structure of human consciousness.

Actions also cast shadows, and the moral shadow that Derrida explicates is quite chilling. He retells the story of Abraham on Mount Moriah, murdering his deeply loved son for the deeply loved other — that is, for God. (Even though God saves Isaac at the final moment, Abraham is still guilty since he was a hair's breadth away from committing the murder.) And Derrida points out that Abraham's story is also my own story: every act of love we do for another, an *other*, is haunted by death: "As soon as I enter into a relation with the other, with the gaze, look, request, love, command, or call of the other, I know that I can respond only by sacrificing ethics, that is, by sacrificing whatever obliges me to also respond, in the same way, in the same instant, to all the others. I offer a gift of death, I betray, I don't need to raise my knife over my son on Mount Moriah for that" (68). This is no abstract claim; it is chillingly concrete. When I use my income to feed and clothe and entertain my spouse, my child, or even my pet, I am "sacrificing and betraying" all those other others to whom I am also obligated,

> the other others whom I know or don't know, the billions of my fellows (without mentioning the animals that are even more other others than my fellows), my fellows who are dying of starvation or sickness. I betray my fidelity or my obligations to other citizens, to those who don't speak my language and to whom I neither speak nor respond, to each of those who listen or read, and to whom I neither respond nor address myself in the proper manner, that is, in a singular manner (this for the so-called public space to which I sacrifice my so-called private space), thus also to those I love in private, my own, my family, my sons, each of whom is the only son I sacrifice to the other, every one being sacrificed to every one else in this land of Moriah that is our habitat every second of every day. (69)

Acting ethically, responsibly toward the other requires a horrific sacrifice of the *other* others. I cannot justify this; it is silent, secret, a shadow haunting every ethical act: "Such, in fact, is the paradoxical condition of every decision. . . . It structurally breaches knowledge and is thus destined to nonmanifestation; a decision is, in the end, always secret" (77). Again we have found a shadow that is not a repressed instinct or drive shoved into a "bag," but rather is part of the very structure of the finite human situation.

Finally, and much more positively, Derrida reverses the horror of the secret sacrifice that haunts every ethical act and finds a secret gift that haunts every sacrifice; this notion of *the gift* is equally unspeakable, invisible — different from what can be measured and named, always deferred, and yet paradoxically part of the (invisible, enshadowed) structure of the human situation. It is the positive shadow that is present by virtue of its absence, and it suggests that the "shadow" is gift as well as curse.

Ruminating on the wildly unpredictable positive ending to the Abraham-Isaac story, Derrida conceives of "gift" as that which is outside a rational economy of measurable costs and benefits. The rational system of cost-benefit analysis is, Derrida says, "the strict economy of exchange, of payback, of giving and giving back, of 'the one lent for every one borrowed'" (102). The economy of exchange is the ordinary realm of calculated human self-interest (the only real human realm, according to tough-minded "enlightened" rationalists), where the reigning code is "the law of the home (*oikos*), of the hearth, of what is one's own or proper, of the love and affection of one's kin" (95). Within this system, Derrida argues, a "gift" is no gift at all; anything that has strings attached — I gave you a birthday present, so you must give me something on my birthday; you treated me to dinner last week, so I "owe you one" — is no "gift." And indeed, Derrida connects this tit-for-tat "economy of exchange" — which, as "the law of the house" and "the love and affection of one's kin" seems benign enough — with "that hateful form of circulation that involves reprisal, vengeance, returning blow for blow, settling scores" (102). This is the disturbing subtext of a system in which love of the other is haunted by the sacrifice and betrayal of the *other* other.

But Abraham's story poetically points toward a gracious impossible possibility. Killing his beloved son for an invisible God is different from the sacrifice of one for another that we have already discussed as endemic to the human situation; if in one sense "this land of Moriah . . . is our habitat every second of every day," in another sense Abraham's world is a radically strange place. Killing a beloved son not for an even more (selfishly) loved other but rather for an invisible God is outside the system of cost-benefit calculation: Abraham is offering "a gift outside any economy, the gift of death — and of the death of that which is price-less — . . . without any hope of exchange, reward, circulation, or communication" (96). And, having renounced any self-interest, Abraham miraculously receives everything back, but only because he expected to receive nothing: "God gives back to him, in the instant of absolute renunciation, the very thing that he had already, in the same instant, decided to sacrifice. It is given back to him because he renounced calculation" (96–97). "Gift," then, *has* to be in the shadow; if Abraham had calculated, even subliminally, that giving up Isaac would somehow be rewarded, "paid back," then this would not be a gift and he would have received no divine reward. Derrida describes, in a passage drenched with paradox (only paradox can point toward this secret, this not-known known, this impossible possibility, this shadow that haunts human exchanges even more darkly than does vengeance, which is obvious and hence not really all that dark) what "the gift" is not and is:

> The moment the gift, however generous it be, is infected with the slightest hint of calculation, the moment it takes account of knowledge [*connaissance*] or recognition [*reconnaissance*], it falls within the ambit of an economy: it exchanges, in short it gives counterfeit money, since it gives in exchange of payment. . . . Once it is tied to remuneration (*merces*), it is counterfeit because it is mercenary and mercantile; even if it is real. . . . One must give without knowing, without knowledge or recognition, without thanks [*remerciement*]: without anything, or at least without any object. (112)

In order for an act toward an other to issue from the invisible "place of the heart . . . the place of true riches" (97) rather than from the calculating reason — and all acts to all others *must* at core issue from this place, since "*tout autre est tout autre*" and therefore every other one is God — the act must take place with this not-knowing. The left hand cannot know what the right hand is doing. This is necessary, and impossible — a shadow.

All of this talk of "gift" and "heart" may sound pious and "heart"-warming. But the reason I connect the idea of gift with the concept of the shadow is that the gift is always deferred; it is always necessary but never present, an impossible possibility, as outside the human situation as unconsciousness is outside consciousness — and yet potent nonetheless. Gift is *structurally* shadowed. The gift is the signified that the word "gift" points toward but of course cannot make present. The gift is an absence, a shadow haunting the word "gift" — indeed, haunting the entire relational human situation.

Derrida's *shadows* are not Platonic ideas that really exist outside the material world, but rather they do *not* exist; and yet in their non-existence they operate as a kind of horizon toward which humans are tilted. As much as the unknown items in the "bag" or "cellar," Derrida's structural secrets — both the negative and the positive ones — are active in their invisibility and in a sense are an operative, deferred difference that is analogous to Hyde in relation to Jekyll and Sula in relation to Morrison's protagonist Nel. Let us now look at these literary works as metaphorical grapplings with the mystery of *shadow* in all dimensions: psychological, spiritual, structural.

Dr Jekyll and Mr Hyde

One of the problems with discussing Robert Louis Stevenson's *Strange Case of Dr Jekyll and Mr Hyde* is that even if we have not read the novella, its story is so familiar that we think we know it and its meaning. And for our purposes it seems obvious what the novella illustrates. Mr. Hyde is the evil half of the human person; pushed into the unconscious, it takes on a life of its own, even an identity of its own, and wreaks havoc. Certainly it is debatable what that evil is made up of — some kind(s) of aberrant, out-of-control sexuality according to popular interpretations, analogous to many of the descriptions of the "shadow" (or the "id" for Freudians). These overly sex-focused views of Hyde have been successfully refuted from time to time — by Stevenson himself originally, as we will see — but the general idea that Hyde personifies the evil side of human nature remains fairly commonsensical.

But just as our theorists about the shadow disagree about whether the shadow is, in itself, wicked, so I suggest that a nuanced reading of *Jekyll and Hyde*, especially aided by Stevenson's statement of his moral position in the essay "Lay Morals," complicates the idea that Hyde directly embodies the evil side of humanity. Indeed, I suggest that Stevenson's "Lay Morals" essay helps us locate true immorality in the respectable Dr. Jekyll rather than in the animal-like Mr. Hyde, and as a result offers us an unexpectedly rich and complex literary reflection on the concept of the shadow. Like Robert Bly, in particular, the novella suggests that wickedness is located not in the Hyde-like shadow dimension of the self but in the mechanism that cuts off this dimension and relegates it to the shadows (in a bag, a cellar, or in this case in a separate ego). But I also think that, by hypothesizing the possibility of a divided self itself, the novella pushes further toward postulating and ruminating on the inescapable and impossible-to-be-"realized" structural shadow discussed by Hillman and Derrida. It is primarily the *story* of Jekyll and Hyde that illustrates and plays with a version of the Jung/Bly shadow, and it is primarily the *design* of the novella itself that illustrates the structural shadow.

The story, as I have said, is quite familiar. Henry Jekyll is a "mad scientist" in the tradition of Mary Shelley's Victor Frankenstein; whereas Frankenstein wants to explore the mystery of life and death, Jekyll's tormenting question is about good and evil — specifically, what he calls "those provinces of good and ill which divide and compound man's dual nature" (52). The tension of living with this self-division is painful: "It was the curse of mankind," Jekyll says, "that these incongruous faggots were thus bound together — that in the agonised womb of consciousness, these polar twins should be continuously struggling" (53). He believes that separating these entities — opening the "bag," if you will, and releasing a shadow with no scrupulous self repressing it — would eliminate this tension: "If each, I told myself, could but be housed in separate identities, life would be relieved of all that was unbearable" (53). Of course, Jekyll finds a potion that will effect exactly this separation, a drug that shakes "the very fortress of identity" (54) by unleashing the shadow in a distilled form: Mr. Hyde. And Jekyll's description of this incarnation of all that has been stuffed in the bag, hidden in the psyche's basement, seems to bear out Jung's and von Franz's more traditional claims that shadow contents are intrinsically wicked: "Edward Hyde, alone in the ranks of mankind, was," says Jekyll, "pure evil" (55). Jung, remember, at least in his more systematic anatomy of the psyche's elements, calls the shadow "the relative evil of [humanity's] nature" (10), and von Franz talks of the true shadow (as opposed to elements that seem shadowy but are actually messages from the wise Self) as "base or evil, an instinctive drive that needs to be overcome" ("Process of Individuation" 234). Yes, the Jungian writers all agree that we need to "realize" the shadow — make it *real*, bring it out of the basement and into consciousness — but that is not the same thing as releasing it willy-nilly, which is what Jekyll does. For Jung and von Franz, at least, "realization" of the shadow means bringing the shadow to consciousness so it will not invisibly control us.

The kind of evil that Hyde seems to represent also appears to match the more traditional notion of wickedness implied by Jung and von Franz, though complicated by Bly and others: instinctual, emotional, especially sexual aspects of the psyche. This is not surprising; if Jung and von Franz reveal the Victorian-era roots of depth psychology, Robert Louis Stevenson was himself actually a Victorian. In Stevenson's story the lawyer Gabriel John Utterson is the primary point-of-view character, and Utterson is almost a caricature of Victorian restraint, a man with no discernible emotional or sexual life whatsoever: he is "never lighted by a smile; cold, scanty and embarrassed in discourse; backward in sentiment," "austere," "undemonstrative," "modest" (5). And into Utterson's world of utter restraint roars all that has been hiding — Hyde: "it was hellish to see . . . like some damned Juggernaut" (7). Hyde's initial action in the story is described somewhat vaguely but it suggests the rape of a little girl: "the man trampled calmly over the child's body and left her screaming on the ground" (7). Hyde's Soho neighborhood is signaled as being a nightmarish version of a red-light district: "a dingy street, a gin palace, a low French eating house, . . . many ragged children huddled in the doorways, and many women of many different nationalities passing out, key in hand, to have a morning glass" (22). Hyde, it seems, incarnates the shadow of seedy sexuality buried beneath Victorian propriety.

But such a reading of Hyde bears reexamination, as Larry Kreitzer points out in an essay relating *Jekyll and Hyde* to the description of moral duality presented in Paul's epistle to the Romans. Kreitzer reviews the early responses to the novella as well as the many stage and film adaptations of the story, and he demonstrates how "a sexually focused interpretation has been dominant" despite the fact that in the actual text Hyde's nastiness is presented with "ambiguous nuances . . . which may or may not have been sexual in the original intention of the author" (140). Indeed, Kreitzer makes reference to a letter that Stevenson wrote complaining about this reduction of Hyde to sex and sensuality: Hyde, says Stevenson, is "not, great gods! a mere voluptuary. There is no harm in a voluptuary; and none, with my hand on my heart and in the sight of God, none — no harm whatever — in what prurient fools call 'immorality.' . . . [P]eople are so full of folly and inverted lust, that they can think of nothing but sexuality. . . . I know . . . that bad and good, even to our human eyes, has no more connection with what is called dissipation than it has with flying kites" ("Letter" 231). There is no doubt that Hyde does wicked things; he eventually kills the harmless Sir Danvers Carew. But Stevenson himself claims — and the text, which really is quite understated about Hyde, showing him to us very minimally, bears this out — that the story's wickedness is not located in sexuality or even passion. Rather, in the same letter Stevenson claims that "The harm was in Jekyll, because he was a hypocrite" ("Letter" 231). *Here*, it seems, is where destructive wickedness has its roots in *Jekyll and Hyde*. The issue is not sensuality but rather its hypocritical repression, and now we are in Robert Bly's territory.

Robert Bly specifically uses Stevenson's novella to illustrate his positive view of the shadow, his neo-romantic idea that the material shoved into the "bag" we drag behind us is intrinsically good, made from slices of the "living globe of energy" (Bly 17) that we originally are. Using his metaphor of a shadow-bag, Bly supplies this thumbnail analysis of *Jekyll and Hyde*:

Suppose the bag remains sealed — what happens then? A great nine-teenth-century story has an idea about that. One night Robert Louis Stevenson woke up and told his wife a bit of a dream he'd just had. She urged him to write it down; he did, and it became "Dr. Jekyll and Mr. Hyde." The nice side of the personality becomes, in our idealistic culture, nicer and nicer. The Western man may be a liberal doctor, for example, always thinking about the good of others. Morally and ethically he is wonderful. But the substance in the bag takes on a personality of its own; it can't be ignored. The story says that the substance locked in the bag feels angry, and when you see it it is shaped like an ape, and moves like an ape.

The story says then that when we put a part of ourselves in the bag it regresses. It de-evolves toward barbarism. (18–19)

In Bly's reading, Hyde is not intrinsically "evil," though he certainly wreaks terrible destruction. The problem according to Bly is that Hyde embodies Jekyll's energies and appetites and spontaneities, which are intrinsically positive but which have "de-evolved" because — in order to appear "nice" (not the same thing as being "good") — Jekyll has segregated them, sealed them off. The result is the stunted, apelike, "troglodytic" (*Jekyll and Hyde* 16) Edward Hyde, a fully separate entity from Henry Jekyll. Bly, we remember, asserts that "Every part of our personality that we do not love will become hostile to us. . . . [I]t may move to a distant place and begin a revolt against us" (20). Hyde is that hostile revolutionary.

For Bly the problem, then — the wickedness, if you will — is not the shadow contents themselves but the forceful diligence with which they are rejected and sealed off. Drawing on the work of William James, Bly describes a snobbish Western respectability that rejects the body and indeed ends up being blind to physical reality (and hence to beauty) of all kinds: "William James warned his students that a certain kind of mind-set was approaching the West — it could hardly be called a way of thought — in which no physical details are noticed, trees in the plural are mentioned, but no particular tree is ever loved, nor where it stands; the hair in the ear is not noticed" (70). What is bagged here, notice, is not in itself sexual; this is not just the Victorian repression of the id. Rather, what is repressed is a certain mindfulness about the rich texture of the world, about the value of attending to this texture. And Bly claims that today's students, hardly Victorian prudes, are as infected as anyone by this kind of bag-stuffing:

We now see this mind-set spread all over freshman English papers, which American students can now write quickly, on utterly generalized subjects; the nouns are usually plurals, and the feelings are all ones it would be nice to have. . . . Since the immense range of color belongs to physical detail — the thatness — of the universe, it is the inability to see color. (70–71)

It is this colorless mindset — a refusal to go down into the dark places that John Dunne calls "the valley" of human "cares and concerns" (14), and of colors and textures and specificities and differences — that Bly condemns as a bland form of idealism, a lazy rather than genuinely philosophical form of idealism. Modern idealists, he says, are

> horrible types, specialists in the One, builders of middle-class castles, and upper-class Usher houses, writers of boring Commencement speeches, creepy otherworldly types, worse than Pope Paul, academics who resemble gray jars, and who would ruin a whole state like Tennessee if put into it; people totally unable to merge into the place where they live — they could live in a valley for years and never become the valley. (73)

By these terms, a culture that values statistics and efficiency and bullet points more than textures and particularities and careful human interactions is as shadow-deprived as any sexually repressed Victorian. And Bly directly links these "horrible types," who refuse to "go down" into the dark side, with Henry Jekyll: "it's clear the idealist is a man or woman who does not want to go down. They plan to go to the grave with the shadow still repressed. The idealists are shadow-haters. They all end as does Dr. Jekyll, with a monkey-like Mr. Hyde scurrying among back buildings elsewhere in the city" (74).

We are a long way, now, from seeing Hyde as the embodiment of evil. It now seems that he is, in a sense, a victim of his alter-ego Jekyll's rejection of all that we are calling "the dark side." All of our theoretical writers about the shadow claim, of course, that the shadow develops without the ego's awareness and that it exists and operates in the unconscious. But Stevenson, as we saw, condemns Dr. Jekyll as a "hypocrite," a *conscious* deceiver. This may be one of the most important aspects of Stevenson's novella, for our purposes. In Jekyll, Stevenson dramatizes and brings into artistic daylight the mechanism of shadow-creating, which in "real" life occurs without conscious ego-awareness; Jekyll's *secret* scientific project of generating Hyde is a kind of analogy for the *unconscious* activity of shadow-making described by Jung, Bly, et al. So the rest of our examination of the psychological shadow in the *story* (as opposed to the deconstructive *structure*) of Stevenson's novella needs to focus not on Hyde but on Jekyll.

If the point-of-view character Utterson is a fairly benign embodiment of Victorian restraint, Jekyll is a more insidious portrayal of this restraint brought to hypocritical, manipulative self-awareness. In his "Full Statement of the Case," Jekyll describes himself as a wealthy, successful man who is "fond of the respect of the wise and good"; thus, he makes it his business to conceal those aspects of his 360-degree ball of energy that would detract from his social respectability:

> the worst of my faults was a certain impatient gaiety of disposition, such as has made the happiness of many, but such as I found it hard to reconcile with my imperious desire to carry my head high, and wear a more than commonly grave countenance before the public. Hence it came about that I concealed my pleasures; and that when I reached years of reflection, and began to look round me and take stock of my progress and position in the world, I stood already committed to a profound duplicity of life. (52)

The point here is that Jekyll's hidden traits are not intrinsically evil — "Many a man would have even blazoned such irregularities as I was guilty of" — but because of his "high views" about himself he has hidden his "gaiety of disposition" with "an almost morbid sense of shame" (52). This is a fairly precise presentation of the mechanism of bag-stuffing described by Bly, but with a *consciousness* about the mechanism that results in Jekyll's sense that the two sides of himself are separated by "a deeper trench than in the majority of men" (52). Jekyll claims he is not a hypocrite, but that is because he is convinced that his socially respectable persona is just as authentic as his hidden "gaiety." His persona, in other words, is not false but merely incomplete, and of this he is fully aware; it is this awareness, and the lengths he goes to hide his Hyde-self, that leads Stevenson himself to say that "the harm was in Jekyll, because he was a hypocrite" ("Letter" 231). Indeed, all the elaborate pseudo-science of the chemical separation of Hyde from Jekyll is a kind of metaphor for this concealment, a removal of Hyde from the mix in order to seal him off. In fact, however, the experiment fails; Hyde is chemically distilled as the undiluted shadow, but Jekyll is still as mixed and divided as ever: "although I had now two characters as well as two appearances, one was wholly evil, and the other was still the old Henry Jekyll, that incongruous compound of whose reformation and improvement I had already learned to despair" (56). Jekyll thinks that he could have distilled pure goodness rather than pure evil, "Had I approached my discovery in a more noble spirit, had I risked the experiment while under the empire of generous or pious aspirations" (55). But by the terms of this study such a claim is more than unlikely. I would assert that the very attempt to divide, to remove the "dark side," is as impossible as the pilgrim Dante's initial wish to escape his midlife despondency by racing straight up to heaven without any detour. The dynamic of Henry Jekyll's story, in other words, is not that Jekyll is the daylight self while Hyde is the shadow; rather, Jekyll is the shadow-*maker*, and that, not the shadow itself, is the location of wickedness for Stevenson, as it is for Bly.

It is in his essay "Lay Morals" that Stevenson lays out this idea most directly. Stevenson is annoyed, as he would likely be even more today, by conflicting scientific and theological views of what humanity is: "Some read his history in a certain intricacy of nerve and the success of successive digestions; others find him an exiled piece of heaven blown upon and determined by the breath of God; and both schools of theorists will scream like scalded children at a word of doubt" (29). In the face of these opposed dogmas, Stevenson opts for a notion of the human person that harmonizes the physical and the spiritual. (This self, this conscious subject, would be dislodged by Freud and "killed" by postmodernism. But Stevenson himself, even in the nineteenth century, recognized its trembling volatility.) Thus we have Stevenson calling for reconciliation of flesh and spirit, not an attempt to separate the two as ego and shadow, angel and demon, Dr. Jekyll and Mr. Hyde:

> All that is in the man in the larger sense . . . we must accept. It is not wrong to desire food, or exercise, or beautiful surroundings, or the love of sex, or interest which is the food of the mind. All these are craved; all these should be craved; to none of these in itself does the soul demur; where there comes an undeniable want, we recognize a demand of nature. (32)

The soul, Stevenson says, "demands that we shall not live alternately with our opposing tendencies in continual seesaw of passion and disgust, but seek some path on which the tendencies shall no longer oppose, but serve each other to a common end" (34).

Stevenson describes two ways or reasons for dividing the self — asceticism and respectability — and he rejects both. An ascetic — a "high character" — will, Stevenson says, "go without food to the ruin and death of the body rather than gain it in a manner which the spirit disavows. Pascal laid aside mathematics; Origen doctored his body with a knife; every day some one is thus mortifying his dearest interests and desires, and, in Christ's words, entering maim into the kingdom of heaven" (33). Stevenson calls instead for "reconciliation, in which the soul and all the faculties and senses pursue a common route and share in one desire" and "in which soul and body may unite like notes in a harmonious chord" (33–34).

But for Stevenson an even worse reason for chopping off and burying distasteful pasts of ourselves is Henry Jekyll's reason: *respectability*, a desire for *profit*. Stevenson describes the Victorian quest for respectability in terms that precisely describe Jekyll's hypocrisy, clearly signaling that the real location of immorality in *Jekyll and Hyde* is Henry Jekyll and not Edward Hyde:

> Now, the view taught at the present time seems to me to want greatness; and the dialect in which alone it can be intelligibly uttered is not the dialect of my soul. . . . We are to regulate our conduct not by desire, but by a politic eye upon the future; and to value acts as they will bring us money or good opinion; as they will bring us, in one word, *profit*. We must be what is called respectable, and offend no one by our carriage. . . . (36)

In *Jekyll and Hyde*, Dr. Jekyll is aware of the ideas that Stevenson records in "Lay Morals." Jekyll's explication of human dividedness in the novella's final section indicates that, unlike either typical ascetics or typical profiteers, he is explicitly purposeful in his manufacturing of a destructive shadow side; he does not create Mr. Hyde unconsciously. That is why I have said that Jekyll is an embodiment not of the ego but of the shadow-making mechanism itself, the mechanism that Stevenson wants to expose in "Lay Morals."

Thus, I agree with Larry Kreitzer's claim that wickedness in *Jekyll and Hyde* is not equated with sexuality. But I believe that Kreitzer's biblical, Pauline reading of Stevenson's novella is wrongheaded in a telling and important way. Kreitzer links *Jekyll and Hyde* with the famous lament in Romans 7:

> For I do not do the good I want, but the evil I do not want is what I do. . . .
> So I find it to be a law that when I want to do what is good, evil lies close at hand. For I delight in the law of God in my inmost self, but I see in my members another law at war with the law of my mind, making me captive of the law of sin that dwells in my members. (Romans 7:19–23, NRSV)

Kreitzer rightly notes that *Jekyll and Hyde* is a meditation on this famous biblical passage, and he quotes a letter from Stevenson verifying this: "Jekyll is a dreadful thing, I own; but the only thing I feel dreadful about is that damned old business of the war in the members" (Kreitzer 130). Kreitzer helpfully argues that the "members" mentioned in Romans are not just a reference to sexuality but rather embody a larger notion of sinfulness that Paul struggles against. By analogy, then, Hyde would seem to be the sinfulness — not just sexual — that Jekyll struggles with. I believe, however, that when we see *Jekyll* rather than Hyde as the locus of "sin" in Stevenson's novella, and reconciliation rather than suppression or transcendence as the goal, we have a rather different model of the spiritual journey from that which Kreitzer seems to be endorsing: one in which the "shadow" contains a great deal that is good — that can be reconciled or embraced or "eaten" (in Robert Bly's sense). Releasing this shadow willy-nilly, as Jekyll does, is analogous to "expressing" it or "acting-out," the flip side of repressing; and suppressing and indiscriminately expressing are equally partial, equally destructive. What Stevenson and our various Jungian theorists are calling for is not a vanquishing of "sin," but some kind of (always elusive, always a journey-toward) enlarging of person and world.

So far I have been writing about *Jekyll and Hyde* almost as if the entire novella consisted of Jekyll's "Statement of the Case." In fact, however, Jekyll's explanation does not appear until the final chapter of the work. But I did mention that in a sense the lawyer Utterson is the story's point-of-view character, and structurally the novella is built on the framework of Utterson's bit-by-bit unveiling of the truth about Jekyll and Hyde; the *design* of the novella is as important as the *story* of Jekyll and Hyde. Utterson first hears about the existence of Edward Hyde from Utterson's friend Richard Enfield, and Utterson initially assumes that Hyde's connection to Jekyll is as a vicious blackmailer, tormenting Jekyll for past (sexual?) peccadilloes. Only after working his way through a series of incidents and documents — a will, letters within letters, and Jekyll's final written "Statement of the Case" — does Utterson assemble the real story of Jekyll and Hyde and their connection. In the words of critic Roger Luckhurst, "The narrative moves from the outer edges of the secret to its final revelation. It unfolds like a sequence of Russian dolls nested inside each other" (xiii). Utterson's need to read all the documents in the correct sequence, even to the point of rather laboriously assembling them, creates "a constant sense of deferral, as if to get the dolls lined up in the right order" (xiii).

All of this may seem like merely traditional devices, building suspense in a typical horror story. The dangerous unseen is used by writers from Shakespeare to Poe to Stephen King. But perhaps the suspense genre is itself effective precisely because of the uncanny power of the shadow. Hyde is frightening largely because he is mysterious; despite many subsequent up-close-and-personal film portrayals, Stevenson's vague and amorphous (non-)description of Hyde is a great deal more effective:

Mr Hyde had numbered few familiars — even the master of the servant maid had only seen him twice; his family could nowhere be traced; he had never been photographed; and the few who could describe him differed widely, as common observers will. Only on one point, were they agreed; and that was the haunting sense of unexpressed deformity with which the fugitive impressed his beholders. (23)

So Hyde's mysteriousness is mirrored by the novella's complicated design. It is here, in the novella's stress on the hidden and unseen, that the psychological/moral shadow bleeds into what I earlier called the structural shadow — a shadow that cannot be "realized," either in the Christian moral sense of knowing sin in order to avoid it or in the Robert Bly holistic sense of retrieving lost energy by "eating" it. I suggest that the Russian-doll design of the novella and the inaccessibility of its key mystery, Edward Hyde, point toward what James Hillman, in his 1994 postscript to *Insearch*, calls "the fateful and ever-present unconscious-ness of all consciousness"; as Utterson searches for light, he keeps finding more shadow — "the penumbral life," as Hillman puts it, "that lives with life as the never-ceasing darkening of the light in every search. . . . Shadow both keeps us searching and prevents us finding" (134). In this sense "shadow," in Stevenson's novella, is not just a word for a Jungian concept that illuminates the "war of the members" that is waged in Henry Jekyll's psyche; it is also a (flawed, shadowy) name for what Stevenson conjures up by telling a story of a divided self and by using a labyrinthine structure for telling the story. Shadow, in this sense, is something like what Derrida calls *différance*.

In his book *Postmodern Narrative Theory*, Mark Currie includes a detailed analysis of *Strange Case of Dr Jekyll and Mr Hyde* as a postmodern text with Derridean undecidability. In doing so he demonstrates James Hillman's point that the Jungian concept of a psychological and moral shadow, an alter-ego carrying characteristics disdained and rejected by the conscious self, spills over into the shadow of *différance*, the structural situation of human knowing as a knowledge only of comparative differ-ences, with real presence deferred, enshadowed. And this structural situation of *différance* is, for Currie, the scaffolding of our very identities, which again brings us back to the self and its opacity to itself. Using a metaphor from Joseph Conrad's *Heart of Darkness*, Currie proposes that our identity is not "inside us, like the kernel of a nut" but rather that it "inheres in the relations between a person and others" (as a play of difference) and it "exists only as narrative" (the self "is" the story of what the self is) (Currie 17); in both cases "I" am a process rather than a stable entity. My attempt to grasp this "I" is a humbling journey with a deferred goal — the chasing of a shadow. Currie's discussion of these ideas in relation to *Jekyll and Hyde* focuses especially on two details: a mirror that Jekyll uses to watch his transformations into Hyde; and the anxiety with which Jekyll attempts to write the unwriteable, the end of the story, his own death.

In the chapter of *Jekyll and Hyde* entitled "The Last Night," Utterson and his friends — prior to learning the secret revealed in "Henry Jekyll's Statement of the Case" — find Hyde's dead body in Jekyll's laboratory, obviously the victim of suicide. And as they investigate the scene, they find a "cheval glass," a full-length mirror, an odd thing for a scientist to keep in his lab. They look into the mirror's "depths" with "an involuntary horror"; it shows them "nothing" except the play of light and "their own pale and fearful countenances stooping to look in" (42). But why do they consider this to be "nothing"? What else would a mirror show? "This glass have seen some strange things, sir," says the servant Poole, and it almost seems that the observers are looking into the mirror expecting to see those strange past events and are disappointed to see only their own faces. The truth, in other words, is deferred. Currie says that as a witness, the mirror

> has seen so much more than Poole realises or than the reader will ever see in full: the face of Hyde as well as the unnarrated events between the end of Jekyll's confession and this moment. As such, the mirror acts as a metaphor for the vision to which the reader has no access through writing. (129)

But Utterson responds to Poole that the strangest thing the mirror has seen is *itself*, and this leads Currie to note: "Even when a mirror is personified as a witness, it would only be capable of witnessing itself by looking into another mirror" (129). A mirror looking into a mirror is as good an image as I can imagine of the infinite regress that we have been toying with here in our discussion of bringing consciousness to the unconscious: the shadow is that which I am not conscious of; I "realize" the shadow, bring it to consciousness, and then it is not shadow but it casts a new shadow; and so on. Shadow is part of the very structure of the human situation, impossible to be "realized" away.

The other "shadow" that Mark Currie points out is the utter mystery of Jekyll/Hyde's own death. "Henry Jekyll's Statement of the Case" attempts to be a full statement, but it leaves a massive lacuna; in his desperate attempt to shine a light on his identity (the difference between and the narrative of Jekyll and Hyde), Jekyll ends up casting a deep shadow.

The final section of third-person narration in the novella is a chapter called "The Last Night"; in this chapter, Utterson breaks into Jekyll's lab, finds Hyde's dead body and a mirror, and wonders what exactly has happened. At the end of the chapter Utterson has a letter from Dr. Hastie Lanyon (who discovered the identity of Jekyll with Hyde) and Jekyll's "Full Statement," and he goes home to read them; the narrator promises that these documents will bring closure and clarity: "Utterson . . . trudged back to his office to read the two narratives in which this mystery was now to be explained" (44). But closure and clarity are not to be found. As Currie argues, Jekyll's statement ends the book with ambiguity — *différance*, shadow.

Yes, Utterson, along with us readers, learns that Hyde was Jekyll's alter-ego, not a separate individual. But that is not all that Utterson had peered into Jekyll's mirror in search of. The mirror had seen how and when Jekyll came to turn into Hyde for the last time, and how Hyde then died, and this is part of the story's mystery, its solution. In his "Full Statement," Jekyll has tried to answer this mystery, but his narrative instead demonstrates that this necessary closure is precisely what is impossible to narrate. Jekyll has frantically attempted to finish his narration before turning into Hyde one more time, and in the Full Statement Hyde becomes a kind of embodiment of the death both of Jekyll and of narrative itself. "Nor must I delay too long to bring my writing to an end," Jekyll has written in a passage quoted by Currie. ". . . Should the throes of change take me in the act of writing it, Hyde will tear it to pieces" (66). So how could Jekyll write in this document about that which will destroy Jekyll and the document? Jekyll was trying, in the act of writing, to outrun time, to write the unwriteable — his and his statement's demise. Currie calls this "the narratological shipwreck: the collision of the past and the present after which narration is no longer possible" (123). Jekyll could not do this, of course, and he ended his written statement by merely speculating on the final events of a story that for him was still unfinished but that has already ended by the time Utterson reads the document: How will Hyde permanently take over? What will then happen to him? These things are over and done with when Utterson reads the "Full Statement of the Case," which is actually anything but "full." These events have all occurred *after* Jekyll's ambiguous and inconclusively conclusive final sentence: "Here then, as I lay down the pen and proceed to seal up my confession, I bring the life of that unhappy Henry Jekyll to an end" (66). How could he simultaneously write *and* lay down the pen and seal up the document?

Jekyll claims to have brought "the life of that unhappy Henry Jekyll" to "an end." But what can that mean? Does "the life" refer to *the story*, the biography, as in "The Life of a Saint"? Or does it refer to the real flesh-and-blood life? If "the life" means "the biography," then Jekyll has failed, because he has not told the whole story; the biography still had further events, the very ones that Utterson longed to be told by the mirror in Jekyll's lab. If "the life" means the actual existence, then Jekyll has simply lied; Jekyll has not narrated the end of his life — he has, rather, reminded us that death cannot be narrated. Death, in other words, is like the unconscious: death that is experienced and described is not death, and an unconscious that is conscious is not unconscious.

The structure of this novella, then, has forced us to butt up against the structural shadow, the unyielding limits of human knowing. For Mark Currie, this is a realization that identity is not some inner essence but only inheres in narrative: "The unknowable and unnarratable perhaps draw attention to the idea that identity is only identity when narration is in process, so that there is a sense in which Jekyll has no existence beyond the end of the writing; his fictionality ensures that he has no existence after writing has stopped" (124). This is a fairly typical postmodern claim, and there are those who dismiss such statements of unknowability as nihilistic. And if these ideas leave us with a facile sense of mere gamesmanship — writing is about nothing but itself — then perhaps such claims are apt. But listened to deeply, this "structural" shadow, as James Hillman points out, can actually be healing:

> Shadow is an inevitable necessity of the human condition, an indelible psychological fact of all perception and all behavior. No mirror reveals it, no insight dispels it. Like ancient Greek fate that keeps us mortal, flawed, humanely limited, shadow guards us from the *hubris* of blindly trusting our own awareness, and as such shadow is a blessing. (135)

Sula

There are many other literary works that we could examine as illuminations of the motif of the shadow. Indeed, if Robert Bly is correct, *all* literature is in a sense created by the dark side; literature is the not-yet-known dressing itself in metaphors that maintain its mystery but suggest its wisdom. Many other works, therefore, could enlarge and deepen the visions of Jung, Derrida, Stevenson, et al.

But Toni Morrison's 1973 novel *Sula* strikes me as a particularly valuable exploration of these ideas. It is a fine contemporary work of fiction written by a great, Nobel-prize-winning novelist. It specifically plays with the theme of shadow-doubleness; its central characters, Nel Wright and Sula Peace, are young women whose friendship is based on the kind of play of difference that marks the relationship between self and shadow. But the novel is vividly and insistently about the *friendship*, not just about the psyche of one character. Sula is not merely a part of Nel, nor is Nel a part of Sula; their spiritual journeys are played out in a real, mutual relationship, reminding us of James Hillman's claim that soul is not only an inner core but is also out in the world beyond our own private subjectivities. And finally, as a depiction of African American experience, *Sula* stands as a warning against slipping into dangerous, racist-tinged imaging in a discussion of "the dark side" and "the shadow." These are conventional terms, and are useful as such. But as we have already seen we need to resist the seduction of light-is-good, dark-is-bad conceptualizing: not only does this polarize what are "shaded differentiations" rather than dialectical oppositions, but it also is part of a system of hierarchical dichotomies that has historically denigrated women (as opposed to men) and black (as opposed to white). A fine African American woman writer like Toni Morrison can help us avoid such systematizing.

Morrison's *Sula* replicates what I have (awkwardly) called the dark-side narrative in several ways. Morrison begins at a macro-level, describing the setting of the story, and in doing so she reminds us of Hillman's concept of soul as something "out there" — of the larger fabric within which the individual spiritual journey takes place. Then she moves to a mythic level, the story of a fairly minor character whose own dark-side experience creates a sort of metanarrative within which the main narrative about Nel and Sula takes place. The bulk of the novel then deals with this narrative: Nel's and Sula's respective developments as young women with parts of their souls lost, in the shadows, repressed, even stolen; their friendship as an encounter with these lost, needed, dangerous aspects of life; and the conclusions of their stories, in which Nel and Sula partially gain the life lost (*honoring* or *eating* the shadow) but also confront the radical mystery of the humbling "structural" shadow that surrounds life and cannot be integrated, circumscribed. Let us look, then, sequentially at these various parts of Morrison's novel — the opening presentations of the town and its myth, and the development and conclusion of the story of Nel and Sula's friendship — to see how gracefully, insightfully, ambiguously Toni Morrison ruminates on the mysterious (no)thing we have been calling "the shadow."

Sula begins with a description of the story's setting that raises the themes of shadow and dark side, but in ironic and paradoxical ways that resist light-dark, up-down hierarchies. The setting is the African American section of the town of Medallion, Ohio, which exists in the narrator's present time — late twentieth century — as an almost-forgotten shadow beneath what is now a white suburb with a swanky new golf course: "It is called the suburbs now, but when black people lived there it was called the Bottom" (3). So the story takes place not on "the top" but in "the Bottom" — but ironically, at the time of the story the Bottom was the top, the neighborhood on the hill above the town. This was not, however, some hill to heaven like the one Dante unsuccessfully attempts to climb at the start of the Inferno; in Medallion, *up* went *down* into the depths of human cares and concerns. It was named "the Bottom," legend has it, as a racist trick: a white farmer offered the land to his former slave, calling it "bottom land, rich and fertile . . . the bottom of heaven — best land there is," when in fact it was "the hilly land, where planting was backbreaking, where the soil slid down and washed away the seeds, and where the wind lingered all through the winter" (5).

So the Bottom, which now exists only as a shadow beneath a golf course, was the top, but was really the bottom — a hard, spirit-crushing place for blacks to live and make a living. And yet, the narrator says, the whites in the valley heard, up in the Bottom, "singing sometimes, banjos sometimes," and saw "a dark woman in a flowered dress doing a bit of cakewalk, a bit of black bottom, a bit of 'messing around' to the lively notes of a mouth organ" (4); there was vitality and joy up in the Bottom. But beneath the music and accompanying laughter — in the shadows, if you will — was "the adult pain that rested somewhere under the eyelids, somewhere under their head rags and soft felt hats" (4). Pain, however, was not the true truth buried beneath an illusion of laughter: the laughter was real too, and "the laughter was part of the pain" (4). The Bottom is the Blues — sadness that is musically transformed into joy while still being sad, a bottom that is the top that is the bottom. This is the kind of paradox that, as we have seen, makes up the shadow: unconsciousness that is made conscious and is intrinsically unconscious. The bluesy people of the Bottom have lived with that kind of disturbing and funny mystery.

During the timeframe of the story, the people of the Bottom celebrate this mystery once a year, on January third: National Suicide Day, instituted by the Bottom's resident mad prophet, Shadrack. The story of Shadrack, told in the book's second chapter, provides a kind of mythic metanarrative that frames the novel. And his story is a prototypical dark-side narrative.

At the start of his story, Shadrack is a good but naive young man, not unlike Young Goodman Brown in Hawthorne's tale: in 1917, Shadrack is "a young man of hardly twenty, his head full of nothing and his mouth recalling the taste of lipstick" (7). It is World War I that provides Shadrack's world-upending dark-side adventure, thrust on this innocent young man who has not consciously chosen the experience and has no categories by which to absorb it, understand it:

> Shadrack had found himself in December, 1917, running with his comrades across a field in France. . . . Shellfire was all around him, and though he knew that this was something called *it*, he could not muster up the proper feeling — the feeling that would accommodate *it*. He expected to be terrified or exhilarated — to feel *something* very strong. In fact, he felt only the bite of a nail in his boot. . . . Wincing at the pain in his foot, he turned his head a little to the right and saw the face of a soldier near him fly off. (7–8)

Shadrack comes to himself, injured, in a hospital back in the States, and he now sees the world and his own body as utterly strange, other, impossible to assimilate. He has to struggle to see that the colors in a tray actually signify food, and especially that his own hands will maintain their stability as human hands: "just as he was about to spread his fingers, they began to grow in higgledy-piggledy fashion like Jack's beanstalk all over the tray and the bed. With a shriek he closed his eyes and thrust his huge growing hands under the covers" (9). Language, Shadrack discovers, is especially slippery. The signifier for himself ("private," his military status) seems to have no connection to the signified (Shadrack); he has stumbled on what we have been calling *différance*, the structural shadow, the gap between words and any substantive, present reality, exposing the *secret* mystery underneath:

> He wanted desperately to see his own face and connect it with the word "private" — the word the nurse (and the others who helped bind him) had called him. "Private" he thought was something secret, and he wondered why they looked at him and called him a secret. (10)

This is the decentered world Shadrack encounters during his dark-side journey, and his return to the Bottom is marked by his ritualistic attempt to digest this frightening, secret shadow.

Released from the hospital because he is considered violent, Shadrack wanders the countryside unselved:

> he didn't know who or what he was . . . with no past, no language, no tribe, no source, no address book, no comb, no pencil, no clock, no pocket handkerchief, no rug, no bed, no can opener, no faded postcard, no soap, no key, no tobacco pouch, no soiled underwear and nothing nothing nothing to do . . . (12)

Arrested and jailed, Shadrack just wants to see his own face, to find a self again, though surely no longer young, innocent, with a lipstick-sweet mouth. The only mirror he has is the water in his jail-cell toilet, and he achieves an unstable stability by recognizing his own blackness, his racial identity but also his combination of self and shadow:

> There in the toilet water he saw a grave black face. A black so definite, so unequivocal, it astonished him. He had been harboring a skittish apprehension that he was not real — that he didn't exist at all. But when the blackness greeted him with its indisputable presence, he wanted nothing more. (13)

Brought back to Medallion and the Bottom, Shadrack institutes National Suicide Day, a once-a-year solitary parade, as a way ritualistically, metaphorically, to capture what cannot be captured, to expect what cannot be expected, and especially to include in life what life cannot include, *death*:

> Shadrack began . . . a struggle to order and focus experience. . . . It was not death or dying that frightened him, but the unexpectedness of both. In sorting it all out, he hit on the notion that if one day a year were devoted to it, everybody could get it out of the way and the rest of the year would be safe and free. In this manner he instituted National Suicide Day. (14)

So the Bottom, the setting of the story of Nel and Sula, is established as a place that has absorbed — that is, in Robert Bly's terms, has "eaten" and "honored" — the shadow:

> As time went along, the people took less notice of these January thirds, or rather they thought they did, thought they had no attitudes or feelings one way or another about Shadrack's annual solitary parade. In fact they had simply stopped remarking on the holiday because they had absorbed it into their thoughts, into their language, into their lives. (15)

It is here — in this Bottom that is the-top-that-is-a-bottom, drenched in the Blues — that Nel and Sula will encounter and absorb their own personal shadows through a complicated dance of friendship with each other.

Nel Wright's back story, the story of her family and childhood, could almost be a case study on Robert Bly's theory of shadow-creation as a paring away of appetites and spontaneities, reducing "a round globe of energy" to "a slice" (Bly 18). This leaves Nel dominated by what Marie-Louise von Franz calls the ego's "utilitarian attitude of conscious planning," which von Franz says needs to be given up "in order to make way for the inner growth of the personality" ("Process of Individuation" 164).

The story of Nel's mother, Helene Sabat, told in the novel's third chapter, could be called an anti-dark-side story, a tale of *flight from* the shadow. Or rather, in fleeing from the appetites and spontaneities of her family heritage (and hence, presumably, of her own nature) Helene constellates a huge shadow of repression in herself and especially her daughter, Nel. Helene was born in a New Orleans brothel, named — shadowily enough — "Sundown House"; her mother, Rochelle, is a "Creole whore" (17). Sundown House is described as lovely rather than wicked — bedecked with "red shutters" and "soft lights and flowered carpets" (17), marks of Bly's vital, beautiful energy globe, but Helene's ultra-respectable grandmother sees this beauty as a signifier of immorality. She initiates the shadow-creating by taking Helene away from Sundown House and raising her "under the dolesome eyes of a multicolored Virgin Mary, counseling her to be constantly on guard for any sign of her mother's wild blood" (17).

Even more forcefully does Helene guard her daughter, Nel, from this "wild blood"; with her husband, Wiley Wright, Helene leaves the eroticism of New Orleans for the cool north of Medallion, Ohio, and lacking the virginal protection of Mary in a Catholic church, Helene "joined the most conservative black church. And held sway" (18). *Holding sway* involves using that "utilitarian attitude of conscious planning" to tamp down any traces of Sundown House in Nel: "Under Helene's hand the girl became obedient and polite. Any enthusiasms that little Nel showed were calmed by the mother until she drove her daughter's imagination underground" (18). If Bly — let alone Jung, von Franz, and others — is correct, pushing Sundown House "underground" will not eliminate it; rather, this will generate a shadow that will need eventually to be *retrieved, realized, eaten.*

The latter part of this third chapter is a portrait in miniature of Nel's retrieval of the shadow, foreshadowing her complex friendship with Sula. But, again, Toni Morrison adds an important consideration of racial identity, reminding us that shadow issues, and the spiritual journey in general, are part of a large cultural framework. On the one hand, in repressing Nel's potential high spirits Helene is happy that Nel is not beautiful by white society's standards, like the light-skinned Creole Rochelle — "that her skin had dusk in it, that her lashes were substantial but not undignified in their length, that she had taken the broad flat nose of Wiley . . . and his generous lips" (18). And yet Helene simultaneously wants to make Nel seem less black and more white, so she will be respectable; hence, throughout the novel she pressures Nel to "improve . . . somewhat" the "broad flat nose" she has inherited from her father by pulling on it. So Helene is caught in an absurd contradiction, fleeing the white society's norms of beauty while also grasping at that same society's norms of respectability. Helene's paradoxical encouragement/suppression of her daughter's racial characteristics demonstrates the complex intertwining of the psychological shadow with the cultural and ethnic shadow, and Nel's ability to relate authentically to her race, her world, and herself is squeezed dry.

But when Helene's grandmother, Nel's great-grandmother, becomes ill, requiring Helene and Nel to travel down to New Orleans to visit, Nel glimpses the truth about her pared-away "globe of energy" in a way that deepens her sense of self and prepares for her friendship with Sula. First Nel sees that her mother's obsession with respectability is futile in the face of cultural racism and is fundamentally self-hating: when Helene and Nel accidentally enter the white section of the southbound train, they are reprimanded by the white conductor, and Helene — rather than taking a stand against degrading treatment — "smiled dazzlingly and coquettishly at the salmon-colored face of the conductor" (21). Nel is ashamed of her mother, especially when she sees that two black soldiers look "stricken" by Helene's subservient demeanor. Perhaps, Nel seems subliminally to realize, there is something self-destructive about Helene's control and repression, and this possibility is underlined when Helene and Nel, in the absence of black-designated restrooms, are forced to urinate in a field. And then for the first time Nel meets, in New Orleans, her grandmother, the "Creole whore" Rochelle, who far from being appalling is quite lovely: she carries a "sweet odor as of gardenias," wears a striking "canary-yellow dress" (25), and speaks a softly exotic French. ("I don't talk Creole," Helene snaps to Nel. "And neither do you" [27].) In the wake of Helene's degrading self-subordination to the racism on the train, Nel infers that Rochelle's self-possession may not be so bad after all, and Rochelle's beauty and sheer sensuousness suggest an alternative to Helene's sterilized relationship with the world.

What the New Orleans visit activates in Nel is a first, tentative awakening to an approach to self and world that differs from her mother's repressiveness — a "realization" of the shadow. When Helene and Nel get back to Medallion, Helene is relieved to have escaped the power of Sundown House, and she thanks her respectable God for extricating her: "Lord, I never thought I'd get back here safe and sound. Whoo. Well, it's over. Good and over. Praise His name" (27). And she immediately pesters Nel to get back to suppressing her blackness: "Don't just sit there, honey. You could be pulling your nose" (28). But Nel instead remembers "the smell and the tight, tight hug of the woman in yellow" (28) — sensory images and feelings rather than the abstract idea of respectablity. And she looks in the mirror and sees something more than the girl who has been diminished by her mother; she sees something richer and more mysterious — the shadow, at least, of a 360-degree ball of energy — leading her to pray to a very different God from her mother's:

> "I'm me," she whispered. "Me."
> Nel didn't know quite what she meant, but on the other hand she knew exactly what she meant.
> "I'm me. I'm not their daughter. I'm not Nel. I'm me. Me."
> Each time she said the word me there was a gathering in her like power, like joy, like fear. . . .
> "Me," she murmured. . . . "I want . . . I want to be . . . wonderful. Oh, Jesus, make me wonderful." (28–29)

Now Nel is ready to befriend Sula, whom previously she "never played with, never knew, because her mother said that Sula's mother was sooty" (29). The narrator insistently points out that the friendship is directly related to the visit with Rochelle, the "whore" of Sundown House, and that Sula will give Nel access to a dimension of life — of Nel herself and of the world beyond — that Helene has tried to push into the shadows: "The trip, perhaps, or her new found me-ness, gave her the strength to cultivate a friend in spite of her mother" (29).

Unlike Nel's rigid world and meticulously kept house, Sula's house is "woolly" and her family wildly spontaneous. Nel is drawn to this energy; Nel, the narrator says,

> preferred Sula's woolly house, where a pot of something was always cooking on the stove; where the mother, Hannah, never scolded or gave directions; where all sorts of people dropped in; where newspapers were stacked in the hallway, and dirty dishes left for hours at a time in the sink, and where a one-legged grandmother named Eva handed you goobers from deep inside her pockets or read you a dream. (29)

Sula, on the other hand, loves Nel's house, which Sula's presence enriches: "Nel, who regarded the oppressive neatness of her home with dread, felt comfortable in it with Sula, who loved it and would sit on the red-velvet sofa for ten to twenty minutes at time — still as dawn" (29). Sula, from a "woolly" house and a rough-and-tumble family, can be "still as dawn" in Nel's house. Clearly she needs Nel's (or Helene's) orderliness as much as Nel needs Sula's spontaneity; in this novel, the dynamics of a "realization of the shadow" are mutual, two-way. But it is important to note the *relationality* in both cases. Nel and Sula do not just offer each other abstract compensatory ideas — spontaneity for Nel and order for Sula — but rather, they fully inhabit each other's very different worlds, signified by the pot on the stove (Sula's house) and the red-velvet sofa (Nel's). This friendship is, for each of them, an immersion in a sensuous otherness; this otherness cannot be absolutely, rationally bridged (*tout autre est tout autre*, says Derrida), but its light and shadow can be bathed in.

The mutual way Nel and Sula enhance each other's 360-degree globe of energy comes to focus to a large degree on sexuality, but in a complex way; the Jungian (and Freudian) stereotype of the shadow being constituted by suppressed sex is complicated here, even more than it was in *Jekyll and Hyde*. Helene Wright's suppression of the Sundown House and its "Creole whore" represents the typical kind of shadow-creating that Jung, von Franz, Bly, and others describe, and with Sula's help Nel opens up the "bag" a bit. When Sula and Nel are twelve years old, Sula takes Nel on walks past titillated and titillating men who make the friends feel their own burgeoning sexual desires, sparked by the men's "cream-colored trousers marking with a mere seam the place where the mystery curled" (50). Sula is bringing Nel back to her own inner Sundown House. But Nel brings Sula to a shadowy sexual place too. Utterly unlike Nel, Sula has grown up surrounded by sexual activity. When Sula's father died, Sula's mother, Hannah, became a "sweet, low and guileless" flirt who "rippled with sex" (42). Hannah has sex lightly, happily, with man after man, implicitly teaching Sula that "sex was pleasant and frequent, but otherwise unremarkable" (44); if sexuality seems nonexistent in Nel's house, it seems flat and mundane in Sula's. So Sula as much as Nel needs acquaintance with "the place where mystery curled" — the awe and wonder of sexuality, and of the world in general. For Sula, "wedged into a household of throbbing disorder constantly awry with things, people, voices and the slamming of doors" (51–52), awe and wonder have to be acquired in a world of quiet and introversion — "in the attic behind a roll of linoleum galloping through her own mind on a gray-and-white horse tasting sugar and smelling roses in full view of a someone who shared both the taste and the speed" (52). It is from the kind of order and quiet she experiences with Nel and Helene (not an idea but a sensuous experience of a vividly quiet attic) that Sula gains depth and soul, not just sexuality but eros. A similar deepening for Nel requires looking out to the exterior world, the world of soul *out there* described by James Hillman, "the inside 'out there': in the trees, in the finches and squirrels in the trees, in the soil and stones, and even in the panes of glass that you see through to the trees, the squirrels, and the stones" (*Insearch* 130). It is this outside-ness that eroticizes Nel's imagination, a "fiery" extraversion she draws from Sula and her family:

"When Nel, an only child, sat on the steps of her back porch surrounded by the high silence of her mother's incredibly orderly house, feeling the neatness pointing at her back, she studied the poplars and fell easily into a picture of herself lying on a flowered bed, tangled in her own hair, waiting for some fiery prince" (51).

A concept of soul as *out there* (in the poplars and finches) as well as *in here* (in the subject's mind) can help us see that Nel's and Sula's encounters with their respective shadows through each other are more than psychological projections. This friendship is a pair of genuine encounters with an *other*, a deepening of self by finding the shadow out there as well as in here:

> Their meeting was fortunate, for it let them use each other to grow on. Daughters of distant mothers and incomprehensible fathers (Sula's because he was dead; Nel's because he wasn't), they found in each other's eyes the intimacy they were looking for. . . .
>
> Their friendship was as intense as it was sudden. They found relief in each other's personality. (52, 53)

This is why the friendship between Nel and Sula is so important. The shadow that these young women need to embrace is not just some repressed inner content that needs to be "integrated" into an "individuated" self. When the "realization of the shadow" is left in these terms, the self is seen as an atomistic subject; in that case, Sula could just as well be Nel's inner "Mr. Hyde" rather than a genuine friend. But in *Sula* what we are calling *the shadow* is an outer other as well as an inner otherness, and indeed it erases easy dichotomies between "inner" and "outer": the novel cannot be reduced *either* to a story of inner spiritual growth *or* one of outer friendship. *Tout autre est tout autre.*

Perhaps the novel's best representation of the enriching effect of an access to the shadow has to do not with sex but with humor, laughter. When the women have grown up and Nel has gotten married, Sula leaves Medallion. During this time, Nel slips back into a more conventional mindset, rather typical, according to Robert Bly, of young people at an early point in their marriages and careers. But then, after a ten-year absence, Sula comes home, and Nel feels the difference — not just internally but in the environment, the soul of the world around her, illuminated by the return of the shadow. The world has "a sheen, a glimmering as of green, rain-soaked Saturday nights (lit by the excitement of newly installed street lights); of lemon-yellow afternoons bright with iced drinks and splashes of daffodils" (94). The difference, Nel knows, is the presence of Sula, who opens Nel's eyes and makes Nel laugh — and who reveals, therefore, that vision and humor are closely intertwined, that what Buddhists call "mindfulness" is somehow related to the ability to laugh:

> She knew it was all due to Sula's return to the Bottom. It was like getting the use of an eye back, having a cataract removed. Her old friend had come home. Sula. Who made her laugh, who made her see old things with new eyes. . . . More than any other thing, humor returned. (95)

A conversation between Nel and the newly returned Sula is an operatic duet. Each melodic line would be partial, but the two together are a musical version of that 360-degree energy globe, throbbing with *the* human embodiment of energy, *laughter*:

> Nel lowered her head onto crossed arms while tears of laughter dripped into the warm diapers. Laughter that weakened her knees and pressed her bladder into action. Her rapid soprano and Sula's dark sleepy chuckle made a duet that frightened the cat and made the children run in from the back yard, puzzled at first by the wild free sounds, then delighted to see their mother stumbling merrily toward the bathroom, holding on to her stomach, fairly singing through the laughter. . . . (97)

This kind of soulful, shadow-deepened laugh is more than "the miscellaneous giggles and smiles" that Nel has been satisfied with in Sula's absence. It is "a rib-scraping laugh," and Nel "had forgotten how deep and down it could be" (98). "Shadow" signifies the gap that always looms when the mind contemplates otherness (signifier vs. signified, ego vs. full self, me vs. friend). A "rib-scraping laugh," however, erases this gap or makes it (at least momentarily) irrelevant. Self-consciousness, with its shadow of separation, vanishes in the ecstasy of deep laughter.

Not surprisingly, the relationship between Sula and Nel has twists and complications, and eventually a rupture occurs when Nel catches Sula having sex with Nel's husband; shadow recovery and deep friendship both are plagued by, well, *shadows*. For our purposes, however, the important thing is the way, in the end, each woman honors (or, in Robert Bly's terms, "eats") her shadow, and yet also the way Morrison leaves us with a sense of the irreconcilability of this friendship and the shadow-integration it facilitates. In James Hillman's terms, the novel leaves us with a powerful sense of the "structural shadow," mournful, necessary, and humbling.

It is Sula, always more fully in touch with the dark side, who most fully and honestly faces the structural shadow, what Derrida writes of as the "goodbye" lurking beneath every "hello." Sula's broken relationships with her family, her involvement along with Nel years ago in the accidental death of a little boy, and now this permanent rupture with Nel make clear to Sula that a deep aloneness shadows human life:

> there was no other that you could count on; . . . there was no self to count on either. She had no center, no speck around which to grow. . . . She was completely free of ambition, with no affection for money, property or things, no greed, no desire to command attention or compliments — no ego. . . .
>
> She had clung to Nel as the closest thing to both an other and a self, only to discover that she and Nel were not one and the same. (118–119)

This post-Nel Sula deepens our sense of the relation between the shadow and sex; conventionally, sex is considered a key to the shadow because sexual appetite is, or used to be, what people are primarily forced to suppress. But Sula discovers a more fundamental shadow in sexual activity, part of the very structure of sex and of human interaction in general. Humor and laughter are intrinsic parts of sex for Sula (she is aware of that humorously ridiculous shadow side to sex, lurking beneath Valentine's Day romanticism), but so, after the rapture of orgasm, is a kind of tragic emptiness, a "postcoital privateness":

> she leapt from the edge into soundlessness and went down howling, howling in a stinging awareness of the endings of things: an eye of sorrow in the midst of all that hurricane rage of joy. There, in the center of that silence was not eternity but the death of time and a loneliness so profound the word itself had no meaning. (123)

None of this is to suggest that Sula is some kind of depressive, let alone nihilistic, character; rather, the insight she brings to the novel (and to Nel) — especially after the end of the friendship that has defined and enlarged both Sula and Nel — is analogous to the realization of radical uncertainty that, as we have seen, Derrida describes so well. Sula's discovery that at base, in the face of loss and death, the other and even the self are not solid objects to be counted on, echoes what Derrida's calls "The question of the self: 'who am I?' not in the sense of 'who am I' but 'who is this "I"' that can say 'who'? What is the 'I,' and what becomes of responsibility once the identity of the 'I' trembles *in secret*?" (*Gift of Death* 92). This lack of an absolutely certain foundation is the version of a "shadow" that for James Hillman is part of the structure of the human situation. And far from being nihilistic, Hillman says that the realization of this shadow is a humbling "gift from Hades" (*Insearch* 135).

Toni Morrison, however, ends her novel not with Sula but with Nel, and we similarly end our discussion of literary reflections on the shadow with Nel's mournful but loving realization of her shadow, and of the friendship that allows her to honor this shadow and that is itself deeply shadowed. Having (appropriately, surely) sacrificed Sula, as Abraham sacrificed Isaac, at the end of the novel Nel discovers the shadow behind the shadow: a *gift* that is outside the economy of tit-for-tat exchange.

Even before Sula's return to the Bottom, there are indications that Nel's husband, Jude, is not a good partner for Nel. Robert Bly warns that when two people's globes of energy have been pared away and pushed into the shadow's "bag," the people make poor marriage partners:

> We'll imagine a man who has a thin slice left — the rest is in the bag — and we'll imagine that he meets a woman. . . . They join each other in a ceremony, and this union of two slices is called marriage. Even together the two do not make up one person! (18)

This is precisely the situation with Nel and Jude. Unlike Sula, Jude does not give Nel access to her repressed spontaneity and energy. Rather, Jude feels rage at the oppression he has experienced as a black man, and he turns to Nel so he can dominate her and at least feel powerful at home; because of her reserve and kindness, Nel helps Jude feel that "the whole venture" of their relationship is "his idea, his conquest" (83): "The two of them together would make one Jude" (83), says the narrator, almost directly echoing Bly. In the absence of Sula, Nel settles in as a wife with no "sparkle or splutter": "Her parents had succeeded in rubbing down to a dull glow any sparkle or splutter she had. Only with Sula did that quality have free reign" (83).

None of this is to justify the eventual affair Jude has with Sula when Sula returns, or to say that Nel is better off without Jude; thus, within a rational value system it is right for Nel to reject Sula as payback for Sula's betrayal of Nel. But this double rupture — broken marriage, broken friendship — leaves Nel with an emptiness that mirrors Sula's own powerful awareness of the "structural" nature of human aloneness, which Nel experiences as a nearly visible shadow, a "gray ball," a "little ball of fur and string and hair always floating in the light near her but which she did not see because she never looked" (109).

This is a shadow that only Sula could make bearable but that Sula now cannot help Nel bear:

> It just floated there for the seeing, if she wanted to. But she didn't want to see it, ever, for if she saw it, who could tell but what she might actually touch it, or want to, and then what would happen if she actually reached out her hand and touched it? Die probably. . . . Here she was in

the midst of it, hating it, scared of it, and again she thought of Sula as though they were still friends and talked things over. That was too much. To lose Jude and not have Sula to talk to about it because it was Sula that he had left her for. (110)

Indeed, when Sula becomes very ill and Nel visits her — feeling coolly self-righteous — Sula further exposes Nel to the structural shadow, the deep uncertainty that shadows human self-confidence, by challenging Nel's chilly sense of nobility. "How do you know?" Sula asks Nel. "About who was good. How do you know it was you?" (146). Maybe, Sula suggests, Nel has not been so good at all; maybe her "goodness" is a false mask. Perhaps "goodness" is not a matter of rational correctness but of relationality itself, and the beautiful Sula — who breaks moral codes but whose rose-shaped birthmark suggests that she, like the "Creole whore" Rochelle, has been touched by Aphrodite — relates like crazy. Speaking so harshly to Nel may be a cruel thing for Sula to do from her own deathbed; it turns out to be her last statement to Nel. Or perhaps this is Sula's "gift" to Nel "from Hades."

This final conversation with Sula foreshadows the final conversation in the novel, between Nel and Eva, Sula's grandmother. Again Nel is feeling noble, self-righteous, visiting Eva in a nursing home called, ironically, Sunnydale ("There was too much light everywhere; it needed some shadows" [167]). And Eva shakes Nel's sense of nobility even more radically than Sula did. As previously mentioned, Sula and Nel were involved years ago in the accidental death of a little boy, but Nel has always told herself that it was Sula's fault. Eva challenges this: "You. Sula. What's the difference? You was there. You watched, didn't you? Me, I never would've watched" (168). And afterward Nel is flooded with a realization of the excitement she actually felt when the boy died, which she has buried deeply. Her friendship with Sula comes back to her as a message that she has a wildness about her too, as Sula did, that her personality is bigger and more complex than she has allowed herself to realize: "All these years she had been secretly proud of her calm, controlled behavior when Sula was uncontrollable. . . . Now it seemed that what she had thought was maturity, serenity and compassion was only the tranquility that follows a joyful stimulation" (170).

This realization of Nel's own hidden, wild self and of her profound but hidden connection with Sula is painful, morally challenging, but filled with depth and soul. As the novel ends Nel has two key experiences, which signal that she is beginning to embrace the shadow — to grieve and to face complex truths, which she draws from her own memory but also from the world around her, "the tops of trees" and the leaves and mud and ripe smells of the natural world:

> Suddenly Nel stopped. Her eye twitched and burned a little.
> "Sula?" she whispered, gazing at the tops of trees. "Sula?"
> Leaves stirred; mud shifted; there was the smell of overripe green things. A soft ball of fur broke and scattered like dandelion spores in the breeze. (174)

That gray ball, which Nel had tried to avoid looking at, has burst and revealed itself to be filled with vitality, living spores. And Nel mournfully keens, finally knowing and feeling the depth of her friendship with Sula and the pain of its loss:

> "All that time, all that time, I thought I was missing Jude." And the loss pressed down on her chest and came up into her throat. "We was girls together," she said as though explaining something. "O Lord, Sula," she cried, "girl, girl, girlgirlgirl."
> It was a fine cry — loud and long — but it had no bottom and it had no top, just circles and circles of sorrow. (174)

Nel's gasp — "girlgirlgirl" — is analogous to her earlier "rib-scraping laugh," an ecstatic break from her calculated, self-conscious moralism and into a place of radical connection in which Nel/world/Sula are somehow all present to each other despite the shadow of disconnection. This is something like the miraculous gift, outside the economy of calculated exchange, that Derrida says Abraham receives at the very moment that he renounces his loved son Isaac: "God gives back to [Abraham], in the instant of absolute renunciation, the very thing that he had already, in the same instant, decided to sacrifice. It is given back to him because he renounced calculation" (96–97). This is not the end of shadow but a deeper shadow, neither just inner nor just outer, an absence of self and other that is a presence of self and other, incalculable, not clarity but just "a fine cry" with "no bottom" and "no top." Nel has "realized" the shadow — personal, moral, structural, breaking down distinctions between "bottom" and "top." And she has begun the long activity of eating it.

Works Cited

Bly, Robert. *A Little Book on the Human Shadow*. San Francisco: HarperCollins, 1988.

Currie, Mark. *Postmodern Narrative Theory*. New York: Palgrave Macmillan, 1998.

Derrida, Jacques. *The Gift of Death*. Trans. David Willis. Chicago: University of Chicago, 1995.

Dunne, John S. *The Way of All the Earth*. New York: Macmillan, 1972.

Hillman, James. *Insearch: Psychology and Religion*. 1967. Woodstock, CT: Spring Publications, 1994.

Himes, Michael J. "'Finding God in All Things': A Sacramental Worldview and Its Effects." *As Leaven in the World: Catholic Perspectives on Faith, Vocation, and the Intellectual Life*. Ed. Thomas M. Landy. Franklin, WI: Sheed & Ward, 2001. 91–103.

Jung, C. G. *Aion: Researches into the Phenomenology of the Self*. Trans. R. F. C. Hull. Princeton: Princeton University, 1959.

Kreitzer, Larry. "R. L. Stevenson's *Strange Case of Dr. Jekyll and Mr. Hyde* and Romans 7: 14–25: Images of the Moral Duality of Human Nature." *Literature and Theology* 6 (1992):125–144.

Luckhurst, Roger. "Introduction." *Strange Case of Dr Jekyll and Mr Hyde and Other Tales*. Robert Louis Stevenson. Oxford: Oxford University, 2006. Vii-xxxii.

Morrison, Toni. *Sula*. 1973. New York: Knopf, 2002.

Stevenson, Robert Louis. "From a Letter to John Paul Bobock." *Robert Louis Stevenson: The Critical Heritage*. Paul Maixner, ed. London: Routledge, 1981.

———. *Lay Morals and Other Papers*. New York: Scribner's, 1911.

———. *Strange Case of Dr Jekyll and Mr Hyde and Other Tales*. 1886. Oxford: Oxford University, 2006.

Von Franz, Marie-Louise. "The Process of Individuation." *Man and His Symbols*. Ed. C. G. Jung. New York: Dell, 1968. 157–254.

———. *Shadow and Evil in Fairy Tales*. 1974. Boston: Shambhala, 1995.

Zweig, Connie and Wolf, Steve. *Romancing the Shadow: A Guide to Soul Work for a Vital, Authentic Life*. New York: Ballantine, 1997.

Illuminating
Family Shadows

"All happy families are alike," Leo Tolstoy famously wrote; "each unhappy family is unhappy in its own way" (1). This may be one reason that literature dealing with family tends to focus on the dark side — the shadows — of family life; unhappy families are simply more interesting than happy ones. But I would suggest another reason, one that I think Tolstoy himself actually agreed with: all families have some pain and shadowiness, and it is often from these darker corners that deep truth emerges. And if Robert Bly is correct, literature always issues from the depths, the dark side, exploring the hitherto unseen (and, most likely, never completely seeable), so the shadow side of family is exactly what literature *would* focus on. In any case, family is the first, and often last, vessel in which *soul* is fermented, and much literature about dark, light, light/dark, dark/light spiritual journeys tends to have a family locus. In this chapter I will survey a few views about the way family relates to the soul journey, even including warnings against excessive attention to the family, at least the literal "nuclear" family. And then I will look at three literary works — William Shakespeare's *King Lear* and two contemporary novels, Jane Hamilton's *Book of Ruth* and Jonathan Safran Foer's *Everything Is Illuminated* — as portrayals of dark-side journeys that are primarily located in the context of family.

"The family holds mythic power — the source of all good, the defense against evil," write Connie Zweig and Steve Wolf, whose thoughts about "romancing" the shadow we examined in the previous chapter. Family, say Zweig and Wolf, is life's "container," and they write about the space family creates: "home: More than a place, . . . a dwelling for the soul" (58). At its best, home is "a natural environment or psychic space that allows for the deepening and unfolding of family members' individual souls" (61). This is a sacred space presided over by the goddess Hestia, "who symbolizes the hearth containing the fires at the center of the household, the city, and the earth. . . . She turns the house into a home, a dwelling place where family members can feel that their own natures are accepted" (61).

But Zweig and Wolf, interested as they are in the shadow, are no dewy-eyed sentimentalists. "Home," they acknowledge, "is also a dwelling for the shadow" (58). They decry the decline of "family soul": a lack of authenticity; a failure to accept conflict and difference; a hiding behind a false persona, whether it be religious uprightness, political correctness, urban toughness, or elitist economic success. This false family persona, Zweig and Wolf claim, pushes qualities that go contrary to the persona out of sight: "In this way, the family persona and the family shadow develop together" (59), say Zweig and Wolf, and hence, "in many homes the *family soul* has been sacrificed to maintain the illusion of the *family persona*. As a result, the *family shadow* erupts, ripping apart the fabric of life for its members" (58).

This painful situation calls for "shadow-work":

> the unconscious wounds of the family can set us on the path toward consciousness. Instead of remaining profane wounds, instilling feelings of bitterness or thoughts of revenge, which restrict awareness from the ego's point of view, they can become sacred wounds from the soul's point of view, opening our awareness to a higher order. Instead of unconsciously learning to bury our wounds, we can consciously learn to carry them, identifying our projections and deepening our empathy for others and for ourselves. In this way, the betrayal and its wound become a vehicle for soul-making. (62)

As we will see, the action of Shakespeare's *King Lear* can be described as exactly such a process of transforming "profane" wounds into "sacred" wounds, and turning cold, unforgiving judgment into compassion.

If Tolstoy is right and only unhappy families are particular and individualized rather than generic, then James Hillman's colleague Thomas Moore might say that it is unhappy families that best nurture the soul. Moore, most famous for his book *Care of the Soul* (subtitled "A Guide for Cultivating Depth and Sacredness in Everyday Life"), claims that the soul needs the particular and quotidian, not the general and abstract: "The soul," he says, "prospers in an environment that is concrete, particular, and vernacular. It feeds on the details of life, on its variety, its quirks, and its idiosyncrasies" (*Care of the Soul* 25). This is why Moore asserts that family is a key vessel for fermenting soul: "nothing is more suitable for care of the soul than family, because the experience of family includes so much of the particulars of life" (25). Tolstoy's "happy families," all "alike," would not do for Moore.

It is ironically fortunate, then, that according to Moore "all families are dysfunctional" (26). What Moore is playfully saying is that "Dis" — the god of the underworld, of the dark side, of the shadow — always stands beside Hestia as a god of the family; Moore is less driven to "fix" the "broken" family than Zweig and Wolf. The family's "functioning," says Moore, "is always soiled by Dis. . . . The sentimental image of family that we present publicly is a defense against the pain," and family "is most truly family in its complexity, including its failures and weaknesses" (27). Since Moore's thesis, much like that of this book, is that "Soul enters life from below, through the cracks" (26), befriending Dis and his shadowy functions rather than fleeing them is how we find illumination in the vessel of family.

The more popular therapeutic approach to family shadows, according to Moore (as well as to Hillman, as we will see), is conquest. Specifically, Moore says, "We may have suffered the excesses of one or both of our parents, and so we make the resolution that *I* am not going to be that way. We make every effort to avoid this parental influence" (31). But conquest or avoidance, says Moore, does not work, even when aided by counseling, cognitive reprogramming, or medication: "the avoidance of parental influence and identification is a sure way to become a carbon copy — the return of the repressed" (31). Moore's prescription for dealing with family shadows is more modest, and it is very relevant to a chapter about literary depictions of family struggles. Because the soul thrives on particulars, quirks, and horrors, Moore recommends a nurturing of *storytelling* about family. "We need," he says, "simply to recover soul by reflecting deeply on the soul events that have taken place in the crucible of the family" (27); by telling and retelling the stories deeply and vividly, one immerses in the "matrix of images by which a person is saturated all through adult life" (29). Moore encourages an immersion in these stories with *negative capability*, which Keats calls an ability to be "in uncertainties, Mysteries, doubts without any irritable reaching after fact & reason": family therapy, says Moore, "might take the form of simply telling stories of family life, free of any concern for cause and effect or sociological influence" (28). Moore complains that, infected by a culture of reductive diagnosing, people too often filter family stories through a generic social-psychological lens: "'My father drank, and as a child of an alcoholic I am prone to. . .' Instead of stories, one hears analysis. The family has been 'etherized upon a table'" (29). It is poetic imagination rather than analytic cognition that, for Moore, brings us into the shadowy depths of family in a way that brings illuminative healing rather than surgical reduction and removal, and I believe that this approach is relevant to literary exploration, which can go deep without imposing rigid analytical paradigms.

And finally, Moore uses his imaginative rather than diagnostic approach to family stories to argue against making the presence of "Dis" in families a reason to cast blame — on parents, say. The shadow, as we have seen, is a structural mystery, not primarily a result of sin that calls for judgment and blame: "Questions about evil and suffering," Moore says, "are the most profound mysteries we can tackle, but blaming our struggling human parents for these utterly deep mysteries distracts us from our own responsibilities" (76). Again, as an alternative to diagnosing, blaming, and extracting, Moore is calling for the more modest, but also more difficult, practice of mindfulness, a steeping of ourselves in the stories.

"If any fantasy," says James Hillman in his book *The Soul's Code*, "holds our contemporary civilization in an unyielding grip, it is that the primary instrument of our fate is the behavior of our mother and father" (63). In psychological practice, not to mention numerous Lifetime television movies, these parental behaviors are imagined as constitutive of children's (dys)functioning, both by the therapy-obsessed left and the "family-values" right:

> The shibboleth "family values," expressed by catch-phrases like "bad mothering" and "absent fathering," trickles down into "family systems therapy," which has become the single most important set of ideas determining the theory of societal dysfunction and the practice of mental health. (63–64)

But Hillman describes a "little elf" — whose alternate take on family informs literary works ranging from the story of Moses to Grimms' fairy tales to *Oliver Twist* to the Harry Potter novels — who tells me that I am not (just) a member of my family, that I have an identity and destiny that are not reducible to familial experiences: this "little elf," says Hillman, "whispers another tale: 'You are different; you're not like anyone in the family; you don't really belong.' There is an unbeliever in the heart. It calls the family a fantasy, a fallacy" (64). Hillman is suggesting that stories about embeddedness in family are counterbalanced by other stories about being from somewhere else, fantasies about *not* being embedded in one's family. Indeed, it is just this kind of fantasy that Hillman unpacks in *The Soul's Code*: a fantasy that my character is primarily influenced not by the past causality of parental dynamics but by the future causality of a spiritual calling, "the call of fate" (5), which is always already present as a beckoning image, much as the oak tree is present, in potential, within an acorn. "For this," says Hillman, "is the nature of an image, any image. It's all there at once" (7). Oliver Twist, for example, is always already a child of wealth and status even while in a workhouse, and Harry Potter is the alter-ego of the powerful Lord Voldemort even while a supposed child of the mediocre Dursleys. We are, according to Hillman, more than mere causal products of our literal parents. And literature dealing with the relation between soul-making and family might well, from Hillman's viewpoint, imagine *beyond* literalistic, parent-blaming family causality.

Among other things, this way of imagining family — breaking free of literal causality — makes human aloneness an existential reality, a "structural shadow," rather than a dysfunction wrought by poor parenting:

> if there is an archetypal sense of loneliness accompanying us from the beginning, then to be alive is also to feel lonely. Loneliness comes and goes apart from the measures we take. It does not depend on being literally alone, for pangs of loneliness can strike in the midst of friends, in bed with a lover, at the microphone before a cheering crowd. When feelings of loneliness are seen as archetypal, they become necessary: they are no longer harbingers of sin, of dread, or of wrong. We can accept the strange autonomy of the feeling and free loneliness from identification with literal isolation. Nor is loneliness mainly unpleasant once it receives its archetypal background. (56)

Alternately, as ecological philosophers remind us, an imaginal rather than literal vision of parenting frees us from limiting nurturance to the literal family and places us in a vital, animated world, a matrix of nurturing forces both human and nonhuman. "Being shaped so fatally by the parental world means having lost the larger world-parents," Hillman argues, "and also the world at large as parent" (86). But in fact the world, not just our parents, "shapes us, nurtures us, teaches us"; the world "affords nesting and sheltering, nourishing and quenching, adventuring and playing" (86). The world is animated with soul — "made less of nouns than of verbs. It doesn't consist merely in objects and things; it is filled with useful, playful, and intriguing opportunities" (86). Hillman points out that this animate, parenting natural world is "buzzing and blooming with information": "The oriole doesn't see a branch, but an occasion for perching; the cat doesn't see a thing we call an empty box, it sees safe hiding for peering. The bear doesn't smell honeycomb, but the opportunity for delicious feeding" (86). All of this leads Hillman to call for a new, bigger, less reductive way of imagining family: "if our children today are disordered, it isn't so much parenting they need as, perhaps, less parentalism, which keeps them from trust and pleasure in the actual, physical world" (87).

Working through the "parental fallacy," says Hillman provocatively, will convert us

> out of our secularism, out of our personalism, out of our monotheism, developmentalism, and belief in causality. It requires a step backward into the old connection with invisibilities and a trusting step out and over the threshold into the rich profusion of influences afforded by the world. "Religion," [Alfred North] Whitehead ... said, "is world loyalty." This could imply disloyalty to a belief long held dear by society as a whole, by therapy in general and by you in particular: the belief in the power of parents. (91)

But by a wonderful twist, this spiritual escape from the literal family beings us back to family in a broader, poetic, imaginal way, not as a dysfunctional system of literal pathologies that we need to eradicate but as a shadowy and illuminating vessel in which we bathe ourselves by telling stories. Thomas Moore, more favorable to family than his mentor Hillman, says that the Hillman turn away from a fixation on family's literal, lifeless facts can reanimate family itself by illuminating family with the shadowy light of the imagination: the power of the family, says Moore,

> is not political or personal, rather it is a power of soul. The capacity of a family to strengthen, educate, and enrich a child or another of its members goes far beyond any measurable authority or influence. By its very nature, family has an inherent power to foster human life. This power ... is "ineffable" — it cannot be spoken, it is so profound and mysterious. (*Soul Mates* 80)

Although she does not write specifically about family and family relations, Buddhist nun Pema Chödrön, whose ideas about "the wisdom of no escape" inform much of my approach to the holding together of shadows and illuminations, adds a further resonance to the points made by Zweig and Wolf, Hillman, and Moore. Chödrön's book *When Things Fall Apart* seems to me particularly apt for a consideration of family, and of literary ruminations on family themes. In this book Chödrön discusses some "shadows" that haunt all human life but perhaps especially family. A sentimental view of family stresses *togetherness*, *permanence*, and *security*; Chödrön, however, points to the reality of *aloneness*, *impermanence*, and *insecurity*, but she claims that befriending these things leads to compassion, the true healer of families.

Chödrön lays the groundwork for her discussion of aloneness, impermanence, and insecurity by endorsing something that might seem anathema to our own consideration of spiritual journeys, but which I think deserves a hearing: *nontheism*. For Chödrön, "nontheism" is not a doctrinal claim but a personal orientation, one that I think even the Catholic priest/theologian Michael Himes, whom we examined in the first chapter, would agree with. Himes critiques a view of "God" as "a great big person out there somewhere, older, wiser, stronger, than you and I. That is Zeus, not God" (94). This is precisely the kind of theism that Chödrön rejects, a God seen as a super-parent — Mom and Dad on steroids — or as a supernatural, always dependable babysitter:

> The difference between theism and nontheism is not whether one does or does not believe in God. . . . Theism is a deep-seated conviction that there's some hand to hold: if we just do the right things, someone will appreciate us and take care of us. It means thinking there's always going to be a babysitter available when we need one. . . . Nontheism is relaxing with the ambiguity and uncertainty of the present moment without reaching for anything to protect ourselves. (39)

In endorsing nontheism, Chödrön is calling for a renunciation of *hope*, which again might seem anathema to a reflection on spiritual journeys but which again deserves a listen. By "hope," Chödrön does not mean a positive, embracing stance toward the world; this she fully encourages. Rather, "hope" is that addictive quest for an absolute fix which James Hillman says has infected our therapy-obsessed culture: "We're all addicted to hope," says Chödrön, " — hope that the doubt and mystery will go away" (40). At bottom, this is a hope that I will not die — that is, a rejection of my very nature as a mortal being:

> it's very hard — no matter how much we hear about it — to believe in our own death. . . . The one thing in life that we can really count on is incredibly remote for all or us. We don't go so far as to say, "No way, I'm not going to die," because of course we know that we are. But it definitely will be later. That's the biggest hope. (43)

As a result of this addictive "hope," Chödrön says, "We can't simply relax with ourselves. We hold on to hope, and hope robs us of the present moment" (41). Chödrön's Buddhist alternative is to "drop the fundamental hope that there is a better 'me' who one day will emerge," to stop trying to "jump over ourselves as if we were not there" (41). And here she gives a preview of how such hope-less acceptance breeds that family-supportive stance, *compassion*, initially toward ourselves but also toward others: "Rather than letting our negativity get the better of us, we could acknowledge that right now we feel like a piece of shit and not be squeamish about taking a good look. That's the compassionate thing to do" (41).

This is the background for Chödrön's call for an acceptance of aloneness, impermanance, and insecurity, and this acceptance turns out to be very relevant to our literary presentations of family as a locus for the soul-making journey through illuminating shadows. "We are fundamentally alone," Chödrön says, "and there is nothing anywhere to hold on to" — including (perhaps especially) family. But, she goes on,

> this is not a problem. In fact, it allows us to finally discover a completely unfabricated state of being. Our habitual assumptions — all our ideas about how things are — keep us from seeing anything in a fresh, open way. We say, "Oh yes, I know." But we don't know. We don't ultimately know anything. There's no certainty about anything. This basic truth hurts, and we want to run away from it. But coming back and relaxing with something as familiar as loneliness is good discipline for realizing the profundity of the unresolved moments of our lives. We are cheating ourselves when we run away from the ambiguity of loneliness. . . .
>
> Cool loneliness doesn't provide any resolution or give us ground under our feet. It challenges us to step into a world of no reference point without polarizing or solidifying. (58–59)

We are often enculturated to think of "family values" as a celebration of permanence, but Chödrön counters that *im*permanence "is the essence of everything." Impermanence is the true story of family: "babies becoming children, then teenagers, then adults, then old people, and somewhere along the way dropping dead. Impermanence is meeting and parting. It's falling in love and falling out of love." This familial life of impermanence is neither giddily happy nor tragic, but rather "bittersweet, like buying a new shirt and years later finding it as part of a patchwork quilt" (60). Furthermore, Chödrön argues that impermanence is "a principle of harmony," a "connectedness" celebrated by traditional cultures, often in a familial context: "There are ceremonies marking all the transitions of life from birth to death, as well as meetings and partings, going into battle, losing the battle, and winning the battle. We too could acknowledge, respect, and celebrate impermanence" (61). Relatedly, Chödrön says that "Seeking security or perfection, rejoicing in feeling confirmed and whole, self-contained and comfortable, is some kind of death. It doesn't have any fresh air. There's no room for something to come in and interrupt all that. We are killing the moment by controlling our experience" (71).

Loneliness, impermanence, and insecurity, if we embrace rather than resist them, shake us free, Chödrön says, of the ego's compulsion to control, and this egolessness provides connection to the world — "a fresh moment, a clear opening to emotions or thoughts rather than closing off into our narrow limited selves. . . . Egolessness is available all the time as freshness, openness, delight in our sense perceptions" (63–64). I suggest that this is what occurs in Shakespeare's *King Lear* when Lear is forced to give up his egoistic identity as King and Father — a shocking, agonizing experience, but a healing one, a giving up of a false persona so he can be merely (and fully) a human being.

In other words, Chödrön's ideas, while not directly focused on the issue of family relationships, are about relationality and connectedness and hence are very relevant to a consideration of family. An embrace of such seeming shadows as loneliness, impermanence, and insecurity helps us, Chödrön says, begin "to befriend and soften toward ourselves," which also allows us to begin to "befriend all human beings and indeed all living things." When we become aware of the silly things we do "because we don't want to dwell in the uncertainty and awkwardness and pain of not knowing, we begin to develop true compassion for ourselves and everyone else, because we see what happens and how we react when things fall apart. That awareness is what turns the sword into a flower" (70). A grasping orientation toward family, one that rigidly upholds "family values" and bemoans a society that lacks these values, is for Chödrön an unnatural attempt to stay in the nest, when in fact, she says, "To be fully alive, fully human, and completely awake is to be continually thrown out of the nest. To live fully is to be always in no-man's-land, to experience each moment as completely new and fresh" (71–72). The attempt to stay hidden in the nest, though it looks like a fear of death, is, says Chödrön, "actually fear of life" (72).

King Lear and the Dark Side

It is audacious, perhaps even foolhardy, to insert a consideration of Shakespeare's *King Lear* into this study of spiritual journeys in literature. I cannot possibly do justice to this massive play — perhaps Shakespeare's masterpiece, which would arguably make it the greatest play ever written in any language — in just a few pages. But *King Lear* does illustrate the ideas I am presenting with a depth and weightiness that make it impossible to ignore. And it does so within a complex and resonant family context, one that ironically supports Connie Zweig and Steve Wolf's claim that family is a key "container" of life as well as Hillman's claim that family's importance, taken too literally, is a "fallacy." And in both of its presentations of family — as container and as fallacy — Shakespeare's play supports our thesis, stated succinctly by

Thomas Moore, that "Soul enters life from below, through the cracks" (*Care of the Soul* 26).

The tragic events of Shakespeare's beautiful, horrifying play all take place within the dynamics of family, or rather, of two families. The main action, the tragic downfall of the once-powerful King Lear, is precipitated by the relationship between him and his daughters. The play begins with Lear, an old man, dividing his kingdom among his three daughters, basing the division on their espoused affection for him. His familial mistake, which launches the drama, is the familiar mistake of judging love superficially rather than deeply and authentically; from this viewpoint the play's action is a journey from surface to depth, along the lines of Paul Tillich's essay/sermon "The Depth of Existence," discussed in our first chapter. Lear undergoes a dark-side journey like that of Young Goodman Brown in Hawthorne's story and Bill Harford in Stanley Kubrick's *Eyes Wide Shut*: the shiny surface of his regal world cracks, and Lear encounters life's underlying depth. And Lear's entire journey takes place within the web of family relationships. Moreover, the play's major subplot, a kind of mirror image of the Lear plot, presents yet another dark-side journey within family: the Earl of Gloucester undergoes an agonizing descent into darkness because of his own failure to see below the surface and understand which of his two sons is genuinely trustworthy and loving. Thus two family stories, Lear's and Gloucester's, embody the dark-side journeys we have been discussing in these pages.

But what of James Hillman's family fallacy? It would appear that *King Lear* is shockingly literal, what with its intense portrayal of madness and violence, even including a graphic scene in which Gloucester's eyes are gouged out. It almost seems that the play is made up of two case studies of dysfunctional families, as literal and detailed as anything recorded by a psychologist or a social worker.

And yet Shakespeare critic Russell Fraser claims that the play's opening scene, in which Lear very theatrically divides his kingdom between evil daughters Goneril and Regan and rejects the good Cordelia, is utterly artificial, not a realistic depiction of character and action at all. After noting that Samuel Johnson, troubled by *King Lear*'s harsh violence, famously found the play "too literal, too realistic for 'dramatick exhibition,'" Fraser goes on to say:

> it is remarkable that this play, in which Shakespeare's unremitting fidelity to fact is almost an occasion for scandal, manifests in its beginning a studied and a deliberate indifference to fact. If subsequent scenes are so realistic as hardly to be endured, the opening scenes have not to do with realism but with ritual and romance. Their abiding character-

istic is a niggling formality. They do not wear the aspect of life so much as the aspect of art. . . .

But there is more than craft to Shakespeare's design in thus introducing his drama. He makes his characters unreal initially because he means them, at least in part, to be symbolic. (lxvii, lxx)

In claiming that *Lear* maintains a "symbolic" dimension amid its generally realistic portrayal of family struggles, Fraser is suggesting that Shakespeare is up to something bigger, more fundamental, than a simple, concrete family case study. Fraser claims that the play explores nothing less than the question of what human nature is: "Lear, as is fitting, is made to enunciate it: 'Who is it that can tell me who I am?'. . . But what is it, to be a man? What is man to profess? To what law are his services bound?" (lxxv). This looming, "symbolic" dimension of *Lear* resonates with James Hillman's claim that modern psychology's fixation on family is a "fallacy": this fixation, Hillman says, narrows our focus to a closed parental causality and hides us from the big world and its deep questions. A focus simply on our individual, biological (or even adoptive) mothers and fathers is, Hillman claims, "misplaced concreteness"; he prefers to talk about "Cosmic mythical parents" (*Soul's Code* 85), an artfully fantastic family who bring us to what Fraser calls a "symbolic" level of imagining. When you imagine only literally, Hillman says,

you believe you belong only to this personal story and your parents' personal influence on it, rather than to the invisible myths parents have displaced. Being shaped so fatally by the parental world means having lost the larger world-parents, and also the world at large as parent. For the world too shapes us, nurtures us, teaches us.

. . . I must make that psychological reconstruction, that leap of faith out of the house of the parents and into the home of the world. (86–87)

By initially giving his family drama a ritualized artificiality, Shakespeare facilitates that "leap of faith."

But the brilliance of *King Lear* is that Shakespeare has it both ways. He portrays two concrete, particular families as vessels for soul-making, but he also — by foregrounding artifice and ritual — subverts the psychological realism of this portrayal of family and points toward deeper religious/philosophical levels of meaning. Let us now look briefly at the trajectories of the two dark-side journeys that Shakespeare presents within his familial and "Cosmic mythical"/"symbolic" framework.

Zweig and Wolf, as we have seen, claim that "the unconscious wounds of the family can set us on the path toward consciousness."

These wounds, an inevitable part of the intimacy of family relations, can remain "profane" — "instilling feelings of bitterness or thoughts of revenge, which restrict awareness from the ego's point of view" (62) — and one need only read a few newspaper advice columns or watch an episode or two of *The Dr. Phil Show* to see what Zweig and Wolf are talking about. But they go on to say that these wounds "can become sacred wounds from the soul's point of view, opening our awareness to a higher order" when, rather than burying the wounds and allowing them to fester (in Robert Bly's "bag," if you will), we consciously carry them (not repressing them, or expressing them willy-nilly, but in Bly's terms "eating" them). I suggest that this is how Lear's story unfolds. Having thought, in his egotistical way, that his kingly and fatherly status inoculated him from being wounded, Lear sees his surface persona crumble and he discovers the *nothing* beneath his regal and parental veneer. But with help from caring supporters — not powerful allies but rather a powerless court jester (the "Fool"), a rejected and ostracized daughter, and others whose statuses have been stripped away — Lear finds that his "profane" ordeal turns into a "sacred" initiation. He travels down into the shadowiest of depths and finds illumination about what it really means to be a human being and a father. This is not to say that the play has a "happy ending"; it surely does not. But as Gloucester's son Edgar famously states, "Ripeness is all" (5.2.11):* the spiritual journey, as Chödrön, Hillman, and others point out, is not about conventional, success-oriented self-improvement but about soul-making, which is a matter not of fixing or curing but rather of cooking what is raw, or digesting, or allowing things to *ripen*.

At the start of the play, Lear is anything but "ripe"; he is harsh, cutting, tart — and naive. In the ritualized, artificial opening scene described by Russell Fraser in the analysis I have already mentioned, Lear comes off as an actor playing at being king and father, in love with the trappings of power and parenthood. He has gathered his courtiers and daughters around him to grandly express his "darker purpose" (1.1.37), the dividing of his kingdom among his daughters so he can experience early retirement, but the scene is all surface theatrics, no depth. "Which of you shall we say doth love us most," he grandiosely and naively asks, "That we our largest bounty may extend / Where nature doth with merit challenge" (1.1.53–55). But like everything in the scene, "love" is a façade to be enacted, not a deep reality to be felt and lived, and so Goneril's and Regan's well-rehearsed proclamations of love are just what Lear is asking for.

---

* *King Lear* exists, of course, in numerous editions, so rather than citing a particular edition I am merely indicating act, scene, and line numbers.

This shiny, false surface needs to be negated in order to open up depth and authenticity, so Cordelia's response needs to be a "no," a negation; Cordelia initiates the play's playfully serious play with the word "Nothing," a necessary fracturing of the theatrics, an insertion of real human love that must at first, from the viewpoint of the façade, look like a lack, a naught. When Lear asks Cordelia what her statement of love is, she simply answers, "Nothing, my lord." "Nothing?" "Nothing." And "Nothing," says Lear, "shall come of nothing" (1.1.89–92), though of course the entire tragic action of this painful play will indeed come from this "nothing."

This is the beginning of Lear's wounding. Cordelia's "nothing" stabs him with a potentially *sacred* wound, an initiatory wound, a nihilation of the theatrical artifice in order to initiate depth and healing. And Goneril and Regan will add the profanest of wounds. Lear naively expects Goneril and Regan to revere and care for him after he has given them his land and wealth, but these wicked daughters instead introduce him to another variant on "nothing": having reliquished his persona as king and the power that goes with it, Lear is *nothing* to his two older daughters, and they soon demonstrate this fact. They deprive him of his retinue of knights, and they deride him as pathetic in his assumption that he still carries intrinsic authority after reliquishing his kingly role and its external trappings, which for these shallow women were the only source of his authority. "Idle old man," sneers Goneril, and her sister fully agrees, "That still would manage those authorities / That he hath given away. Now, by my life, / Old fools are babes again" (1.3.17–19). In a way Goneril is right; she sees the sham of Lear's former kingly persona. But her cruelty does not help Lear to digest this insight, to turn it into soulful wisdom, but only drives him into a reactive posture. Lear rails defensively, even vengefully, praying that Nature will punish Goneril (and Regan too) with sterility or at least with children as ungrateful as herself, so "she may feel / How sharper than a serpent's tooth it is / To have a thankless child" (1.4.294–296). This is precisely how "profane wounds" work, in Zweig and Wolf's terms — "instilling feelings of bitterness or thoughts of revenge, which restrict awareness from the ego's point of view" (62). Lear is not digesting the insight that his royal status is a "nothing," and his bitterness slams against Goneril and Regan's selfish power-mongering until the cruel daughters toss their father out onto the storm-ravaged heath like a bundle of trash. "Blow, winds, crack your cheeks," Lear roars in mad, desperate fury at these not-yet-ripened "profane" wounds. "Rage, blow! / You cataracts and hurricanoes" (3.2.1–2).

But there is an alternate, "sacred" action that begins after Lear's defrocking, one that does help him "eat" his shadow, digest the pain of

his situation, really take in the truth that his grand role and its accoutrements are *nothing* — the first step toward discovering and embracing
his own underlying humanity and the authentic humanity of others.
After Lear relinquishes his kingdom, his entourage at first is a coterie of
one hundred knights, but when Goneril and Regan strip these knights
away from him his entourage shrinks to a small team of other *nothings*:
the Fool, someone with no status at all; the disgraced, exiled, and now
disguised Earl of Kent; and eventually Edgar, son of the Earl of
Gloucester, falsely accused of treason by his evil brother and now under-
cover, pretending to be a madman named Tom. Lear's interactions with
this motley crew, especially with the truly motley-wearing Fool, playfully, sadly, and profoundly illuminate Lear's story and — without
"fixing" anything in a measurable, assessable way — engender ripeness,
healing.

The most effective therapist (if you will) of this odd team is the Fool,
who in a sense rubs Lear's nose in his own painful situation but does so
in a way that Lear can digest, through songs and jokes and play. And
playacting: the Fool and his comrades redeem the theatrical artifice of
King Lear's opening scene by demonstrating that artful dramatics can be
healing as well as deceptive. The Fool, for example, jokily says that he
needs extra fool's caps to pass around — to Kent, for following a loser
(Lear), and to anyone else who has given away property to ungrateful
daughters. And then he sings:

> That lord that counseled thee
>   To give away thy land,
> Come place him here by me,
>   Do thou for him stand.
> The sweet and bitter fool
>   Will presently appear;
> The one in motley here,
>   The other found out there. (1.4.144–151)

"Dost thou call me fool, boy?" asks Lear, to which the Fool answers, "All
thy other titles thou hast given away; that thou wast born with" (1.4.152–
154), a joke with a serious point: now lacking the titles "king" and
"father," Lear is being brought down to his fundamental humanity. The
Fool's critical portrayal of Lear is not substantially different from that
leveled by Goneril and Regan. But the Fool's tone — playful and affec-
tionate — is altogether different; thus, where the daughters provoke
only Lear's defensiveness and rage, the Fool is, in the Keatsian way we
have been discussing in these pages, facilitating "soul-making."

Most effectively, the Fool makes Lear revisit the word "nothing" that pervaded the play's first scene; by poetically and jokingly twisting the word, however, the Fool illuminates it. The Fool's jokes and songs are "nothing," says Kent; the Fool, however, asks Lear, "Can you make no use of nothing, Nuncle?" "Why, no, boy," says Lear, and adds, much more gently and playfully than he said the same words in the earlier scene: "Nothing can be made out of nothing" (1.4.131–136). But Lear's playfulness here shows he is beginning to be able to deliteralize, to poeticize, to mine the mysteries of "nothing," which are the mysteries of his own self stripped of egoistic frills. When an angry Goneril enters the scene, the Fool tells Lear, "Thou wast a pretty fellow when thou hadst no need to care for her frowning" — that is, Lear used to be "pretty" in his regal finery, and that prettiness shielded him. But, the Fool goes on, "Now thou art an O without a figure," a zero with no added digits to inflate its value; "I am better than thou are now: I am a Fool, thou art nothing" (1.4.197–200). This may sound harsh, especially as it echoes that painful word "nothing" from the play's first scene and applies it directly to Lear. But again, the Fool's playful, verbally dexterous tone makes these important revelations palatable, digestible. After Goneril most unplayfully rails at Lear, Lear shows how much he really is getting the message: "Does any here know me? This is not Lear. . . . Who is it that can tell me who I am?" (1.4.232, 236). The Fool answers tellingly, as if he had read Jung: "Lear's shadow" (1.4.237).

This is only one of several such playful and painful exchanges between Lear and his tiny band of disenfranchised supporters; the play continues to proceed dialectically, swinging between cruel-serious interactions between Lear and his wicked daughters and playful-serious ruminations on these events by Lear, Kent, Edgar, and especially the Fool. These scenes carry Lear deeper and deeper into the dark side, the horror of facing the falseness of his ego persona — the "nothing" beneath that persona — and of confronting the twistedness of his family situation. The presence of his compassionate companions does not shield Lear from the pain of visiting the dark side; indeed, Lear goes fully, dreadfully mad. As we have seen throughout these pages, the dark-side journey cannot be skipped or smoothed over, and "symptoms" cannot be escaped or "fixed" or "cured." But at his nadir, aided by the imaginative, therapeutic play of the Fool and the others, Lear does begin to experience what Pema Chödrön says can be found "when things fall apart": a heart-softening — *compassion*.

Lear initially thinks that compassion is something owed *to* him, by a God whom Lear regards as a "babysitter" in the way Pema Chödrön disparages. "O heavens!" Lear prays in this mode, "If you do love old men, . . . Make it your cause. Send down, and take my part" (2.4.188–191). But at the nadir of his dark-side journey, when he has become an utter *nothing* without kingship or family or even sanity, drenched and shivering from exposure to a raging storm, Lear discovers compassion not as something owed to him by a God who favors kings, but as something *he* owes to others: "Poor naked wretches," he says,

> wheresoe'er you are,
> That bide the pelting of this pitiless storm,
> How shall your houseless heads and unfed sides,
> Your looped and windowed raggedness, defend you
> From seasons such as these? O, I have ta'en
> Too little care of this! (3.4.28–33)

"Take physic, pomp," he proclaims — telling the pompous ones (kings, for instance) to take medicine. The medicine (the "physic") that he prescribes for "pomp" is this: "Expose thyself to feel what wretches feel" (3.4.34). Being exposed to wretchedness, and feeling the pain deeply, is a medicine, Lear now thinks, a kind of homeopathic cure undertaken in order "That thou mayst shake the superflux to them, / And show the heavens more just" (3.4.35–36).

So it is human compassion that effects heavenly justice, not some external Zeus-like god. To the extent that *King Lear* presents a theology, it is this: a kind of Chödrön-like nontheistic move away from the transcendent babysitter god who favors the mighty and toward an immanent feeling of compassion toward those who suffer. Along these lines, Gloucester, who undergoes a familial dark-side journey parallel to Lear's, famously says this about the transcendent gods of traditional religion: "As flies to wanton boys, are we to th'gods, / They kill us for their sport" (4.1.36–37). But Gloucester also prays to the heavens to let those who are "superfluous and lust-dieted" feel God's harsh power, which he thinks will provoke these superfluously advantaged people to redistribute their wealth — "So distribution should undo excess, / And each man have enough" (4.1.69–73). Again, the play is suggesting that sinking to nothing can effect a heart-softening whereby, in Chödrön's words, we "befriend and soften toward ourselves" and then "befriend all human beings and indeed all living things" (*When Things Fall Apart* 70).

But in Gloucester's story, just as in Lear's, this heart-softening is not automatic. It occurs only when the suffering has been worked over therapeutically — and the therapy is not (psycho)analysis, a psychosurgical removal of symptoms, but rather a poetic, imaginative, playful, painful intensification of the suffering, an imaginal immersion in the valley of darkness rather than an escape from it. In Lear's case, as we have seen, the primary "therapist" is the Fool, though the good daughter, Cordelia, ultimately takes over this role; in Gloucester's case, the therapist is Gloucester's disguised, unrecognized son Edgar.

Like Lear, Gloucester has judged his children's love foolishly, superficially. He has renounced his good son, Edgar, as Lear renounced Cordelia, and has thrown his lot in with the deceitful Edmund. And also like Lear, Gloucester is condemned by his naivete to a horrendous darkside experience: he is brutally blinded by henchmen of Edmund, and then is thrown out into the cold by Regan, who is now allied with Edmund: "Go thrust him out at gates," Regan tells a servant, "and let him smell / His way to Dover" (3.7.94–95). This is a dark-side experience par excellence: Glouceser, blinded, is literally in the dark, and yet he is also painfully enlightened about his sons' respective virtuousness. In this state, he faces the emptiness of the cosmos — "As flies to wanton boys, are we to th'gods" — but he unknowingly falls in with Edgar, who still is pretending to be mad Tom. And rather than reveal his true self to his father, Edgar engages in therapeutic theatrics similar to those employed by the Fool with Lear. The disguised Edgar leads his father to Dover, where Cordelia and the French army are waiting to aid Lear and his followers and to fight the usurpers (Goneril, Regan, Edmund, et al). And at Dover, Edgar leads his father to commit a mock-suicide in a way that might seem bizarre and sadistic but in fact is healing in exactly the way we have been investigating in these pages: rather than acting as an anitdepressant, comforting his father and raising his spirits, Edgar leads his father down into his depression, even to the point of (seeming) suicide. Though they are actually on the beach at Dover, Edgar tells the blind Gloucester that they are standing atop the Dover cliffs: "you are now within a foot / Of th' extreme verge," he says, warning his father not to jump but actually tempting him to do just that. And in case the audience wonders what kind of sadistic trick Edgar is playing, Edgar tells us in an aside, "Why I do trifle with his despair / Is done to cure it" (4.6.33–34). So, manipulated by Edgar, Gloucester leaps from what he thinks is the Dover cliff, and he is surprised to find himself still alive.

This is exactly the way that James Hillman, in his early, controversial book *Suicide and the Soul*, recommends working with suicidal feelings. Rather than practice "suicide prevention," which he says does not work anyway, Hillman says that he brings the suicidally depressed deeply into their own suicidal feelings and especially images: entering into the suicidal images is a way of traveling *through* the dark valley of depression rather than trying to jump out of it. It is soul-making rather than soul-anaesthetizing. It is extraordinary to discover that Shakespeare presents exactly the same strategy for caring for the soul of the suicidally depressed Gloucester. The Gloucester who survives his imaginal leap into death is not "cured," not made "happy"; after surviving — miraculously, he thinks — his imagined suicide, he comes upon a scene of deep sorrow: the broken Lear. But he is now, we might say, serenely rather than desperately depressed, and Lear is struck by Gloucester's newly found saturnine wisdom: "No eyes in your head," Lear says when he and Gloucester are reunited, "nor no money in your purse? . . . yet you see how this world goes." To this Gloucester strikingly replies, "I see it feelingly" (4.6.147–151). Gloucester is ready to acknowledge what is likely the key insight of this play: "Men," Edgar says to him, "must endure their going hence, even as their coming hither: / Ripeness is all." "And that's true too," says Gloucester (5.2.9–12).

"Ripeness is all" — this could stand as a motto for our entire study of illuminating shadows. Things fall apart, Pema Chödrön says; they always do. But rather than trying to grab onto an idolatrous hope — the kind of all-is-fixed certainty that assumes that the family nest can be absolutely stable and, most importantly, that I and my loved ones will never die — Chödrön recommends "giving up hope of getting ground under our feet" (*When Things Fall Apart* 42), reliquishing our addiction to things that anaesthetize our knowledge of mortality, "making friends with our jumpiness and dread" (57). Yes, we have moments of great bliss; when Lear and Cordelia, for example, are reunited in the play's final act, we watch some of the sweetest scenes in all of Shakespeare's works, a literal *and* symbolic portrayal of the tender love between parent and child. But then Cordelia is killed and Lear dies of anguish; these things cannot be prevented. Ripeness is all: "when the tables are turned," says Chödrön, "and we feel wretched, that softens us up. It ripens our hearts. It becomes the ground for understanding others. Both the inspiration and the wretchedness can be celebrated. We can be big and small at the same time" (*When Things Fall Apart* 62).

The Book of Ruth

Jane Hamilton's 1988 novel *The Book of Ruth* might seem wildly different from *King Lear*. Whereas *Lear* is a grand tragedy about a king who discovers the limits of his power, beginning with an elevated, highly ritualized, unrealistic opening scene, *The Book of Ruth* is an earthily realistic portrayal of dirt-poor, struggling American Midwesterners, with a main character who is a seemingly powerless victim from the start. Yet Ruth, Hamilton's narrator and protagonist, undergoes a dark-side journey as surely as King Lear does. And although she may seem powerless, utterly determined by and trapped in her dreary family circumstances, her story is not finally a clinical portrayal of inescapable family dysfunction. Her vigorous imagination helps Ruth to persevere through the horrors of her family story, allowing her to acknowledge and honor her family shadows while also — in a way that James Hillman might applaud — exposing the fallacy of family determinism. Neither entirely rejecting the family "vessel" in which she exists nor drowning in its wretchedness, Ruth survives by telling her story, staying with its images, affirming the plain truth that "the way through grief is grieving" (316).

In the novel's first chapters, Ruth lays out the facts about her dreary little town and fractured family. About the town she says, "Honey Creek is way up in the very north of Illinois. . . . You will miss the town if you drive through listening to your favorite song on the radio or telling a story about your neighbor" (2). Her father, though a gentle man, was mostly an absence: "I don't have too many clear memories of Elmer. He stayed out of the way" (15). And then, "I was ten," she says, "when my father climbed into the Ford one morning, in the dark. . . . Goodbye to Illinois, he probably said to himself" (7). Ruth's mother, May, is a wounded, disappointed woman, whose beloved first husband died in World War II, whose second husband, Elmer, left her, and who seems to have indelibly stamped her looks and meanness on Ruth. Ruth describes May as looking "very much the same" as Ruth herself, "except she's older and uglier and heavier than I am, and she has a wart on her nose" (8). Though May is now deceased, her presence still haunts Ruth: "She's so clear and radiant she hurts my eyes" (8). And Ruth's bookish brother, Matt, simply torments Ruth by making her feel inferior: "Matt had the words, but my gift was the strong muscles in my arms to put him flat on his face, and when I socked him I had joy in my heart. . . . The meanness that some people have in great quantities came to me early, because Matt became a prodigy" (13).

All these details add up to a narrowness, a constriction, a sense of family as suffocating fate and Ruth as victim. Thomas Moore, as I noted, talks of the way people's family stories are too often psychologized away in reductive, clinical terms: "'The subject is a male who was raised in Judeo-Christian family, with a narcissistic mother and a codependent father.' The soul of the family evaporates in the thin air of this kind of reduction" (*Care of the Soul* 29). And Ruth's family details could easily add up to exactly such a psychological prison: subject is the product of a broken home with an absent father and a depressed mother; possesses an inferiority complex due to successful brother; has signs of being learning disabled.

But there is an alternate story that subverts the easy, obvious psychosocial victim narrative. This alternate story is like a Tillich *depth* beneath a flatly factual surface, or like James Hillman's myth of an acorn within our souls that points forward toward the oak-tree-we-are-to-be rather than backward toward our parents' behavior. Over against the seemingly inexorable story of Ruth's victimhood are early snippets or images that point toward a soul that will survive beyond all the family horrors that will transpire. These images and mini-narratives emerge from Ruth's own contemplative practice — she retreats to a plateau to meditate — and from her friendships with the book-loving blind woman Miss Finch and the music teacher Aunt Sid, two mentors who help Ruth see beyond her narrow familial horizons.

The plateau is Ruth's version of the harsh heath in *King Lear*, where Lear — drenched, nearly naked, stripped of all the trappings of kingship and parenthood — experiences his own *nothing*ness, which engenders his newfound compassion toward himself, others, and the world. It may not seem that Ruth needs such an exercise in humility, since everything about her experience already is self-diminishing. But as we have seen, the dark-side journey is always about depth, about dipping beneath the ego-bound surface of life to something larger and darker, and low self-esteem is as ego-trapped as kingly pride is. So Ruth, too, benefits from a negation, a nothing-ing, and that is what she experiences when she withdraws from May and Matt and walks up to a nearby plateau "where there are a few cedar trees and long wild grasses":

> I lay on the ground looking up to the sky and sometimes I got the queerest feeling. I could sense the earth spinning around, and I felt small, probably how a midget feels in a room with regular people. For a split second I had the sensation all through my body that there wasn't a reason for our being on the planet. We were hurtling through space and there wasn't any logic to it. It was all for nothing. (60)

This is Ruth's experience of the power of the *nothing*, and as with Lear it leads Ruth away from her literal self and family and out, compassionately, to what James Hillman calls "the larger world-parents, and also the world at large as parent" (*Soul Code* 86). The thought that "It was all for nothing" makes Ruth

> feel so lonesome I had to turn over on my stomach and cry for all the world. I cried for the little lamb we had once that lost its hind leg in a dog attack. It had to hobble around the yard bleating, waiting for someone to feed it corn. I cried for it, and the hungry people on top of Starved Rock, and Miss Finch's blind eyes, and how long and soft the grasses were that I lay in. I cried for the loveliness in the night. I couldn't stop the flow. . . . (60)

The visit to the plateau, which Ruth repeats frequently over the course of her story, takes her to a shadow realm beyond that of her own narrow, suffocating story; she experiences what we called in the previous chapter a *structural* rather than merely personal shadow, and this joins Ruth to a world larger than that of her literal family.

Miss Finch and Aunt Sid also help usher Ruth into a larger world, a world that goes beyond the reductive "parental fallacy." In eighth grade, Ruth begins a job playing taped audio books for the blind Miss Finch, and the experience broadens Ruth's world and deepens her imagination: "It took Miss Finch," she says, "to show me all the colors in the world, such as the people who live in jungles without clothes, hunting for berries and nuts" (55). In particular, Miss Finch introduces Ruth to Charles Dickens, whose novels feed what Hillman would call Ruth's *acorn*, that image of one's calling or future potential, which for Hillman fuels one's life as surely as past, literal family experiences. Ruth starts a tape playing and then, she says,

> I couldn't help getting sucked into the book. It was called *Oliver Twist.*
> . . . In the story there were evil people and exceptionally good ones also.
> I figured that must be like life, good and evil, otherwise people wouldn't listen to blind tapes so hard. I wished I could meet Oliver Twist. I knew we'd have a million things to talk over. I pretended I had a cudgel and I beat up Bill Sikes and his little dog, too. Afterwards Nancy and Fagin and all the boys had a party to celebrate. (55)

The story of Oliver Twist, an orphaned pauper who is actually part of a kind, wealthy family, activates in Ruth a fantasy that she is from somewhere else, that in a deep way she, the real she, is not identical with her literal family and social circumstances.

It is storytelling itself that Miss Finch is actually introducing Ruth to, the way a crafted narrative transforms raw facts into something deep and resonant. When Miss Finch wants to talk rather than listen to tapes, Ruth is initially resistant ("I hated for her to start in her slow, tired voice about how great it all was back when she was a girl in New England"), but "pretty soon the book magic occurred — that is, I sat there with my mouth hanging open, greedy for what she was talking about" (57). From Miss Finch, Ruth learns the transformative, healing power of narrative, the way artfully working over raw facts can make shadows illuminative, can turn an orphan like Oliver Twist into a hero: "In Charles Dickens's books I had to admire the way the meanest enemies spoke to each other, with what seemed to me to be the greatest civility" (63).

But even before Miss Finch introduces Ruth to good books, Ruth learns about storytelling — and constructs her secret fantasy about being from somewhere else — from May's sister, Ruth's Aunt Sid. May and Sid are estranged, which is part of Sid's attractiveness to Ruth, and Sid lives forty miles away, a huge distance for this family. A third-grade pen-pal project spurs Ruth to begin exchanging letters with Sid, and this letter-writing to a mentor instills in Ruth a love of language that she has not learned at home, where "May's harsh talk" has been "particularly well suited to describing the varieties of barnyard manure" (23). For her letters to Sid, Ruth says, "I longed to understand what was correct, for her eyes alone; I wanted to write everything as precisely as a Queen might, transcribing from her gold-bound grammar rule book" (23). Ruth learns to fabricate in these letters to Sid, to spin fantasies — "I made up stories about how May went to the Sears store in Stillwater and bought me one hundred dresses all in different colors . . . I wrote her how I wished I could be a bloodroot flower" (24) — and this exercise in imaginative creativity prepares her to embrace the Oliver Twist fantasy of being more than her predetermined family circumstances: "I stared at May and Elmer and Matt, when they weren't looking, trying to figure out how I was going to explain that the nurse in the hospital made a mistake and I wasn't their baby" (46). But this talent for imagining also carries her *into* the real; the entire novel is predicated on Ruth's need — and painful ability — to enter imaginatively into the viewpoints of the story's various actors, especially her mother, May, and her lazy and eventually violent husband, Ruby: "I know the only way to begin to understand is to steal underneath May's skin and look at the world from behind her small eyes. I shudder when I think about the inside of Ruby's head, but I know I have to journey there too, if I'm going to make sense of what's happened" (2). Her ability to fabricate *and* her ability to see clearly, compassionately, and truly are the same skill, which she develops by writing (made-up) stories for Aunt Sid.

What Aunt Sid has done for Ruth is what all good mentors do: she has helped Ruth to see beyond the literal present facts, plainly visible to the physical eye, and to glimpse the coming-to-be possibility that is already visible to the loving other. "Mentoring," says James Hillman, "begins when your imagination can fall in love with the fantasy of another" (*Soul Code* 121). And as we have already seen, "fantasy" does not mean untruth; *fantasy* can point to a depth, to shadows brought to illumination by the eye of one who loves. "You are a displayed phenomenon," says Hillman. "'To be' is first of all to be visible. Passively allowing yourself to be seen opens the possibility of blessing. So we seek lovers and mentors and friends that we may be seen, and blessed" (122). An unimaginative, affectionless eye sees flat facts, quantifiable and typical — Ruth as product of a broken home, learning disabled, victim. But, Hillman says, "The mentor perceives the folds of a complexity, those convex-concave, topsy-turvy curves of implication that are the truth of all imagination" (123). These "curves of implication" are the location of what Hillman calls the "acorn" — the possibility, the soul — of a person (or of any being), not the flat objective *what* but the visible-invisible *how*:

> This invisibility of the acorn occurs in the how of a visible performance — in its traces, if you will. The invisible is thoroughly visible all through the oak and is not elsewhere or prior to the oak but acts like an implicate order folded all through the visible, like the butter in a French croissant or the fragrant air in risen bread: invisible, not literally as such but the invisible visible. (123–124)

Only a loving eye sees this specific specialness, a particular "each" rather than a generic type (Ruth as *Ruth* rather than as *abused victim*): "The eye of the heart," Hillman says, "sees 'eaches' and is affected by eachness, to borrow a term from William James. The heart's affections pick out particulars.... We fall for *this* one, not anyone" (124). And Hillman goes on, quoting John Keats, "Perception brings into being and maintains the being of whatever is perceived; and when perception sees in 'the holiness of the Heart's affections,'... things are revealed that prove the Truth of the Imagination" (127).

So what Aunt Sid writes at the end of a vividly detailed letter about her own life experience is key to Ruth's very being: "You have a very special place in my heart, my dear," Sid writes, "and I think of you every day" (48). This affirming sentence explodes in Ruth's imagination; indeed, it makes her imagination explode with possibility:

> That's what she said, "You have a very special place in my heart, my dear..." I almost laughed out loud.... I thought about what that special place must look like in Aunt Sid's heart. I thought it must be a garden with all the kinds of flowers there are in the world, in every color. It would be a place where I could walk and smell the sweet air. I sat picturing the spot, where I could live if I wanted. I thought about it all day long sometimes. (49)

Interestingly, immediately after sending Ruth this imagination-nurturing letter, Aunt Sid does something that seems to demolish Ruth's religious faith; in fact, however, she merely demolishes Ruth's faith in the *literal*. In church at Christmastime, the family's minister — whom Ruth, like her mother, calls "the Rev" — asks the children in the congregation what makes Christmas special. "Pretty soon the baby Jesus is going to be born," Ruth answers, and for once she is praised for being correct. So Ruth begins to await this spectacular birth — "I wanted the baby Jesus to come in the worst way, with his curds and honey, choosing the good, refusing the evil. It seemed that surely he would come soon" (50) — and she describes her great expectations in a letter to Aunt Sid. But Aunt Sid "wrote right back and asked did I know what the word *symbol* meant, or the word *myth*? She said the Jesus story was a celebration of life but that an actual flesh and blood child wasn't going to appear" (51). This is a crushing blow to Ruth, and her new skepticism is reinforced by her church's cheesy, unbelievable Christmas pageant: "It came upon me suddenly that Jesus was in the same league as the tooth fairy and the Easter rabbit, not to mention Santa himself. . . . I was furious with the deacons and the Rev and the Sunday school teachers and the imaginary God who made the whole story unfold" (51–52). The problem, of course, is that Ruth is still caught in the trap of literalism: either Jesus will literally be born as a baby this Christmas, or his story is an utter lie. As we have seen, though, the drift of this novel, and of dark-side journeys in general, is toward *symbol* and *myth*, which Aunt Sid tells Ruth about in her letter but which Ruth will fully grasp only as she matures: the idea that healing is not about getting and analyzing the facts, but about mythologizing, storytelling.

Sherry, the social worker who deals with Ruby, the troubled and ultimately destructive young man whom Ruth eventually marries, sees therapy as involved with rational interpretations of the literal, the factual: "Sherry explained that a professional has to go way back to the family, to the start, to get the answers" (168). (This is precisely what James Hillman calls "the parental fallacy.") But the kind of healing that Ruth will find, aided by Miss Finch's and Aunt Sid's story- and image-saturated mentoring, will be informed by symbol and myth rather than by facts and rational interpretation; Thomas Moore describes this kind of healing:

> I spent many summers in my childhood on a farm with an uncle who told stories endlessly. This, I now see, was his method of working the raw material of his life, his way of turning his experience round and round in the rotation that stories provide. Out of that incessant storytelling I know he found added depths of meaning. Storytelling is an excellent way of caring for the soul. It helps us see the themes that circle in our lives, the deep themes that tell the myths we live. It would take only a slight shift in emphasis in therapy to focus on the storytelling itself rather than on its interpretation. (*Care of the Soul* 13)

Let us leap to the end of *The Book of Ruth* to see the way Ruth, when things fall apart in her fiercely brutal dark-side journey, cares for the soul through symbol and myth, by turning her experience "round and round in the rotation that stories provide" and finding her own "deep themes."

As the novel's late, catastrophic climax approaches, Ruth has married Ruby and they have a young son, Justy. Since Ruby — though he loves Ruth and Justy — is a childish man lacking the discipline to work regularly, and since Ruth's job in a dry cleaner's pays poorly, Ruth, Ruby, and Justy are all living with May in the Honey Creek family house; despite her mentoring from Miss Finch and Aunt Sid, Ruth is still trapped in her mother's little world, which is all the more suffocating due to Ruby and May's loathing for each other. Even this dreary circumstance, though, is enriched and enlivened by Ruth's vivid storytelling, her way with "symbol" and "myth": "I don't know what materials scientists put in bombs but it seems as if they wouldn't need anything more than two personalities who don't get along so wonderfully," Ruth says, precisely capturing in an image the family's latent explosiveness.

Furthermore, Ruth has found, on her own, a wisdom that resonates with Pema Chödrön's spiritual teaching, a kind of "nontheistic" acceptance of loneliness that ripens people, softens them, makes them compassionate. "Nontheism," as we noted before, is not a doctrine of atheism but simply a "relaxing with the ambiguity and uncertainty of the present moment without reaching for anything to protect ourselves" (*When Things Fall Apart* 39). This relinquishing of addictive metaphysical protections, says Chödrön, changes the experience of loneliness; we usually see loneliness as an "enemy," but "When we can rest in the middle, we begin to have a nonthreatening relationship with loneliness" (*When Things Fall Apart* 55). And this openness to uncertainty and loneliness, Chödrön says, makes us compassionate: "when we don't close off and we let our hearts break, we discover our kinship with all beings" (*When Things Fall Apart* 88). This "kinship with the suffering of others, this inability to regard it from afar," leads, Chödrön says, to

> the discovery of our soft spot, the discovery of *bodhichittu*. *Bodhichitta* is a Sanskrit word that means "noble or awakened heart." It is said to be present in all beings. Just as butter is inherent in milk and oil is inherent in a sesame seed, this soft spot is inherent in you and me. (*When Things Fall Apart* 86)

It is exactly such a softening that Ruth experiences during the Easter season, prior to her story's horrendous catastrophe. "Around Easter," Ruth says, the Rev "kept shouting out, daring me to meet his gaze: 'We will actually feel the nails coming into our flesh as we approach Good Friday'" (274). At first Ruth rejects the Rev's message — because she tries to literalize it: "I never felt anything like that. I didn't feel nails. I wanted to say, 'Hey, Rev, I don't have nails! Give me a break.' I couldn't feel very sorry for Jesus and his poor bloody hands, because he lived one trillion years ago" (274). But then, while Ruth is working at the dry cleaner's, she finds what for her is the essence of the Rev's message. Ironically, she first infers a message of nontheism: the Rev, she thinks, "was actually trying to say, despite all the talk of God and Jesus, that there's no one looking after us, that we are alone, and each of us singular" (274). But at the core of this nontheistic aloneness, Ruth finds "*bodhichitta*," the "soft spot" in all of us:

> And still, all of us are miraculously the same in our aloneness, with our red blood cells streaming through our veins. . . . The only blessed way there is, I realized, is for all of us to feel deeply with a wounded, or sick, or even dead person. What the Rev meant to say, if he could ever have spoken plainly, without all the paraphernalia of the Gospel, was, "*Each man's struggle is mine.*" (274–275)

Pema Chödrön says that "this bodhichitta, this tenderness for life," awakens "when we can no longer shield ourselves from the vulnerability of our condition, from the basic fragility of existence" (*When Things Fall Apart* 87). And, for all its fierce violence, the novel's explosive climax and painful denouement really illustrate just that awakening on Ruth's part. In the chapter immediately following her description of her Easter illumination, Ruth reaches the nadir of her dark-side narrative. She tells of May's relentless ridicule of Ruby and then of Ruby's psychotic explosion during which, with a fireplace poker, he pummels Ruth and ferociously murders May, and after which, Ruth says, "He lost interest in killing, seeing it's such an easy thing to do. He dropped his poker and walked inside. I leaned on the fence crying, not with tears, but with my voice" (298).

How Ruth digests such an indigestible event, makes soul from it, is the earthy and unmiraculous miracle with which the book concludes. The novel ends with traces of affirmation and some enduring sense of family, but it is an affirmation founded on staying with the grief, sticking to the images: eating the shadow rather than jumping up and out to some redemptive illumination.

As Ruth begins to narrate this most horrific incident, she stops and wonders why she should tell such a tale. Her first reason is utilitarian:

> I'm about to tell how it went so everyone will know. I'd like to think it won't happen again. Once is enough for the whole earth. It shouldn't recur and if I tell about the day, step by step, people can understand

certain warning signs. Then nothing like it will take place again, not ever. (284)

But then Ruth backs away from this utilitarian approach to storytelling. "This is not an improvement plan," says Chödrön of her spiritual practices (*No Escape* 14–15), echoing Moore's and Hillman's resistance to *fixes* and *cures*, and Ruth comes to something like the same realization: "to tell the truth," Ruth says, "I also know that it isn't very often that people change their ways" (284). Things fall apart, Chödrön thinks, and then they come together, and then they fall apart again. But like Chödrön, Ruth is not dispirited by this realization. "Still," she says, "I have to ring the bell, keep it sounding" (284): she has to tell her story, even if the telling will not simply fix flawed human nature. There is a value, she finds, in telling the story — in ringing the bell — even if that value is not clearly, literally measurable. Somehow Ruth has inferred Thomas Moore's idea that storytelling, "going over and over the material of life" (13), is intrinsically valuable — "Storytelling is an excellent way of caring for the soul," says Moore. "It helps us see the themes that circle in our lives, the deep themes that tell the myths we live" (*Care of the Soul* 13). Terrible things have happened, do happen, will happen. Ripeness, it seems, really is all.

In any case, Ruth fully, honestly tells the story of Ruby's violent rampage, neither withholding nor sensationalizing. And in the aftermath, when she returns from her dark-side experience, physically and emotionally battered, finding herself in the care of Aunt Sid, Ruth finds and articulates a deepened understanding, a modest but genuine realization that pain and grief cannot be escaped but must be lived through.

Ruth's illuminations occur largely in a series of oppositional interactions with the Rev, who visits Ruth as she recovers from the wounds that Ruby has inflicted on her. In each visit, the Rev mouths Christian platitudes, and Ruth rejects them but in the process dives more deeply into an understanding of the human world and even, perhaps, of true Christian wisdom. "We shall not die but live," the Rev tells Ruth when he first visits her, but Ruth says, "I didn't want to hear one thing about our heavenly father. I said to the Rev, '*Beat it*'" (302–303). And yet, she goes on to say, "I felt slightly closer to Jesus now, with my bloody hands" (303); what Jesus now means to Ruth has to do not with doctrinal assertions but with compassion. The next time the Rev comes — during the week before Christmas — he prays, "Whoever believes and lives in Jesus shall never die," to which Ruth responds, "Sure, yeah, leave me alone, go to hell, you big old fart" (304). But after the Rev leaves, this visit somehow triggers a flood of horrible but necessary memories in Ruth; the Rev is a catalyst bringing Ruth down into her story, precisely the place of Chödrön's compassionate *bodhichitta*, and of what we have been calling "soul."

The Rev's next visit sparks one of Ruth's most crucial insights — again, seemingly in opposition to him, but nonetheless catalyzed by him. "Our kingdom on earth is not complete," the Rev says, trying to raise Ruth's thoughts to heaven. But he provokes just the opposite response; he makes Ruth realize the sacredness of what is below, down here, what Hillman might call the soul in the world around us and not just in the (flawed) human self: "Don't tell me," she says, "our kingdom ain't complete. Don't be one of them big fat greedy assholes, Rev. If those chubby knees of yours can hold your weight, kneel down sometime in early spring and sniff a bloodroot. Just because you can't take it all in with your senses doesn't mean the earth is half-baked. It's ideal, if you don't count the humans" (309).

Ruth's final recorded interaction with the Rev is gentler, and it contains what I believe is Ruth's key realization. Again the Rev parrots a Christian teaching — "Trust in the Lord with all thine heart, and lean not into thine own understanding" (315) — and Ruth demurs, but she does so silently this time, and with a "smile" (315). Ruth has come to believe, in opposition to the Rev, that pain cannot be simply skipped over or ignored through blind trust in God: "The Rev merely closes his eyes and trusts," she thinks, "when he runs smack into a thorn bush" (316). Instead, Ruth has come to realize, the "thorn bush" — which stands for all the dark side and its shadows — needs to be faced (eaten and digested, in the terms we have discussed in these pages): "you have to learn where your pain is. You have to burrow down and find the wound" (316). But Ruth is not endorsing some kind of superhuman heroism; her story has been fueled, after all, by caring mentors. Thus, she says, "if the burden of it is too terrible to shoulder you have to shout it out; you have to shout for help. My trust, even down in that dark place I carry, is that some person will come running" (316). And then comes what I consider Ruth's key statement, the *deep theme* that emerges after Ruth has turned her story round and round. Out of context her statement might sound like a mere truism, but in context it has a thick, soulful richness: "And then finally the way through grief is grieving" (316).

The way through grief is grieving. This simple statement joins "*Ripeness is all*" as a motto for soul-making dark-side stories. Here is Thomas Moore's explanation of a similar James Hillman motto, drawn from the poet Wallace Stevens:

> Observance of the soul can be deceptively simple. You take back what has been disowned. You work with what is, rather than with what you wish were there. . . . Therapy sometimes emphasizes change so strongly

that people often neglect their own natures and are tantalized by images of some ideal normality and health that may always be out of reach. In "Reply to Papini," Stevens put the matter . . . in lines that James Hillman has taken as a motto for his psychology. "The way through the world is more difficult than the way beyond it." (*Care of the Soul* 9)

And this brings us back to the theme of *family*. Ruth rejects the "parental fallacy" as derisively as Hillman does: "I'm thinking," Ruth says, "about going into social work because all you have to do is say, 'Tell me about your parents . . . *Oh!* That explains why you're a wreck.' Then you look mournful and say, 'Sorry, there's no hope for you'" (325). But it is only this kind of deterministic, reductive use of family that Ruth rejects; her compassionate immersion in the world, with all its quirks and grief, is an immersion in family. Family is the web of connection that binds people to the here and now — a way *though* the world, not *beyond* it — and Ruth embraces this. At the end of the novel, Ruth is pregnant with a second son, conceived before Ruby's rampage — "It's a boy. I get another chance" (310) — and after her terrible ordeal Ruth makes a simple, profound familial pledge that especially resonates with Thomas Moore's praise of storytelling: "The only fact I knew for sure," says Ruth, "was that someday it would be up to me to tell a long story to both my boys" (310).

Everything Is Illuminated

Near the end of *The Book of Ruth,* narrator Ruth realizes that truth is a primary principle for her: "I looked up *truth* the other day. . . . The word has a lot to do with seeing clearly, and with things that are honest and beautiful. Perhaps I should change my name to Ruth Truth" (326). Seeing clearly is also, for Pema Chödrön, a Buddhist for whom *mindfulness* is key, a primary virtue: "the reason," she says, "that we're here in this world at all is to study ourselves" (*When Things Fall Apart* 73), not for narcissistic reasons but because, for a Buddhist, "by looking directly into our own heart, we find the awakened Buddha, the completely unclouded experience of how things really are" (*When Things Fall Apart* 74).

How things really are: the truth. This truth includes, says Chödrön, "every nook and cranny, . . . every black hole and bright spot, whether it's murky, creepy, grisly, splendid, spooky, frightening, joyful, inspiring, peaceful, or wrathful. We can just look at the whole thing" (*When Things Fall Apart* 74). This really does seem to be Ruth Truth's project: looking at "the whole thing."

But *Ruth Truth* has two parts — not just "truth" but "ruth": "Ruth. Ruth. To say my name," Ruth says, "I have to shape my lips as if I'm going to kiss someone. Ruth means pity and compassion, so that figures" (325). The combination "of pity and compassion with honesty and beauty," says Ruth, "would be a real knockout. . . . Ruth Truth. It has a nice ring to it" (326–327). And again Ruth's rumination resonates strikingly with Chödrön's:

> along with clear seeing, there's another important element, and that's kindness. It seems that, without clarity and honesty, we don't progress. We just stay stuck in the same vicious cycle. But honesty without kindness makes us feel grim and mean, and pretty soon we start looking like we've been sucking on lemons. . . .
>
> So the challenge is how to develop compassion right along with clear seeing, how to train in lightening up and cheering up rather than becoming more guilt-ridden and miserable. Otherwise, all that happens is that we all cut everybody else down, and we also cut ourselves down. Nothing ever measures up. Nothing is ever good enough. Honesty without kindness, humor, and goodheartedness can be just mean. From the very beginning to the very end, pointing to our own hearts to discover what is true isn't just a matter of honesty but also of compassion and respect for what we see. (*When Things Fall Apart* 74–75)

This ruthful truth, Chödrön claims, though it begins with humorously compassionate honesty toward ourselves, carries us outward beyond ourselves — to community, to *family*: "We're not just talking about our individual liberation, but how to help the community we live in, how to help our families." And this movement outward toward family goes even farther, to "our country, and the whole continent, not to mention the world and the galaxy and as far as we want to go" (*When Things Fall Apart* 76). Compassionate truth, in other words, takes us to what James Hillman calls *soul*, something beyond the inner self: "the inside 'out there': in the trees, in the finches and squirrels in the trees, in the soil and stones, and even in the panes of glass that you see through to the trees, the squirrels, and the stones" (*Insearch* 130). This is the way an authentic, truly imaginal journey into family for Hillman negates literal family — exposes it as a "fallacy" (*Soul's Code* 64) — and brings us to our "Cosmic mythical parents," our mythic "ancestors," the "formative powers and mysteries" that are bigger and deeper than "personal mothers and fathers" (*Soul's Code* 85) and that help us take "the leap of faith out of the house of the parents and into the home of the world" (*Soul's Code* 87). This is Hillman's archetypal psychological way of describing what Chödrön calls "an interesting transition" whereby "the willingness to look, to point directly at our own hearts" with both honesty and kind compassion leads us to "actually forget ourselves and open to the world" (*When Things Fall Apart* 76). That, says Chödrön, is "the beginning of growing up.... Finally there's room for genuine inquisitiveness, and we find we have an appetite for what's out there" (*When Things Fall Apart* 77). This notion of *growing up* — as a journey from *self* to *family* to mythic *ancestors* to the world "out there," fueled by ruthful (compassionate, and also humorous) truth — not only is the vision that Jane Hamilton's narrator in *The Book of Ruth* comes to espouse but also is, I believe, the vision that fuels the shadowily illuminating narrative in Jonathan Safran Foer's 2002 novel *Everything Is Illuminated*.

Foer's novel begins with an individual journey, that of the book's protagonist, who happens to be named "Jonathan Safran Foer." Jonathan is a twenty-year-old Jewish man from New York who is on a pilgrimage in the Ukraine, which the novel's Ukrainian travel agent describes this way: "He is looking for the town his grandfather came from, ... and someone, Augustine he calls her, who salvaged his grandfather from the war. He desires to write a book about his grandfather's village. ... The name of the town is Trachimbrod" (6–7). So right away we can see how this rather conventional American excursion — college kid travels abroad — might link up with Pema Chödrön's "growing up" journey: Jonathan, budding writer, is traveling abroad alone as a kind of *self*-exploration, but he is investigating a *family* location, his grandfather's home town, which will perhaps connect him with the larger family of his *ancestors*. And through this "Augustine" who "salvaged" his Jewish grandfather from the Nazis in World War II, Jonathan may also become connected with the larger world "out there."

For Chödrön, Jonathan will grow up and encounter the world "out there" only if his journey is more than a self-indulgent excursion and is truly infused with what she calls *paramitas*, "transcendent actions . . . going beyond the conventional notions of virtue and nonvirtue" (*When Things Fall Apart* 99): "the word paramita means 'going to the other shore.' These actions are like a raft that carries us across the river of samsara [the profane rather than sacred world]" (*When Things Fall Apart* 98–99). Going to "the other shore," says Chödrön, requires flexibility and *humor* (*When Things Fall Apart* 99).

As we have seen, growing up in this sacred way and encountering the world out there requires, for Chödrön, seeing the whole truth, inward and outward — "every black hole and bright spot." *Everything* must be illuminated. But fierce honesty, grim truth, is not all that one needs; quoting Thich Nhat Hanh, Chödrön says that "Suffering is not enough" (*When Things Fall Apart* 75). Ruthful, compassionate truth requires "lightening up and cheering up ... kindness, humor, and goodheartedness" (*When Things Fall Apart* 75). And indeed, Jonathan's adventure, which will become as grim as the Holocaust itself, commences with great humor.

The novel unfolds through three different narrative forms, and two of these are voiced by the book's other major character, Alex Perchov, a young Ukrainian who serves as Jonathan's translator during Jonathan's journey through the Ukraine in a car driven by a third major character, Alex's grandfather. Alex's narrative, written in mauled English, is, at least early in the book, hilarious:

> I was sired in 1977, the same year as the hero of this story. . . . I dig Negroes, particularly Michael Jackson. I dig to disseminate very much currency at famous nightclubs in Odessa. Lamborghini Countaches are excellent, and so are cappucinos. Many girls want to be carnal with me in good arrangements, notwithstanding the Inebriated Kangaroo, the Gorky Tickle, and the Unyielding Zookeeper. If you want to know why so many girls want to be with me, it is because I am a very premium person to be with. I am homely, and also severely funny, and these are winning things. (1–2)

It is Alex's severely funny writing — ridiculous but immediately endearing, winning our affection, our "ruth" — that first hooks the reader and that spurred some of the book's most enthusiastic initial reviews. "It's hard," wrote Francine Prose in the *New York Times*,

> to get through the first chapters of *Everything Is Illuminated*. The problem is, you keep laughing out loud, losing your place, starting again, then stopping because you're tempted to call your friends and read them long sections of Jonathan Safran Foer's assured, hilarious prose. For me this difficulty was compounded by the fact that I was reading the novel on a trans-Atlantic flight. My inappropriate laughter (the film being shown on the plane was sad, or at least melodramatic) was clearly making several of my fellow passengers wonder if my behavior was the sort that, these days, requires that the flight attendants be notified at once. And even as I eyed the phone in the console beside my seat, I realized that indulging the temptation to call the folks back home and tell them about this wonderful first novel might cost far more than I was likely to earn from writing this review.

Foer — or at least the "Jonathan" who is a character in the novel — appears to reject his own sense of humor late in the narrative, when the book turns deadly serious: "I used to think," Jonathan tells Alex, "that humor was the only way to appreciate how wonderful and terrible the world is, to celebrate how big life is. . . . But now I think it's the opposite. Humor is a way of shrinking from that wonderful and terrible world" (158). But this is an ironic claim in a novel that itself has been very funny, and Jonathan later corrects his corrected view of humor (though the passage actually appears earlier in the book) by telling Alex that "*humorous is the only truthful way to tell a sad story*" [53]). I believe that Pema Chödrön precisely describes why Jonathan is correct to see humor as an essential part of an appreciation of the world's wonder and terror and bigness: "lightening up" with "kindness, humor, and good-heartedness," Chödrön says (*When Things Fall Apart* 75), is necessary in order for us to keep our relation to truth open and flexible, so we are porously connected to the world rather than closed off in moralistic egoism. Humor, in other words, is part of "bodhichitta," the softly awakened heart that is needed for an openness to the dark-side journey, the journey into the world: "The poet Jalaluddin Rumi," Chödrön says, "writes of night travelers who search the darkness instead of running from it, a companionship of people willing to know their own fear. Whether it's in the small fears of a job interview or the unnameable terrors imposed by war, prejudice, and hatred" — and what could be more unnameable than the terror of the Holocaust? — ". . . in the tenderness of the pain itself, night travelers discover the light of bodhichitta" (*When Things Fall Apart* 91). By using elaborate narrative techniques that mythologize Jonathan's family, looking beyond his literal parents and grandparents to "Cosmic mythical" ancestors, and by journeying all the way to the Holocaust, with ruthful truth drenched in pathos but also in playfulness and hilarious humor — that is, with bodhichitta — Foer turns a conventional college-kid-travels-abroad story into a family-based dark-side narrative that dissolves the duality between shadows and illuminations.

Foer's novel is designed as a kind of conversation between Jonathan and Alex, and I would suggest that their relationship — their brotherhood, to put it in familial language — is a key theme of the work. The text exists in a series of small sections, each of which reflects an ongoing correspondence between Jonathan and Alex that has been taking place subsequent to Jonathan's visit to the Ukraine in the form of writings mailed back and forth. The first part of each section is a chapter narrated by Alex and sent to Jonathan for editorial advice, telling, bit by bit, the story of Jonathan's "VERY RIGID [i.e., difficult] JOURNEY" in the Ukraine searching for Augustine and Trachimbrod; each section's next part is made up of one or more chapters of the book Jonathan is supposedly writing, narrated by Jonathan and sent to Alex, which convey Jonathan's fanciful history of Trachimbrod and the saga of his ancestors, covering years from the eighteenth century through World War II; and each section (save the last) ends with a letter from Alex to Jonathan commenting on the materials they have just exchanged and we have just read.

This framework and especially the letters from Alex give *Everything Is Illuminated* aspects of a metanovel, a novel about its narrators' own writing process. In many cases, a metanovel's design annihilates the apparent content and makes a text self-referential — makes it a text in which the meaning is how-texts-mean. But in this case, the metanovel elements actually *add* content: they make this a novel about how friendship works, how Alex and Jonathan grow from strangers to brothers; they become as close, in a way, as Dr Jekyll and Mr Hyde — alter egos or doppelgängers or mutual shadow figures, but in a positive rather than negative way. The novel is really about two "rigid journeys" rather than one: Jonathan's journey *away from* America and *into* his family and its history, and Alex's would-be journey *to* America (his dream is to move to the United States) and *away from* his family and its history. In both cases, however, the "rigid" journeys soften (in Pema Chödrön's terms); adolescent individualism and egoism matures — along Chödrön's lines of "growing up" — into mutuality, connectedness, bodhichitta, ruthful truth. Let us look at that process in three places in the novel: early in the book where we see both Jonathan and Alex, well-meaning but naive, commence their respective dark-side journeys; the middle of the book, where we learn the story of Jonathan's fabricated, fictionalized, mythical ancestors and their own dark-side journey into love, relationship, and family; and late in the book, where everything is (ironically, darkly, with horror and deep, unsolvable mystery) illuminated.

The novel opens with the first of the chapters written by Alex, which will mesh and meld with the book Jonathan is writing until the two texts together become the volume we are holding. Alex's initial chapter title is "AN OVERTURE TO THE COMMENCEMENT OF A VERY RIGID JOURNEY" (1), and Alex's general naivete is signaled by his naive use of the English language (this despite Alex's claim to the contrary: "I had performed recklessly well in my second year of English at university. This was a very majestic thing I did because my instructor was having shit between his brains" [2]). He brags about his mentoring of his brother, Little Igor — "I have tutored Little Igor to be a man of this world" (3) — but his tutoring, of course, turns out to be amusingly uninformed, about sex especially.

But despite his ridiculous malapropisms and other mistakes, Alex does reveal in this first chapter an ability to learn, and even more importantly a devotion to his family. He is somewhat able, for example, even in this initial, funny chapter to rise above his anti-Semitic bigotry:

before the voyage I had the opinion that Jewish people were having shit between their brains. This is because all I knew of Jewish people was that they paid Father very much currency in order to make vacations *from* America *to* Ukraine. But then I met Jonathan Safran Foer, and I will tell you, he is not having shit between his brains. He is an ingenious Jew. (3)

Beneath the comic foolishness here, there is an important point: Alex has been brought up with racist attitiudes about Jews, but he is capable of getting past them, and this will happen because of a deepening relationship with Jonathan — and ultimately because of a dark-side journey into the heart of Jewish persecution.

And despite his mistaken tutoring of Little Igor in all things sexual, we can infer that Alex genuinely cares about his brother:

he is a first-rate boy. It is now evident to me that he will become a very potent and generative man, and that his brain will have many muscles. We do not speak in volumes, because he is such a silent person, but I am certain that we are friends, and I do not think I would be lying if I wrote that we are paramount friends. (3)

More generally, Alex expresses the compassion, the reaching beyond ego, that characterizes family at its best; the fact that he does so in a funny and seemingly shallow way merely creates the possibility of his achieving more depth (in Paul Tillich's sense) as the novel progresses. Here is Alex's funny but potentially touching description of his mother:

Mother is a humble woman. Very, very humble. She toils at a small café one hour distance from our home . . . and says to me, "I mount the autobus for an hour to work all day doing things I hate. You want to know why? It is for you, Alexi-stop-spleening-me! One day you will do things for me that you hate. That is what it means to be a family." What she does not clutch is that I already do things for her that I hate. . . . But I do not do these things because we are a family. I do them because they are common decencies. . . . I do them because I am not a big fucking asshole. (2)

In our discussion of family as the locus for illuminating dark-side journeys, we have seen no more amusingly provocative definition of "what it means to be a family" than Alex's mother's: *doing for someone things that you hate*. And Alex's expansion of this definition to the community at large — "I do them because they are common decencies" — shows him pushing beyond familial literalism to a larger vision that James

Hillman and Pema Chödrön might applaud. Dipping below the mala-propisms, we can see that family for these characters points toward something beyond ego; here is the "ruth" (with plenty of humor to keep us from getting too pious) in Ruth Truth. All of this will enter into Alex's journey into his family's dark secrets: the truth behind the seeming anti-Semitism that Alex has drawn from his grandfather and behind the not-at-all-comic meanness of Alex's father.

Meanwhile, we also encounter Jonathan in Alex's initial bits of writing — in this and subsequent early chapters as well as in Alex's first letter to Jonathan — and Jonathan too is a naive young man whose smug-seeming surface needs to be shattered both to facilitate his own growth and to open Alex's eyes to the ruthful truth of who Jonathan is.

Alex idolizes America and its people, but his first meeting with Jonathan is a letdown, leaving him "underwhelmed to the maximum":

When we found each other, I was very flabbergasted by his appearance. This is an American? I thought. And also, This is a Jew? He was severely short. He wore spectacles and had diminutive hairs which were not split anywhere, but rested on his head like a Shapka. . . . He did not appear like either the Americans I had witnessed in magazines, with yellow hairs and muscles, or the Jews from history books, with no hairs and prominent bones. He was wearing nor blue jeans nor the uniform. In truth, he did not look like anything special at all. (31–32)

This passage reveals Alex's naivete, certainly (his only image for Jews is drawn from concentration-camp photographs), but it reveals Jonathan's plain, unheroic youthfulness as well. Alex has been calling Jonathan "the hero," both because of Alex's worship of things American and because he is self-consciously, and ironically, trying to write a story about a grand romantic quest. That the real Jonathan lacks the heroic qualities Alex has imagined nicely sets up the story as a dark-side narrative, of the sort we have been describing in these pages, rather than a heroic romance; Jonathan, like Goodman Brown, Bill Harford, et al, is a decent chap but a callow, limited one. He needs some shadows and illuminations.

Jonathan deflates Alex's heroic expectations even further when he reveals that he is a vegetarian, which Alex and his grandfather find unimaginable:

"How can you not eat meat?" "I just don't." "He does not eat meat," I told Grandfather. "Yes he does," he informed me. "Yes you do," I like-wise informed the hero. "No. I don't." "Why not?" I inquired him again. "I just don't. No meat." (65)

A gap of incomprehension initially looms between Jonathan and his Ukrainian hosts, and neither Alex nor Jonathan tries very hard to bridge it. "What is wrong with you?" Alex asks Jonathan, translating a question from Grandfather. "It's just the way I am," Jonathan dismissively answers. And then, writes Alex, "'You are a schmuck,' I informed the hero. 'You're not using the word correctly,' he said. 'Yes I am,' I said" (65). Not much truth is being shared here, and certainly no ruth.

It is laughter that introduces a hint of connection, and a deepening of Jonathan's, Alex's, and Grandfather's stories. When Jonathan, Alex, and Grandfather go to a restaurant for their first meal together, the only way that Jonathan can purchase a vegetarian meal is to order pork and potatoes and then eat only the potatoes. But Alex and Grandfather's dog — named Sammy Davis, Junior, Junior — "became sociable with the table, and also made the plates move. One of the hero's potatoes descended to the floor. When it hit the floor it made a sound. PLOMP" (66). Alex goes on to write:

> We laughed with violence, and then more violence. I witnessed that each of us was manufacturing tears at his eyes. It was not until very much in the posterior that I understanded that each of us was laughing for a different reason, for our own reason, and that not one of those reasons had a thing to do with the potato. (67)

This strange laughing reminds Alex of a painful, deeply sad laughing fit he experienced when he discovered his brother, Little Igor, crying (Igor, we learn, has been suffering abuse at the hands of his and Alex's cruel father): "I am able to understand now that it was the same laugh that I had in the restaurant in Lutsk, the laugh that had the same darkness as Grandfather's laugh and the hero's laugh" (69). Laughter filled with darkness: this is the vehicle of ruthful truth, a beginning of a linkage among Jonathan, Alex, and Grandfather, the basis of which we will not come to understand until much later in the novel.

This narrative that Alex is writing describes events that occurred just a few weeks earlier, when Jonathan visited the Ukraine in search of Augustine and the shtetl of Trachimbrod. But while Alex writes this story, Jonathan is also writing his own book inspired by his experience in the Ukraine. And his text breaks free of literalism altogether, telling the story of his ancestors in comic, mythic, magical-realistic terms. He describes the genesis of Trachimbrod at the site of the drowning, in the Brod River, of a man named Trachim B. This site is a locale that comically dramatizes Pema Chödrön's *paramitas*, actions that cross the border between the secular and the sacred: "The accident," writes Jonathan, had happened by the small falls — the part of shore that marked the current division of the shtetl into its two sections, the Jewish Quarter and the Human Three-Quarters. All so-called sacred activities — religious studies, kosher butchering, bargaining, etc. — were contained within the Jewish Quarter. Those activities concerned with the humdrum of daily existence — secular studies, communal justice, buying and selling, etc. — took place in the Human Three-Quarters. Straddling the two was the Upright Synogogue. (The ark itself was built along the Jewish/Human fault line, such that one of the two Torah scrolls would exist in each zone.) (10)

Right at this "Jewish/Human fault line," Trachim B's wagon seems to have toppled into the river, pinning him to the bottom, but releasing to the surface all sorts of "curious flotsam" (8), including Trachim B's baby daughter. This mythical, magical girl is adopted by the money-lender Yankel D, a disgraced pariah due to some undisclosed past crime, who names her "Brod" after the river, and she — whom Jonathan claims is his great-great-great-great-great-grandmother — reigns over the shtetl, and over the center of the novel, as a kind of comic, overwhelmingly attractive river goddess.

Brod is the shtetl's Venus (even her magical birth reflects Venus's), envied by all the women and adored by the men: she is, Jonathan writes, "Loved by everyone, even those who hated her" (77). Most of all she is loved by Yankel, her adoptive father, and yet theirs is a love with a huge blight, a shadow: Yankel never tells Brod the truth about her origins, and so their relationship is a tapestry of falsehoods, fabrications. So this goddess of love is a goddess of shadows — indeed, of what James Hillman describes as the *structural* shadow, the shadow that is endemic to the human condition: "Shadow," says Hillman, "is the penumbral life that lives with life as the never-ceasing darkening of the light in every search, a darkening of the light of certainty, the light's own sense that however an 'I' searches for soul, that same 'I' is inherently biased against the object of its searching" (*Insearch* 134). This inherent shadow is the aloneness that haunts us all, the aloneness that is the goblin right at the center of love and family, the voice that whispers that family itself is a fallacy. Foer's, or Jonathan's, description of the "love" between Yankel and Brod is a powerful evocation of this structural shadow that haunts the human condition, turning love itself into a journey rather than a goal, a fabricated story rather than a fact:

> if there is no love in the world, we will make a new world, and we will give it heavy walls, and we will furnish it with soft red interiors, from the inside out, and give it a knocker that resonates like a diamond falling

to a jeweler's felt so that we should never hear it. Love me, because love doesn't exist, and I have tried everything that does.

... [M]y very-great-and-lonely grandmother didn't love Yankel, not in the simple and impossible sense of the word. In reality she hardly knew him. And he hardly knew her. They knew intimately the aspects of themselves in the other, but never the other. . . . They were strangers, like my grandmother and me.

. . . They reciprocated the great and saving lie — that our love for things is greater than our love for our love for things — willfully playing the parts they wrote for themselves, willfully creating and believing fictions necessary for life. (82–83)

Fictions necessary for life: this is the structural shadow *and* its antidote at the very same time, an endorsement of family *and* a proclamation of the family fallacy. Rather than writing a literal history of his family, Jonathan is writing this mythic history of his ancestors, a fiction necessary for life, an acknowledgement of "the penumbral life that lives with life as the never-ceasing darkening of the light in every search, a darkening of the light of certainty" — the *not*, the dark side that cannot be analyzed away but that must be accepted tenderly, humorously, with bodhichitta.

Indeed, this shadowy story includes grand illumination — everything is illuminated, in an image that is fictive (a shadow) but marvelously, evocatively imaginal (an illumination). The novel draws its title from a variety of sources, but the most central is Jonathan's elaborate poeticization of the electrically illuminative power of human connection (despite his equal assertion that there is no absolute connection between people — "They were strangers, like my grandmother and me" [82]). Every year, Jonathan writes, on the anniversary of Trachim B's drowning and Brod's emergence from the river, the shtetl of Trachimbrod celebrates "Trachimday" with a festival, which ends with the people of the shtetl making "wild, urgent love in the dark corners where houses met and under the hanging canopies of weeping willows" (95). And then Jonathan breaks off and spins a tale that with outrageous humor accomplishes what James Hillman calls for in *The Soul's Code*: the tale widens his focus from familial literalism, which the Trachimbrod mythology has already begun to do, to a sweeping "Cosmic mythical" (*Soul's Code* 85) scale that makes us contemplate the soul in the world out there, "the larger world-parents, and also the world at large as parent. For the world too shapes us, nurtures us, teaches us" (*Soul's Code* 86). "From space," Jonathan writes, "astronauts can see people making love as a tiny speck of light. Not light, exactly, but a glow that could be mistaken for light — a coital radiance that takes generations to pour like honey through the darkness to the astronaut's eyes" (95). What? we find ourselves asking. How does such a crazy claim relate to Trachimbrod and its story? Well, it takes "about one and a half centuries — after the lovers who made the glow will have long since been laid permanently on their backs" (95) — for the honey-thick glow to ooze out to outer space. Furthermore, any glow seen from so far away must be "born from the sum of thousands of loves": "metropolises will be seen from space. . . . Smaller cities will also be seen, but with great difficulty. Shtetls will be virtually impossible to spot. Individual couples, invisible" (95). On certain days — Valentine's Day in New York City, St. Patrick's Day in Dublin, Chanukah's eight nights in Jerusalem — the glow intensifies because of a great deal of love-making, and on Trachimday enough illumination is generated even to make little Trachimbrod visible:

> Trachimday is the only time all year when the tiny village of Trachimbrod can be seen from space, when enough copulative voltage is generated to sex the Polish-Ukrainian skies electric. *We're here*, the glow of 1804 will say in one and a half centuries. *We're here, and we're alive.* (96)

Trachimday of 1804 is a crucial day in Jonathan's narrative because that is the day that Yankel dies and Brod meets her future husband, a man named Shalom from the neighboring shtetl of Kolki (yet another illumination: "A wink of light illuminated the Kolker at [Brod's] window" [97]). The Kolker, who will change his name to "Safran," and Brod become Jonathan's great-great-great-great-great-grandparents, and one hundred sixty-five years later, in 1969, Jonathan's mother and grandmother watch the moon landing on television:

> *Look et diz*, my grandmother says into the television's glow. *Look.* She puts her hand on my mother's hand and feels her own blood flow through the veins, and the blood of my grandfather (who died only five weeks after coming to the States, just half a year after my mother was born), and my mother's blood, and my blood, and the blood of my children and grandchildren. . . . They cry together, cheek to cheek. And neither of them hears the astronaut whisper, *I see something*, while gazing over the lunar horizon at the tiny village of Trachimbrod. *There's definitely something out there.* (98–99)

This is as audacious, playful, ridiculous, grand a celebration of blood and heritage and "Cosmic, mythical parents" (*Soul's Code* 85) as we are likely to find in literature. Everything is indeed illuminated . . . and yet, the story that Jonathan proceeds to tell about his ancestors, Brod and the Kolker, is riddled with shadows, a love story about the structural impossibility of love. In brief, Brod finds herself married to a kind man and his cruel doppelgänger, Dr Jekyll and Mr Hyde both.

At first this is not the case; rather, Brod *had* been living a "once removed life" (80), loving the idea of loving her apparent father, Yankel, but not loving him himself because their relationship has been riddled with unknowing. But with the Kolker, Brod finally, happily lives in "the primary world" (122), a world of immediacy, based on pure, gapless knowledge, which equates with simple, gapless love: "She always felt that she knew everything about [the Kolker] that could be known — not that he was simple, but that he was knowable, like a list of errands, like an encyclopedia" (122). So Brod is "in love" (123) with the Kolker. It turns out that this is a mixed blessing, however; Brod's not-love for Yankel had texture, play, story, but this primary, immediate, unselfconscious love with the Kolker is flat. *"We've only had six conversations, Brod,"* the Kolker complains. *"Six in almost three years."* Brod blithely, unselfconsciously replies, *"I never noticed"* (124). "All she wanted from him," Jonathan writes, "was cuddling and high voices. Whispers. Assurances. Promises of fidelity and truth she made him swear to again and again: that he would never kiss another woman, that he would never even think of another woman, that he would never leave her alone" (125). An assurance that he would never leave her alone: this is (or Brod wants it to be) a relationship without the structural shadow of aloneness, the inherent shadow haunting self-conscious human nature. But Jonathan, who is designing Brod and the Kolker's story as the prototype, the cosmic myth, of love, and as the prototypical dark-side/illumination story, is merely setting them up in this Eden of a primary, immediate world (with which already the Kolker is expressing impatience). The blow is about to fall, the blade that will slice into this immediacy and create distance, plunging these naive lovers into a dark-side adventure within which self-enclosed, immediate love will complicate and thicken into marriage, procreation, family . . . suffering but also depth.

The Kolker begins working in the Trachimbrod flour mill, and there his dark-side journey commences. On a lunch break in the mill, the Kolker is in his happy, naive Eden, eating a cheese sandwich, ruminating on Brod, "oblivious to the chaos around him," when a disk-saw blade spins out of control, flies around the mill, and embeds itself "perfectly vertical, in the middle of his skull" (125). The blade does not kill the Kolker, but it splits off his shadow side, causing unpredictable "malicious eruptions" (127), especially at Brod. He now has violent outbursts at Brod and even sometimes uses physical brutality: "The Kolker hated himself, or his other self, for it. He would pace the bedroom at night, arguing savagely with his other self at the top of the two lungs they shared, often beating the chest that housed those lungs, or boxing their face" (129). As James Hillman, Thomas Moore, and Pema Chödrön would say, this dark side cannot be removed, cured: "all agreed that the only possible cure for his disposition would be to remove the blade from his head, which would certainly kill him" (129). So the pure, immediate love between Brod and the Kolker has been sliced, thrust back by a blade that works as an image, a comic-tragic exaggeration, of the self-consciousness that distances a human subject from the outside world and even from itself — doppelgänger not as personal flaw but as structural shadow. The Kolker knows that the blade severely qualifies their love and forces the reality of (his) death into consciousness, and he discovers the necessity of fabrication: "*I wonder if you could just pretend for a while, if we could pretend to love each other. Until I'm gone*" (133).

So they create a living situation that is simultaneously functional (it protects Brod physically from the Kolker's violent outbursts) and symbolic (it conveys a vivid image of the connection/disconnection that is endemic to conscious human relatedness): the Kolker has himself locked in a bedroom that adjoins Brod's, with a small hole cut in the wall through which Brod and the Kolker can see and communicate with each other. This situation becomes iconic of human structural aloneness, which the Kolker and Brod had not been aware of in their young naivete. And, like the other dark-side journeys we have seen, this one combines pain with new depth:

> They had never seen one another from afar. They had never known the deepest intimacy, that closeness attainable only with distance. . . .
>
> They removed their underwear and took turns gazing through the hole, experiencing the sudden and profound joy of discovering each other's body, and the pain of not being able to discover each other at the same time. (134–135)

This experience of absent presence is powerfully erotic. Erotic love is predicated on *longing*; in their previous Edenic immediacy they never had to experience longing but only a perfect present, but now they long for each other passionately, with the realities of separation and death always before them, not suppressed but carried mindfully:

> They lived with the hole. The absence that defined it became a presence that defined them. Life was a small negative space cut out of the eternal solidity, and for the first time, it felt precious — not like all of the words that had come to mean nothing, but like the last breath of a drowning victim. (135)

When the Kolker, renamed "Safran," dies, his body is bronzed and placed in the shtetl square, where it becomes a symbol of luck — fate, really, the structural shadow as limit, which cannot be evaded but can only be known and accepted ("eaten," in Robert Bly's terms). Casting a shadow, the bronzed body becomes the Dial, a sundial for keeping time, time itself being a concept based on limitedness, fate. And the Dial becomes an image of the myth of family — the *story*, not the literal fact, of familial connection. The statue, we are told, looks just like Jonathan's grandfather Safran, whose story Jonathan has come to the Ukraine in pursuit of. But this resemblance is due not to literal genetic determinism but to myth, story, art: the statue is so venerated that over the years the bronze has been rubbed away — negated — by the hands and lips of visiting pilgrims, and then rebronzed by artisans who use the Kolker's descendents as models: "He was a changing god," Jonathan writes, "destroyed and recreated by his believers, destroyed and recreated by their belief. . . . So when my grandfather thought he saw that he was growing to look like his great-great-great-grandfather, what he really saw was that his great-great-great-grandfather was growing to look like him" (140). This influence not of the past on the future but of the future on the past makes the Dial a powerful image of James Hillman's "acorn theory" (6), the "call of fate" (5). In the image of the Dial, as Hillman says of his "acorn," "It's all there at once" (7): a future potentiality calls forth, pulls the world forward, at least as much as past fact causes and determines what follows. The Dial points forward toward Jonathan's grandfather, Safran, as much as it looks backward toward Jonathan's great-great-great-great-grandfather, the Kolker.

The story of Brod and the Kolker is, as I have said, a prototypical dark-side narrative that Foer has placed at the center of his novel. It follows the dark-side form we have seen again and again; its protagonists begin as naive and limited people (living in an Edenic, immediate present) and then undergo a disturbing, shadow-ridden experience that leaves them sadder but wiser. In this case, the dark-side story even leaves Shalom-Kolker-Safran divinized as the Dial, the mythic patron of Trachimbrod, who shapes and limits Jonathan's family in a non-literalistic, poetic way — not as a parent-induced psychopathology that needs to be analyzed and expunged, but as a myth that needs to be imagined deeply and that already carries, as the "acorn" does, the mysterious soul-filled call of the future. This is how the story affects Alex, whose reaction we hear in his subsequent letter to Jonathan. *"One could learn very much from the marriage of Brod and Kolker,"* Alex writes. *"I do not know what, but I am certain that it has to do with love"* (143). Alex infers that the story relates love and family to the structural shadow, the deep unknowing that haunts all knowing; apparently Jonathan has made such a point in his own letter to Alex (which is not included in the text), and Alex responds: *"One part of your letter made me most melancholy. It was the part when you said that you do not know anybody, and how that encompasses even you. I understand very much what you are saying"* (144). And Alex then realizes the collaborative nature of his and Jonathan's artistic enterprise, realizing the illuminative nature of their friendship: *"With our writing, we are reminding each other of things. We are making one story, yes?"* (144). Perhaps, Alex seems to be realizing, humans do not know anything or anybody, including themselves — but *together* they can weave stories that point toward some approximate, poetic truth.

Then Alex comes to what I take to be the central "illumination" of the novel, analogous to the realization in *King Lear* that the facts of family and self and world cannot be changed, but only one's relationship with those facts: "Ripeness is all." Alex's version of this insight combines fatalism — family cannot be escaped, his dream of flight to America is illusory — with gentle, forgiving bodhichitta.

"Everything," Alex writes, *"is the way it is because everything was the way it was. Sometimes I feel ensnared in this, as if no matter what I do, what will come has already been fixed"* (145). He accepts this limit for himself — *"For me, OK"* — but bristles at the thought that Little Igor is fated to live with violence (*"and I mean more than merely the kind that occurs with fists"* [145]). The source of this violent fate is Alex and Igor's cruel father, who himself was fated by an act committed by his own father, Alex and Igor's grandfather, during the grim, hidden, dark World War II situation that Foer will illuminate only near the end of the novel. But even before we learn this hidden story, we are given a glimpse of Alex's "ripeness," his gentle bodhichitta, the product of the journey to Trachimbrod that he has gone on with his grandfather and with Jonathan. We have not yet seen the dark place this journey took them to, but we read here the softening and "growing up" that it has engendered in Alex:

> *Father is never home because then he would witness Grandfather crying. . . . (This is why I forgive Father. I do not love him. I hate him. But I forgive him for everything.) I parrot: Grandfather is not a bad person, Jonathan. Everyone performs bad actions. I do. Father does. Even you do. A bad person is someone who does not lament his bad actions. Grandfather is now dying because of his. I beseech you to forgive us, and to make us better than we are. Make us good.* (145)

"Make us good," Alex says; this is a metafictional moment — an admission by Alex that he is a character created by Jonathan who himself is a creation of the actual Jonathan Safran Foer. There is the possibility of goodness in this family-based dark-side story, but it is not a goodness

fought for heroically by grappling analytically and medically with pathologies engendered by literal fathers and mothers. Rather, it is a more modest goodness achieved by fabricating stories with care and ripeness, listening to the call of the beautiful acorn as much as acknowledging the fact of the past abuse; indeed, in this case the "acorn" is the sad but beautiful story itself, which calls forth its own writing. The action of *Everything Is Illuminated*, then, is shaped not just by the terrible past events but also by the emergence of the beautiful book that will incarnate these dark, terrible past events. This is the kind of family therapy recommended by Thomas Moore, which takes "the form of simply telling stories of family life, free of any concern for cause and effect or sociological influence" (*Care of the Soul* 28). It is up to Foer, the novelist, Alex says, to "Make us good."

One way *not* to create familial goodness, it appears, is to tell the stories sentimentally, to purge the dark side and replace it with a coating of sugar. In the chapters that follow the letter by Alex quoted above, Alex writes of the woman whom he, his grandfather, and Jonathan find at the end of their odyssey, initially thinking that she is the longed-for Augustine but then discovering that she is only a minor former girlfriend of Jonathan's grandfather Safran, descendent of Brod and the Kolker; and then Jonathan writes fancifully of his grandfather's withered arm, which strangely leads to his having many sexual affairs, especially with a "Gypsy girl" and even with his new wife's sister on his and his wife's wedding day. "*We are being very nomadic with the truth, yes? The both of us?*" says Alex in his subsequent letter to Jonathan. "*Do you think that this is acceptable when we are writing about things that occurred?*" (179). If such fictionalizing of true events is not acceptable, then why are they doing it? wonders Alex, and if it *is* acceptable to fictionalize,

> *Why do we not make the story more premium than life? It seems to me that we are making the story even inferior. We often make ourselves appear as though we are foolish people, and second rate. We could give your grandfather two arms, and could make him high-fidelity. We could give Brod what she deserves in the stead of what she gets. We could even find Augustine, Jonathan, and you could thank her, and Grandfather and I could embrace, and it could be perfect and beautiful, and funny, and usefully sad, as you say. . . . I do not think that there are any limits to how excellent we could make life seem.* (179–180)

This is not how Alex's and Jonathan's artful stories will go, however. Rather, they become darker and darker, intersecting with each other, Alex's present-day story moving backward to the horrendous "illumination" of his grandfather's betrayal, during a Nazi purge, of a Jewish friend named Herschel, and Jonathan's family history moving forward to the destruction of Trachimbrod by the Nazis. But these terrible stories create deep, profound connections — connections that sugar-coated versions would not effect: *"We are talking now, Jonathan,"* writes Alex,

> *together, and not apart. We are with each other, working on the same story, and I am certain that you can also feel it. Do you know that I am the Gypsy girl and you are Safran, and that I am Kolker and you are Brod, and that I am your grandmother and you are Grandfather, and that I am Alex and you are you, and that I am you and you are me? Do you not comprehend that we can bring each other safety and peace? . . . Do not present not-truths to me. Not to me.* (214)

The connection Alex is describing between himself and Jonathan — and indeed, between each person and everyone else — is presented in the text as tragic, a shared guilt in the face of atrocities that go beyond "dark-side stories" to a level of absolute evil. ("It is not a thing that you can imagine," says the Holocaust survivor, who is not Augustine, whom they find at the end of their journey. "It only is. After that, there can be no imagining" [188]. This is the naught, the *Lear*-ish *nothing* that stands as a limit to Alex's, Jonathan's, and Jonathan Safran Foer's storytelling.) In the face of this evil, Alex's grandfather pointed to his friend Herschel, betraying him to the Nazis as a Jew, trying to save his family but blighting them in the process; and Alex asserts that this blight is itself the connection of all humans. There is, Alex says, no separate "I" and "you" and "he" and "she":

> Grandfather said that I am I but this could not be true the truth is that I also pointed at Herschel and I also said he is a Jew and I will tell you that you also pointed at Herschel and you also said he is a Jew and more than that Grandfather also pointed at me and said he is a Jew and you also pointed at him and said he is a Jew and your grandmother and Little Igor and we all pointed at each other so what is it he should have done he would have been a fool to do anything else but is it forgivable what he did can he ever be forgiven for his finger for what he pointed to and did not point to for what he touched in his life and what he did not touch he is still guilty I am I am I am Iam Iam I? (252)

This passage expresses the "soul" that emerges from *Everything Is Illuminated*: a shared reality beyond self. It is tragic, marked by profound horror and guilt, but when its story is told fully — with humor at first, eventually with brutal honesty, but always with soft-hearted bodhichitta — the result is beautiful.

"[B]ut is it forgivable?" Alex asks of the terrible acts that humans commit, seemingly holding up to question his previous claim, which I described as his embrace of "ripeness" and soft-heartedness ("bodhi-chitta"): "*I forgive Father. I do not love him. I hate him. But I forgive him for everything*" (145). Now he seems to suggest that all humans are connected by their *unforgivable* guilt, a tragic place indeed to leave a discussion of the family locus of dark-side stories. Near its conclusion, however, the novel adds a more serene anecdote, a kind of coda to the Brod-Kolker story, that reaffirms the value of ripeness — calm, mature acceptance of family stories rather than heroic surgical removal of family dysfunctions. Near its conclusion the novel presents a small but striking image of the kind of healing relationship with the dark side that we have seen repeatedly in these pages: what Robert Bly calls *eating the shadow*, Pema Chödrön calls *bodhichitta*, and James Hillman calls *being true to your depression*.

The story is told — appropriately enough, in this fanciful book — by the Dial itself, the godlike statue of Shalom-Kolker-Safran. The Dial is speaking to his, or its, great-great-great-grandson Safran, Jonathan's grandfather, who has just married his new wife Zosha, whom he has just impregnated after having, despite years of sexual promiscuity, his first actual orgasm. His checkered life, complicated by a withered arm, and now his unsought rush of love for his not-yet-born child have left Safran feeling pummeled, and he throws himself at the feet of this statue that looks like him and moans, "*I am a dupe of chance*" (263). And the Dial speaks to him ("with the unmoving lips of a ventriloquist" [263]), pointing out that Safran's fate, driven by love for a future child, is the kind of fate imaged by Hillman's acorn, and by the Dial itself — a call from the future: "*The others are being pulled back, and you're being pulled forward*" (264), the Dial says. "*In both directions!*" Safran answers (264), thinking of events of the mythic familial past (Trachim's wagon, Brod's story) and the Jews' political past (the pogroms) and also imagining "his possible futures":

> life with the Gypsy girl, life alone, life with Zosha and the child who would fulfill him, the end of life. The images of his infinite pasts and infinite futures washed over him as he waited, paralyzed, in the present. He, Safran, marked the division between what was and what would be. (264)

This is a rich, detailed presentation of the kind of "soul" that James Hillman uses his acorn metaphor to describe in *The Soul's Code*; it is what "fate" looks like when imagined deeply, with texture, which happens after a truly digested dark-side journey. That this "growing-up" journey has taught Safran love, but has actually increased his suffering, is the irony of a dark-side journey, and it explains why writers as different as Paul Tillich, Pema Chödrön, and James Hillman do not say that this movement to depth is an antidepressant.

And it is Safran's pain that leads the Dial — Safran's ancestor, his "Cosmic mythical" parent, a familial mentor but not his literal father or mother — to tell his parable-like story about serenity, ripeness, eating the shadow, being true to one's depression:

> *Let me tell you a story, the Dial went on. The house that your great-great-great-grandmother and I moved into when we first became married looked out onto the small falls, at the end of the Jewish/Human fault line. It had wood floors, long windows, and enough room for a large family. It was a handsome house. A good house.*
>
> *But the water, your great-great-great-grandmother said, I can't hear myself think.*
>
> *Time, I urged her. Give it time. (265)*

At first, says the Dial, he and Brod *"couldn't stand to be alone in the house for more than a few hours at a time"* (265). The noise of the waterfall embodied and accentuated the anxieties, angers, and depressions — all those symptoms — of life, especially life for people living together familially. Brod and the Kolker got little sleep, could hardly eat, and quarreled incessantly. But after a couple of weeks things got *"a little better,"* with more sleep, less anxiety, less constant irritation from the noise, until,

> *after a little more than two months: Do you hear that? I asked her on one of the rare mornings we sat at the table together. Hear it? I put down my coffee and rose from my chair. You hear that thing?*
>
> *What thing? she asked.*
>
> *Exactly! I said, running outside to pump my fist at the waterfall. Exactly!*
>
> *We danced, throwing handfuls of water in the air, hearing nothing at all. We alternated hugs of forgiveness and shouts of human triumph at the water. Who wins the day? Who wins the day, waterfall? We do! We do! (265)*

"And this is what living next to a waterfall is like," says the Dial, and he drives home the meaning of his parable — how the ability to live with grief, pain, depression, shadows emerges when one stays in the dark place without trying to leap out of it:

> *Every widow wakes one morning, perhaps after years of pure and unwavering grieving, to realize she slept a good night's sleep, and will be able to eat breakfast, and doesn't hear her husband's ghost all the time, but only some of the time. Her grief is replaced with a useful sadness. Every parent who loses a child finds*

*a way to laugh again. The timbre begins to fade. The edge dulls. The hurt
lessens. Every love is carved from loss. Mine was. Yours is. Your great-great-
great-grandchildren's will be. But we learn to live in that love.* (265–266)

What the Kolker and Brod do in this parable is both tiny and huge. It
is tiny in that all they do is stay there by the waterfall, when their instinct
is to escape. But resisting this urge to escape is a significant achievement.
"We're so used to running from discomfort," says Pema Chödrön, "and
we're so predictable. If we don't like it, we strike out at someone or beat
up on ourselves. We want to have security and certainty of some kind"
(*When Things Fall Apart* 117). But wisdom, says Chödrön, is a recognition
that such security and certainty are illusory: "actually we have no
ground to stand on," she says, and an experience that sharpens our
awareness of this groundlessness — for instant, living adjacent to a
waterfall, which bombards us with the harsh, uncontrollable noise of life
— "could soften us and inspire us. Finally, after all these years, we could
truly grow up" (*When Things Fall Apart* 117). The waterfall teaches Brod
and the Kolker about Chödrön's wisdom of no escape. Ripeness is all.
It is just such wise maturity that James Hillman ascribes to those who
are true to their depression, living with it but not identifying with it.
(Initially, in their rage and sleeplessness, Brod and the Kolker *identify
with* the noisy waterfall, but eventually they learn just to live with it, to
relax and lighten up.) "Did you ever think," Hillman writes, "what a
relief to be with someone who knows how to live in the depression
without being it. That's a master to learn from, like old people can sometimes be. Depression lets you live down at the bottom" (*Inter Views* 21).
This is a quieter, less exultant prescription for dealing with family
pathologies than we are perhaps used to: living with family pathologies
is like living next to a waterfall; grief is *"replaced with a useful sadness"*
(Foer 266).
But the waterfall parable ends with a disorienting final detail, which
jars us back to Chödrön's always-uncertain groundlessness. After
seeming to end his story with a comforting moral — *"we learn to live in
that love"* — the Dial adds that this is *"not the entire story"*:

*I realized this when I first tried to whisper a secret and couldn't, or whistle a
tune without instilling fear in the hearts of those within a hundred yards, when
my coworkers at the flour mill pleaded with me to lower my voice, because, Who
can think with you shouting like that? To which I asked, AM I REALLY
SHOUTING?* (266)

The dark side can be embraced; the shadow can be eaten; depression can
be bearable if we are "true" to it; family pathologies can make soul when

we tell the stories deeply, without sentimentalizing them. But none of these stances ends the journey, erases the wounding. The Kolker, without even realizing it, is now SHOUTING. He has become a disturbing presence. And he is soon going to have that disk-saw blade embedded in his skull.

Works Cited

Chödrön, Pema. *When Things Fall Apart: Heart Advice for Difficult Times*. 1997; Boston: Shambhala, 2000.

——. *The Wisdom of No Escape and the Path of Loving-Kindness*. 1991; Boston: Shambhala, 2001.

Foer, Jonathan Safran. *Everything Is Illuminated*. New York: Houghton Mifflin, 1992.

Fraser, Russell. "Introduction." *King Lear*. William Shakespeare. 1963; New York: Signet, 1998. Lxiii-lxxvi.

Hamilton, Jane. *The Book of Ruth*. 1988; New York: Anchor Doubleday, 1990.

Hillman, James. *Inter Views*. 1983. Dallas, TX: Spring Publications, 1992.

——. *The Soul's Code: In Search of Character and Calling*. New York: Random House, 1996.

Himes, Michael J. "'Finding God in All Things': A Sacramental Worldview and Its Effects." *As Leaven in the World: Catholic Perspectives on Faith, Vocation, and the Intellectual Life*. Ed. Thomas M. Landy. Franklin, WI: Sheed & Ward, 2001. 91–103.

Moore, Thomas. *Care of the Soul: A Guide for Cultivating Depth and Sacredness in Everyday Life*. New York: HarperCollins, 1992.

——. *Soul Mates: Honoring the Mysteries of Love and Relationship*. New York: HarperCollins, 1994.

Prose, Francine. "Back in the Totally Awesome U.S.S.R." Rev. of *Everything Is Illuminated*, by Jonathan Safran Foer. *New York Times*. NYTimes.com. 14 April 2004. Web. 6 March 2010.

Tolstoy, Leo. *Anna Karenina*. Trans. Richard Pevear and Larissa Volokhonsky. New York: Viking Penguin, 2001.

Zweig, Connie and Wolf, Steve. *Romancing the Shadow: A Guide to Soul Work for a Vital, Authentic Life*. New York: Ballantine, 1999.

The Better Story

In these pages I have been telling stories, spinning fictions. Or rather, since I am a commentator here, not a creative writer myself, I should put it differently: I have been spinning fictions about fictions, telling stories about these literary texts as narratives of spiritual, soul-making, healing journeys. But to describe them this way is itself to fictionalize; obviously these works can be, and have been, analyzed differently, so we ought to explore what makes my idiosyncratic description valid. I will conclude this book by enlisting James Hillman and novelist Yann Martel to help me examine the way fictionalizing can in itself be a healing activity, a move beyond the deadness of literal facts to soul-making imagination. The "only possible perfection that the soul can want," says Hillman, "is perfection of its fictional understanding, the realization of itself in its images, itself a fiction among fictions" (106). Dissolving "substantiations" — considerations of *just the facts*, as our unimaginative inner Joe Friday might say — into the multiplicity of "perspectives," which is the way of fiction (with its multiple viewpoints and genres), is, for Hillman, a "method of as-if" that "keeps the way open" and "comes closest to the religious idea that the final goal is the way itself, in this case, the way of fiction" (106). It is this imaginal, perspective-shifting method of fabricating that Yann Martel dramatizes in his Man Booker-award-winning *Life of Pi*; the novel's protagonist, Pi Patel, tells a story that proposes to "*make you believe in God*" (x), and the way it purportedly creates religious faith is by explicitly illustrating the value of fictionalizing, fabricating, image-making.

Pi's story is framed by an external narrator, a fictionalized persona of Yann Martel himself. While struggling to write a novel during a visit to India, this narrator meets an elderly man who tells him about Pi and his story; it is this man who informs the narrator that the story will make him "*believe in God*" (x). So the narrator seeks out Pi, an Indian now living in Canada, and Pi tells him his boyhood story, which details Pi's quest for God in Hinduism, Christianity, and Islam and especially his adventure at sea: when the Japanese ship carrying Pi, his family, and his father's zoo animals sinks in the ocean, Pi spends 227 days in a lifeboat with no other humans but only (for a short time) with a zebra, an orang-utan, and a hyena, and for the entire 227 days with a Bengal tiger.

It is at the novel's end that the story lays claim to making us *"believe in God,"* as it becomes a parable about faith itself. Finally washed ashore in Mexico, Pi is interviewed by representatives of the Maritime Department in Japan's Ministry of Transport, who wish to learn about the sinking of the ship. When Pi tells them, however, his detailed, colorful, deeply imagined story about spending 227 days in a lifeboat with a tiger, the interviewers find this "hard to believe" (297). But, says Pi, "If you stumble at mere believability, what are you living for? . . . Love is hard to believe, ask any lover. Life is hard to believe, ask any scientist. God is hard to believe, ask any believer. What is your problem with hard to believe?" (297). The men plead that they are "just being reasonable" (298), but Pi quarrels with this. Reason, he says, is a good "tool kit" — especially "for keeping tigers away" (298). But an excess of reason, he argues, risks "throwing out the universe with the bathwater" (298); Pi is suggesting that telling one's story cannot be reduced to "reason." "But for the purposes of our investigation," says one of the interviewers, "we would like to know what really happened" (302). What *really* happened: the interviewer sees this as outside and beyond perspective, invention, imagination, genre, storytelling. "We don't want any invention. We want the 'straight facts', as you say in English" (302).

But Pi answers, "So you want another story?" "Uh . . . no," says one of the interviewers; they do not want a story, they want reality. However, Pi responds, "Doesn't the telling of something always become a story? . . . Isn't telling about something — using words, English or Japanese — already something of an invention? . . . The world isn't just the way it is. It is how we understand it, no? And in understanding something, we bring something to it, no? Doesn't that make life a story?" (302). Pi claims that the demand for discourse stating "what really happened" without "invention," the "straight facts," is code for simply wanting a *different* kind of story from the colorful, imaginal one he has told: "I know what you want. You want a story that won't surprise you. That will confirm what you already know. That won't make you see higher or further or differently. You want a flat story. An immobile story. You want dry, yeast-less factuality" (302). And Pi proceeds to tell "another story" of his survival at sea, one that has no zebras or orang-utans or hyenas or tigers but only familiar (if grim, cruel) human behaviors. "What a horrible story," says one interviewer to the other when Pi is finished with this second version (311).

And then (most apropos to our discussion) Pi gets the Japanese interviewers to agree that the first version of his story — the version with the tiger — is "the better story" after all (317). This claim demands explaining, and it is what I want to unpack throughout this final chapter: what are the criteria for claiming that the more colorful, image-rich story is "better"? Prior to hearing the second version of the story, believable but grim, the interviewers assumed that "better" would mean *truer*, more *factual*, but Pi has nudged them away from that viewpoint; their criterion for truth was that it must consist of a collection of data and reasonable analysis without "invention" — the "straight facts" — but Pi has undermined that concept, arguing that the translating of any raw data into language involves fabrication ("Doesn't the telling of something always become a story? . . . something of an invention?"). In terms of the factual information that the interviewers are seeking — how and why the ship sank — both stories are equally valid. "Neither explains the sinking of the *Tsimtsum*," Pi says.

> "That's right."
> "Neither makes a factual difference to you."
> "That's true."
> "You can't prove which story is true and which is not. You must take my word for it."
> "I guess so."
> "In both stories the ship sinks, my entire family dies, and I suffer."
> "Yes, that's true." (317)

Having removed pragmatic fact-gathering from the enterprise, Pi now offers different criteria, those of *preference*: "So tell me, since it makes no factual difference to you and you can't prove the question either way, which story do you prefer? Which is the better story, the story with animals or the story without animals?" (317). And the interviewers agree that "the story with animals is the better story" (317). Not only that, but they even validate Pi's "better story" by referring to it in what is very much a different kind of discourse, their report to the Japanese Ministry of Transport, in which they call Pi's story *"an astounding story of courage and endurance"* and conclude that *"Very few castaways can claim to have survived so long at sea as Mr. Patel, and none in the company of an adult Bengal tiger"* (319).

"And so it goes with God," says Pi when the interviewers acknowledge that the story with animals is "the better story" (317). For Pi, "God" (which, as we will see, Pi places beyond any one narrative, since he embraces Hinduism, Christianity, and Islam sequentially and eventually simultaneously) is not an element of some sort of non-contextual factual truth — but pure factuality is not accessible anyway since all "truth" is grasped by humans relatively, perspectively, in invented stories. Rather, "God" is a kind of value-added element of "better" stories, preferable stories, which is why I raise this issue and why I am looking at *Life of Pi*: retelling stories as narratives of spiritual journeys, of soul-making, is not factual but is, in Pi's terms, a good thing to do. But mere *preference*, though it is the concept that Pi invokes, does not quite explain why such stories are "better"; preference can be merely whimsical and random, a choice of what feels good rather than of what has any sort of deeper validity.

Perhaps choosing this "better" story is something like a wager; the story with animals, as far as we know, is as true as the story without them, but it is "better" to take a risk on the story with animals, which is what the Japanese interviewers end up doing in the final report to the Ministry of Transport. Let us briefly play this idea through the discourse — the story, if you will — of the seventeenth-century philosopher Blaise Pascal's famed wager for God. Ultimately, neither feel-good whim nor Pascal's Wager quite gets at the way Pi's imaginal story is "better" than his "flat" story; for example, for some reason Pi *cries* after suggesting that "God" is related to "the better story," so God and better stories appear to lead to weeping — neither an obvious winning wager nor a good-feeling whim. So we will first glance at Pascal, but it is James Hillman who will truly help us grasp what Pi means by "the better story."

Pascal's Wager is built from probability theory as applied to gambling.* God either exists or does not exist, and this "wager" explains how we decide whether or not to believe. As far as God's objective, factual existence is concerned, "Reason cannot decide anything," Pascal says (153) — and for him, reason is the only faculty that we can appeal to (this will ultimately differentiate Pascal's argument from both Pi's and Hillman's). Lacking rational proof one way or another about God's existence and yet having only reason to work with, "towards which side," Pascal asks, "will we lean?" (153). Pascal decides to "weigh up the gain and the loss by calling heads that God exists," and Pascal claims that "if you win, you win everything; if you lose, you lose nothing. Wager that he exists then, without hesitating!" (154). In other words, if I bet on God's existence and God actually does exist, I win big; and if I bet on God's existence and God actually does not exist, I do not really lose anything. And in case that is not convincing enough, Pascal — still using a gambling concept, and a rational cost-benefit analysis — expands on what the "everything" is that "you win" if you bet on God and God actually exists. "Since there is an equal chance of gain and loss," Pascal says,

---

* I am indebted to "Pascal's Wager" in the online Stanford Encyclopedia of Philosophy <http://plato.stanford.edu/entries/pascal-wager/#1> for help with the explication of Pascal's ideas.

"if you won only two lives instead of one, you could still put on a bet" (154). In other words, in betting my life on God or not-God, a fifty-fifty proposition, it *could* be worth betting even if the possible payoff were merely two lives rather than one. And if the payoff were *three* lives, "you would have to play . . . and you would be unwise . . . not to chance your life to win three in a game where there is an equal chance of losing and winning" (154). So with the odds at fifty-fifty, and the payoff three times the bet, reason says I definitely should make the wager, Pascal claims. But in fact the payoff for this wager is much bigger: "there is an eternity of life and happiness," says Pascal, if I bet on God and God exists (154). The payoff would be not just two or three times the bet, but infinite: "here there is an infinitely happy infinity of life to be won, one chance of winning against a finite number of chances of losing, and what you stake is finite" (154). Since the loss, if I bet on God and it turns out that there is no God, is negligible ("if you lose, you lose nothing" [154]), and the gain, if I bet on God and God does in fact exist, is infinite ("an infinitely happy infinity of life" [154]), then reason commands me to bet on God.

On the face of it, this sounds quite a bit like Pi's argument. Both of his stories have a chance of being true, so must it not be reasonable to choose the more agreeable one, the one with animals, adventure, and color rather than the one with grim cruelty? And yet, the terms of that statement ("must it not be reasonable . . . ?"), like the rational cost-benefit analysis of Pascal's argument, are precisely the terms that Pi eschews. So for all its resemblance to Pascal's Wager, Pi's way to "*make you believe in God*" is something different.

This is where Hillman's claim that fictions heal supersedes Pascal's Wager, at least for our purposes (and, I think Pi's). Early in his book *Healing Fiction*, Hillman describes fictionalizing as a ubiquitous activity, much along the lines that Pi takes in his dialogue with the Japanese interviewers. For instance, Hillman — a psychologist writing to psychologists, yet saying things very relevant to this study — argues that psychological case histories, which aspire to be empirical and scientific (just the facts), are works of fiction in the way that Pi's life story is constructed, fabricated. Under the paradoxical heading "*Empirical Fiction*," Hillman argues that "Case history as factual history . . . is a fiction in the sense of a fabrication, a lie. But it is only a lie when it claims literal truth. Freud found that he was not recording a true account of historical events" — and neither is Pi, at least in one of the two mutually exclusive versions of his story — "but fantasies of events as if they had actually happened" (12). A case history — like, I suggest, any biography or autobiography, including Pi's (which is doubly fictional, since Pi is a made-up character who tells two made-up stories about his life)

— is fashioned from what Hillman calls "not historical facts but psycho-logical fantasies, the subjective stuff" (12). Fictions, says Hillman, "are mental constructs, fantasies by means of which we fashion or 'fiction' (*fingere*) a life or a person into a case history" (13). Hillman is applying fictional categories to supposedly empirical psychological works, but I believe that his point goes both ways: if empirical accounts are really fictions-in-hiding, so must literary fictions create some level of empir-ical appearance in order to foster a willing suspension of disbelief. The interpenetration of data ("dry, yeastless factuality") with fantasy ("God," the yeast), is deep and inextricable.

One way that Hillman, then, helps people heal is by developing their fictional sense — their sense of yeast, of God, of the fictive dimension of their imaginal stories. This is analogous to that journey down into Paul Tillich's "depth" that we have been examining in these pages, and to the sense of metaphor that for Catholic theologian Michael Himes is the only way we can name what "God" refers to. Hillman facilitates such a move-ment to imaginal depth by helping people flip their stories from one fictional genre to another. This practice differentiates Hillman from most conventional psychotherapists, who tend to utilize one masterplot; for instance, Freud took his patient Dora's story "and gave it a new plot, a Freudian plot: and part of this plot is that it is good for you, it's the best plot because it cures" (17). (By these terms, a contemporary biomedical diagnosis, complete with a regimen of prescription drugs, is also a fictional masterplot, not absolute fact.) But Hillman suggests that a more healing approach is to fictionalize more variously and intentionally — not to assert that there is only one correct, curative plot (that is another version of the absolutism and literalism of Pi's Japanese interviewers) but to discover that a more healing approach is to see that

> case histories have different fictional styles and may be written in a variety of fictional genres. And therapy may be most helpful when a person is able to place his life within this variety, like the polytheistic pantheon, without having to choose one against the others. For even while one part of me knows the soul goes to death in tragedy, another is living a picaresque fantasy, and a third engaged in the heroic comedy of improvement. (19)

The problem with any one genre is that it privileges the ego, that shallow surface that we ride on which needs to crack open to bring us, in Paul Tillich's terms, *down* to depth and, in Hillman's sense, *out* to world and soul. Of course, this journey to depth and soul is yet another fictional genre, one that has dominated my own discussion, but my point is that it is a valid, healing genre. And this particular genre is largely based on the value of *multiple* genres, of genre-flipping itself; flipping genres — which is, metaphorically, a shift from one masterplot, one God-narrative, to another — can jar us out of brightly lit but shallow egoism into dark, mysterious soul: "Thus we would open ourselves," says Hillman, "to the idea that were the story written in another way, by another hand, from another perspective, it would sound different and therefore *be a different story*. I am suggesting the poetic basis of therapy, of biography, of our very lives" (21).

In a variation on his call for literary-genre-shifting, Hillman suggests that we break open our shallow limitation to ego by reimagining our lives not as singular, heroic master narratives but as plays with a multiplicity of characters. To do this is to embrace Dionysos, the god not so much of hysteria and drunkenness but of theater: "Healing begins when we move out of the audience and onto the stage of the psyche, become characters in a fiction (even the God-like voice of Truth, a fiction), and as the drama intensifies, the catharsis occurs; we are purged from attachments to literal destinies, find freedom in playing parts, partial, dismembered, Dionysian" (38). Dionysos is often seen as absolutely chaotic, without logos; Hillman, however, claims that Dionysos has a form, a logos, but that it is a poetic, theatrical logos, a logos freed from the narrowness of a singular, certain, literal-minded ego:

> Dionysian logos is the enactment of fiction, oneself an as-if being whose reality comes wholly from imagination and the belief it imposes. The actor is and is not, a person and a persona, divided and undivided — as Dionysos is called. The self divided is precisely where the self is authentically located.... Authenticity is the perpetual dismemberment of being and not-being a self, a being that is always in many parts, like a dream with a full cast. We all have identity crises because a single identity is a delusion of the monotheistic mind that would defeat Dionysos at all costs....
>
> ... His is the viewpoint which can take nothing as it is statically, nothing literalistically, because everything has been put literarily into dramatic fictions. (39)

It is these ideas — the healing flipping of genres, the embrace of poetic polytheistic variety rather than "dry, yeastless" literalism and absolutism, the trying-on of various theatrical roles as a kind of playful Dionysian flow — that link together the beginning and ending of *Life of Pi*. The beginning and end of Pi's narrative, separated by the lengthy sea adventure, may seem to have little to do with each other: prior to the sea adventure Pi tells of his boyhood love of biology and his embrace of three different religious traditions, and then at the novel's end he describes his interview with the Japanese bureaucrats and his two incompatible ways of telling them his sea story. But the linking clue is provided by Pi's elderly mentor, who says "*I have a story that will make you believe in God*" (x), and by Pi himself, who tells the Japanese interviewers when they express preference for the more colorful version of his story, "And so it goes with God" (317). Pi's initial embrace of apparently irreconcilable religious traditions and his eventual telling of his story in two different genres are two sides of the same coin, two ways of exploring the question of what constitutes "the better story" (or, in Hillman's terms, the "healing fiction").

Pi plays with the value of disparate storytelling genres from the very beginning of his tale: he tells us right from the start that what has brought him "back to life" after suffering left him "sad and gloomy" is a combination of an "[a]cademic study" of science "and the steady, mindful practice of religion" (3). Implied here is the juxtaposition of two modes (or genres) for understanding the world, and Pi has been drawn to both: as an undergraduate student at the University of Toronto he

> took a double-major Bachelor's degree. My majors were religious studies and zoology. My fourth-year thesis for religious studies concerned certain aspects of the cosmogony theory of Isaac Luria, the great sixteenth-century Kabbalist from Safed. My zoology thesis was a functional analysis of the thyroid gland of the three-toed sloth. (3)

Kabbalistic mysticism and science: Pi sees the world through both frameworks, considering neither framework as absolutely factual. Zoology itself is more than a collection of scientific data; it has a healing poetic dimension for Pi: "I chose the sloth because its demeanor — calm, quiet and introspective — did something to soothe my shattered self" (3). Pi, although always religious ("Since when I could remember, religion had been very close to my heart" [27]), values the passionate master narrative of scientific atheism as much as he values religious master narratives. "Reason is my prophet," says his revered biology teacher Mr. Kumar when Pi is a boy in India, "and it tells me that as a watch stops, so we die. It's the end. If the watch doesn't work properly, it must be fixed here and now by us. One day we will take hold of the means of production and there will be justice on earth" (28). This is a paradoxically spiritual view of scientific materialism; with Mr. Kumar, says Pi, "I felt a kinship. . . . It was my first clue that atheists are my brothers and sisters of a different faith, and every word they speak speaks of faith. Like me, they go as far as the legs of reason will carry them — and then they leap" (28).

This "leap" of faith may sound, again, like a version of Pascal's

Wager; although Pi acknowledges the necessity of doubt as a temporary phase, he prefers both atheists and believers to lifelong agnostics because both atheists and believers make a choice (a *wager*?), whereas maintaining "doubt as a philosophy of life is akin to choosing immobility as a mode of transportation" (28). But behind Mr. Kumar's choice of reasoned, matter-bound atheism is not an analytical account of a rational wager but a personal story of suffering and healing. "Some people," Mr. Kumar says, "say God died during the Partition in 1947. He may have died in 1971 during the war. Or he may have died yesterday here in Pondicherry in an orphanage. That's what some people say, Pi. When I was your age, I lived in bed, racked with polio. I asked myself every day, 'Where is God? Where is God? Where is God?' God never came. It wasn't God who saved me — it was medicine" (27–28). Mr. Kumar embraced science not as "dry, yeastless factuality" but as a healing practice.

So it is contextualized, personal, image-filled stories that draw Pi's homage — his faith — not literal propositions: for Pi, beliefs are part of a theater of vital stories, not a list of flatly certain dogmas. And Hillman, remember, describes the psyche as theater rather than as a mere passive receptacle of facts, and then he describes memory — *memoria* — as this very theater. For Platonists, Hillman says, "*reminiscence* is never only of facts that happened in your or my lifetime, imprinted on the wax tablet of the mind, stored and retrieved through links of association" (41). Rather, *memoria* refers to "a great hall, a storehouse, a theatre packed with images," and "all images and the mental activity that summons them is in some direct but obscure relation with the mind of God" (41). Hillman's words illuminate *Life of Pi*'s external narrator's description of Pi's remembering: "*At times he gets agitated. It's nothing I say (I say very little). It's his own story that does it. Memory is an ocean and he bobs on its surface. I worry that he'll want to stop. But he wants to tell me his story. He goes on*" (42). This is the context in which Pi tells his faith-instilling story: *memoria* for him is an active ocean of images or a vital storytelling theater. And prior to taking us to his main theater or sea of memory (populated by colorful animals or cruel humans), Pi tells the multigenred story of his own religious belief(s).

The grown-up Pi swims in this ocean of religious images, or lives in a theater well stocked with religious props. "*His house is a temple*," says the narrator, and he proceeds to list the images that pervade the house. Notice how the juxtapositions of one tradition with another, and of religious iconography with ordinary household furnishings, blur the lines between religious genres and between sacred and secular:

> *In the entrance hall hangs a framed picture of Ganesha, he of the elephant head. . . . On the wall opposite the picture is a plain wooden Cross.*
>
> *In the living room, on a table next to the sofa, there is a small framed picture of the Virgin Mary of Guadalupe, flowers tumbling from her open mantle. Next to it is a framed photo of the black-robed Kaaba, holiest sanctum of Islam, surrounded by a ten-thousandfold swirl of the faithful. On the television set is a brass statue of Shiva as Nataraja, the cosmic lord of the dance, who controls the motions of the universe and the flow of time.* (45–46)

And on and on throughout the house: there are Hindu images, "*another Virgin Mary*," "*a wooden Christ on the Cross from Brazil*," a Koran covered by a cloth ("*At the center of the cloth is a single Arabic word, intricately woven, four letters: an* alif, *two* lams *and a* ha. *The word* God *in Arabic*"). And a Bible (46).

It is in this image-drenched context that Pi tells the narrator of his religious faith(s). His faith story begins, fittingly, with images, theatrical (Dionysian) props:

> I am a Hindu because of sculptured cones and red kumkum powder and baskets of turmeric nuggets, because of garlands of flowers and pieces of broken coconut, because of the clanging of bells to announce one's arrival to God, . . . because of colourful murals telling colourful stories, because of foreheads carrying, variously signified, the same word — *faith*. I became loyal to these sense impressions even before I knew what they meant or what they were for. It is my heart that commands me so. I feel at home in a Hindu temple. (47–48)

Pi then explicates the "Presence" that these props mediate — "The universe," says Pi, "makes sense to me through Hindu eyes" (48) — and in doing so he sounds much like Michael Himes describing God as what *cannot* be talked about and as what *must* be talked about (but only with metaphors, which themselves are Dionysos' theater props). Pi's God who cannot be talked about is "Brahman nirguna, without qualities, which lies beyond understanding, beyond description, beyond approach; with our poor words we sew a suit for it — One, True, Unity, Absolute, Ultimate Reality, Ground of Being — and try to make it fit, but Brahman nirguna always bursts the seams. We are left speechless" (48). But there is also "Brahman saguna, with qualities, where the suit fits. . . . Brahman saguna is Brahman made manifest to our limited senses, Brahman expressed not only in gods but in humans, animals, trees, in a handful of earth, for everything has a trace of the divine in it" (48). Using his Hindu categories — inspired by images, theater, not by factual analysis — Pi suggests what Hillman claims about the soul, that it is "out there" as well as "in here": if Brahman is the *world* soul, the

> truth of life is that Brahman is no different from atman, the spiritual force within us, what you might call the soul. The individual soul touches upon the world soul like a well reaches for the water table. That which sustains the universe beyond thought and language, and that which is at the core of us and struggles for expression, is the same thing. The finite within the infinite, the infinite within the finite. (48–49)

But Hinduism is only the beginning, the first "genre," of Pi's religious pilgrimage. "A plague upon fundamentalists and literalists!" he says (49). He counters literalism not with a literalistic rebuttal but with images and a story. When Lord Krishna was a cowherd, says Pi, he invited milkmaids to dance with him. "The night is dark, the fire in their midst roars and crackles, the beat of the music gets ever faster — the girls dance and dance with their sweet lord, who has made himself so abundant as to be in the arms of each and every girl" (49). But Krishna vanishes when a milkmaid becomes possessive, thinking "that Krishna is her partner alone" (49). God eludes; metaphors should not rigidify; genres need to be flipped to keep a single genre from becoming dogma. Pi now flips genres, shifting to his Christian narrative.

Pi begins his take on Christianity by claiming that at fourteen years old he "met Jesus Christ" (50), but that is the only time he uses such evangelical language, and the rest of his discussion of Christianity — which is made up of images and narrative — provides an important context for this seemingly literal claim. During a family visit to Munnar, Pi encounters a Catholic church, and right away his focus is on the church's sense images, at first blank in meaning but increasingly illuminating: "It was a building unremittingly unrevealing of what it held inside, with thick, featureless walls pale blue in colour and high, narrow windows impossible to look through. A fortress. . . . The vestibule had clean, white walls; the table and benches were of dark wood; and the priest was dressed in a white cassock — it was all neat, plain, simple. I was filled with a sense of peace" (51–52). It is from this priest, Father Martin, that Pi learns of Christianity, but the imagined context is important: "He was very kind. He served me tea and biscuits in a tea set that tinkled and rattled at every touch; he treated me like a grown-up" (53). Only now, amid all these sense images, these theater props, does a narrative intrude: "he told me a story," Pi says. "Or rather, since Christians are so fond of capital letters, a Story" (53).

The capital letter is telling. For Father Martin, this will not be *a* story but rather *the* Story, the *only* Story: "Father Martin made me to understand that the stories that came before it — and there were many —

were simply prologue to the Christians. Their religion had one Story, and to it they came back again and again, over and over. It was story enough for them" (53). Pi, however, sees things differently, Dionysianly, theatrically. "Surely," he thinks, "this religion had more than one story in its bag — religions abound with stories" (53). But Father Martin, benign but a literalist, tells him otherwise: Christ and the Cross are the only story. Pi's theatrical, multi-genred approach, then, differs from Father Martin's, and yet it does not deter Pi from being deeply affected by the Christian story and its central image, the Cross. Pi is scandalized by the story and image of Christ's violent execution, as St. Paul says he ought to be. How could a god allow his son to die? Pi is moved by this religious story that carries death right into the heart of what "God" refers to:

> It was wrong of this Christian God to let His avatar die. That is tantamount to letting a part of Himself die. . . . But once a dead God, always a dead God, even resurrected. The Son must have the taste of death forever in His mouth. The Trinity must be tainted by it; there must be a certain stench at the right hand of God the Father. The horror must be real. Why would God wish that upon Himself? Why not leave death to the mortals? Why make dirty what is beautiful, spoil what is perfect?
> Love. That was Father Martin's answer. (54)

This Christ, this Christian story of a God who out of love takes on humanity and even death, infiltrates Pi's imagination, deepens it — "I couldn't get Him out of my head. Still can't" (57). Pi becomes a Christian, adds Christian props to his religious theater. He has a new religious genre, but it is neither literal not exclusive: "I offered prayers to Christ, who is alive. Then I raced down the hill on the left and raced up the hill on the right — to offer thanks to Lord Krishna for having put Jesus of Nazareth, whose humanity I found so compelling, in my way" (58).

And then, says Pi, "Islam followed right behind, hardly a year later" (58). He flips religious genres again. And again the story begins with sensory details: "A small, quiet neighborhood with Arabic writing and crescent moons inscribed on the façades of the houses. . . . I had a peek at the Jamia Masjid, the Great Mosque. . . . The building, clean and white except for various edges painted green, was an open construction unfolding around an empty central room. Long straw mats covered the floor everywhere. Above, two slim, fluted minarets rose in the air" (58). Though these details attract his imagination, Pi is not inclined to get too close because "Islam had a reputation worse than Christianity's — fewer gods, greater violence, and I had never heard anyone say good things about Muslim schools" (58). But a nearby bakery intrigues him with a display of "some sort of unleavened bread. I poked at one. It flipped up stiffly" (59). A kind Muslim baker invites Pi to taste the bread, and then, called to prayer by the crier, the muezzin, the baker unrolls his carpet and prays. Now this new genre of religion appears to Pi not to be imbued with violence and ignorance but rather to be "an easy sort of exercise. . . . Hot weather yoga for the Bedouins," and it adds yet another layer of possibility to Pi's view of how to encounter God, yet another perform-ance for his Dionysian theater: "Next time I was praying in church — on my knees, immobile, silent before Christ on the Cross — the image of this callisthenic communion with God in the middle of bags of flour kept coming to my mind" (60).

As Pi gets to know this Muslim baker, he learns that Islam is more than "an easy sort of exercise," that it has a profound and sophisticated theology — "It is a beautiful religion of brotherhood and devotion" (61) — but theory is always embedded for him in the ritual, the theatrics: "The mosque was truly an open construction, to God and to breeze. . . . It felt good to bring my forehead to the ground. Immediately it felt like a deeply religious contact" (61). And the baker brings together Pi's two largest genres, the scientific and the religious; the baker's name, like that of the atheist biology teacher, is Mr. Kumar, and, Pi says, "it pleased me that this pious baker, as plain as a shadow and of solid health, and the Communist biology teacher and science devotee, . . . sadly afflicted with polio in his childhood, carried the same name. Mr. and Mr. Kumar taught me biology and Islam. Mr. and Mr. Kumar led me to study zoology and religious studies at the University of Toronto. Mr. and Mr. Kumar were the prophets of my Indian youth" (61).

Not surprisingly, Pi's family and community are not willing to allow him to travel so comfortably among traditions. When Pi and his atheist parents encounter a priest, an imam, and a pandit, Pi's religious genre-flipping is exposed, and none of these grownups is willing to tolerate Pi's non-literal, Dionysian approach to faith. "In these troubled times," Pi is told, "it's good to see a boy so keen on God. . . . But he can't be a Hindu, a Christian, *and* a Muslim. It's impossible. He must choose" (69). The adult Pi, who now lives with his eclectic assortment of religious images, complains to the narrator about literalistic orthodoxy defenders in terms that James Hillman, praiser of metaphorical polytheism, would approve. The fact that a rejection of literal-minded orthodoxy provokes not compassion but anger suggests that there is ego-control, not soul, operative here: "There are always those," says Pi,

who take it upon themselves to defend God, as if Ultimate Reality, as if the sustaining frame of existence, were something weak and helpless. These people walk by a widow deformed by leprosy begging for a few paise, walk by children dressed in rags living in the street, and they think, "Business as usual." But if they perceive a slight against God, it is a different story. Their faces go red, their chests heave mightily, they sputter angry words. The degree of their indignation is astonishing. Their resolve is frightening. (70)

These defenders of orthodoxy, who cannot tolerate a metaphorical approach to language about God, are like the bureaucratic Japanese interviewers at the end of *Life of Pi*, who are not willing to accept Pi's fanciful story of survival for 227 days in a lifeboat with a tiger: "We want a story without animals that will explain the sinking of the *Tsimtsum*" (303). This, then, is the linkage between the beginning and the end of the novel, between Pi's childhood Dionysian theater, filled with science and Hinduism and Christianity and Islam, and his later flipping of genres in the two ways he tells his sea story. At issue is not a wager, a singular choice of one genre *or* the other, but an embrace — a both/and. Indeed, Pi's second version of the sea adventure, in which the animals are replaced by struggling humans, though not presented as the "better" story, is nonetheless a powerful story: brutal, sad, desolate rather than heroic, a legitimate but different genre of narrative. Indeed, this second version of the tale deepens the first, cracks open its storybook vitality and glimpses something dark and dreadful beneath the surface; without the second version, the tiger adventure would seem richly imagined but just slightly cartoonish. By these terms, "God," the yeast, is present not just in the full-bodied textures of the tiger story but also — perhaps primarily — in the interface between the two stories, in the very genre-flipping itself.

Such a claim is exactly what diminishes the novel for some religious readers. In a review in the conservative religious journal *First Things*, for example, Randy Boyagoda criticizes what he calls *Life of Pi*'s protagonist's "eclectically tacky approach to religion." Boyagoda, noting Pi's peregrinations among various religious traditions, claims that author Yann Martel lacks an "appreciation for the intensity and particularity of religious devotions," offering instead "a confusing pastiche of devotions brought into unity by the sincerity of individual intention and action, rather than by virtue of the singular truth inherent in any of the religions Pi purports to follow." So Pi's God, for Boyagoda, is nothing more than a feel-good, individually invented conglomerate of pleasant bits and pieces assembled from three major religions; that is how this "God," for Boyagoda, is linked to the adventure story Pi tells, which we believe in — instead of the grim version — because it is more fun. Martel's "God," Boyagoda thinks, is a kind of fiction-as-colorful-entertainment. "Of course," Boyagoda says, "Martel wants us to believe in the original version" of Pi's survival story, complete with animals and heroic exploits, rather than the "more comprehensible but less enjoyable" version. "In his [Martel's] view," Boyagoda asserts, "to do so is a leap of faith, which in turn is a leap towards God: the God brought into existence by the novel itself, a strange mishmash of religious notions and figures that together comprise the deity that Pi creates and celebrates. In short, a God of fiction." Martel's "invitation to believe in God through his novel," says Boyagoda, "is too individualized to be reasonable. We do not turn to fiction to find the true God, and we should not turn to it to find a recipe for making a God agreeable enough to our personal tastes to believe in." Martel, according to Pi, implies "that we can find God by using our imaginations freely. But we can only hope to find God by using our imaginations wisely. Fiction, on its own, cannot create truth. The finest books can at best sound the depths of the human condition and bring rumors of the highest truths."

In defending the Martel from Boyagoda's charges I am not trying to claim that *Life of Pi* is a towering literary masterpiece and that Boyagoda has failed to appreciate this. I actually agree with Boyagoda's assessment that *Life of Pi* lacks the imaginative brilliance of such literary depictions of India as Salman Rushdie's *Midnight's Children*, in which the protagonist, in Boyagoda's words, dashes "from one end of India to another, experiencing the nation's religious panoply as it must be — as frenzied, vital, occasionally terrifying — rather than as a well-meaning Canadian might imagine it: as polite, passive, frequently meek." Nor will I argue that Boyagoda has completely misunderstood Martel's linkage of the religious and the fictive; I suggest, rather, that the brand of Christianity that Boyagoda reveres really does differ from the more pluralistic, metaphorical, open-ended view of the divine that Martel suggests and that I have endorsed in these pages — but with some Christian theological authority (Paul Tillich, John S. Dunne, Michael Himes). I wish to conclude by arguing that a religious vision founded on imagination and "fiction" cannot be facilely dismissed as an individualistic, anything-goes faith in a "God agreeable enough to our personal tastes to believe in." As I have tried to demonstrate throughout these pages, and especially to illustrate using Martell's imperfect but imaginative novel, James Hillman's idea of "Healing Fiction" suggests that truly vital spiritual journeys take place in a kind of Dionysian theater: a metaphorical space that resists rigid literalism and ego-driven religious triumphalism by periodically flipping genres, keeping the God question open rather than shutting it down. The purpose of such open, play-full (in both the dramatic and childlike senses) fictionalizing is not to offer "a recipe for making a God agreeable enough to our personal tastes to believe in" but rather, I would suggest, to keep surfaces from hardening and to maintain access to depth (in Paul Tillich's Protestant Christian sense), or to maintain the humbling mystery and rich, sacramental metaphoricity of the divine (in Michael Himes' Catholic Christian sense). Seeing God as "the better story," in other words, need not reduce the religious to a good-feeling whim or to a rational cost-benefit wager. But it does, I suggest, render the religious as less interested in a Static Object ("God is the Supreme Being, infinitely perfect, Who made all things and keeps them in existence," says the old Catholic Baltimore Catechism) than in an ongoing journey; "God," in this sense, is more verb than noun.

And as a verb, this goal of the spiritual journey is the seeking itself; it is a journey to journey. The light and the dark, the shadows and illuminations, are always inextricably intertwined; any "disjunctive move" is indeed "contra-indicated" (Hillman 102). Though Boyagoda would perhaps fault me for leaping from Tillich and Himes to Pema Chödrön, I suggest, as Pi Patel might, that she is an entirely valid dialogue partner and that her suggestion at the end of *When Things Fall Apart* that "the path is the goal" and that we are invited to enter ambiguity with openness rather than bitterness is entirely relevant to our exploration of "the better story" as "the journey story":

> When we realize that the path is the goal, there's a sense of workability. Trugpa Rinpoche said, "Whatever occurs in the confused mind is regarded as the path. Everything is workable. It is a fearless proclamation, the lion's roar." Everything that occurs in our confused mind we can regard as the path. Everything is workable. . . .
>
> It's an insecure way to live. . . . Basically, the instruction is not to try to solve the problem but instead to use it as a question about how to let this very situation wake us up further rather than lull us into ignorance. We can use a difficult situation to encourage ourselves to take a leap, to step out into the ambiguity. . . .
>
> This is our choice in every moment. Do we relate to our circumstances with bitterness or with openness?
>
> That is why it can be said that whatever occurs can be regarded as the path and that all things, not just some things, are workable. (145–146)

Aren't the sacramental imagination, the descent to depth, the making of soul, the resistance to dichotomizing shadows and illuminations, all attempts to grasp the way "all things, not just some things, are workable"?

Works Cited

Boyagoda, Randy. Rev. of *Life of Pi*, by Yann Martel. *First Things*. FirstThings.com. May 2003. Web. 6 March 2010.

Chödrön, Pema. *When Things Fall Apart: Heart Advice for Difficult Times*. 1997. Boston: Shambhala, 2000.

Hillman, James. *Healing Fiction*. 1983. Woodstock, CT: Spring Publications, 1996.

Martel, Yann. *Life of Pi*. Orlando, FL: Harcourt, 2001.

Pascal, Blaise. *Pensées*. Trans. Honor Levi. In Blaise Pascal, *Pensées and Other Writings*. 1995; Oxford: Oxford University Press, 2008.

Index